Russian Multinationals

Russian multinationals are playing an increasingly important role in the world economy, particularly in some key sectors such as oil, gas and metallurgy. At the same time, Russian multinationals differ in many respects from multinationals from other countries in that they often receive special treatment from the Russian government, and, because of past experiences, international investors are often reluctant to invest in them. This book presents a comprehensive overview of Russian multinationals. It discusses the rise of Russian multinationals, examines Russian multinationals' activities in key sectors, analyses the relationship between Russian multinationals and the Russian government and between Russian multinationals and international counterparts, and concludes by assessing how Russian multinationals are likely to develop in the future.

Andrei Panibratov is Professor of Strategic and International Management at the Graduate School of Management (GSOM), St. Petersburg State University (Russia) where he teaches contemporary strategic analysis and international business strategy courses. He holds a first doctoral degree (Candidate of Sciences in Economics) from St. Petersburg State University, an MBA degree from the University of Wales (UK) and a second doctoral degree (Doctor of Sciences in Economics) from Moscow State University of Management (Russia). Professor Panibratov has participated in consultation and research projects for the World Bank, Manchester University (UK), Aalto University School of Economics and Tampere University of Technology (both Finland), and many international and Russian companies. He is a visiting professor at Lappeenranta University of Technology in Finland where he teaches corporate strategy in emerging markets for international masters students. Professor Panibratov's research interests include the strategy of western multinational enterprises in Russia, marketing decisions when going abroad, international expansion of emerging economy companies, outward FDI from Russia and the internationalisation of Russian firms. He is the author and co-author of a number of books, case studies and articles published in Russia and abroad.

Routledge Contemporary Russia and Eastern Europe Series

1 Liberal Nationalism in Central Europe
Stefan Auer

2 Civil–Military Relations in Russia and Eastern Europe
David J. Betz

3 The Extreme Nationalist Threat in Russia
The growing influence of Western Rightist ideas
Thomas Parland

4 Economic Development in Tatarstan
Global markets and a Russian region
Leo McCann

5 Adapting to Russia's New Labour Market
Gender and employment strategy
Edited by Sarah Ashwin

6 Building Democracy and Civil Society East of the Elbe
Essays in honour of Edmund Mokrzycki
Edited by Sven Eliaeson

7 The Telengits of Southern Siberia
Landscape, religion and knowledge in motion
Agnieszka Halemba

8 The Development of Capitalism in Russia
Simon Clarke

9 Russian Television Today
Primetime drama and comedy
David MacFadyen

10 The Rebuilding of Greater Russia
Putin's foreign policy towards the CIS countries
Bertil Nygren

11 A Russian Factory Enters the Market Economy
Claudio Morrison

12 Democracy Building and Civil Society in Post-Soviet Armenia
Armine Ishkanian

13 NATO–Russia Relations in the Twenty-First Century
Aurel Braun

14 Russian Military Reform
A failed exercise in defence decision making
Carolina Vendil Pallin

15 The Multilateral Dimension in Russian Foreign Policy
Edited by Elana Wilson Rowe and Stina Torjesen

16 Russian Nationalism and the National Reassertion of Russia
Edited by Marlène Laruelle

17 The Caucasus
An introduction
Frederik Coene

18 Radical Islam in the Former Soviet Union
Edited by Galina M. Yemelianova

19 Russia's European Agenda and the Baltic States
Janina Šleivytė

20 Regional Development in Central and Eastern Europe
Development processes and policy challenges
Edited by Grzegorz Gorzelak, John Bachtler and Maciej Smętkowski

21 Russia and Europe
Reaching agreements, digging trenches
Kjell Engelbrekt and Bertil Nygren

22 Russia's Skinheads
Exploring and rethinking subcultural lives
Hilary Pilkington, Elena Omel'chenko and Al'bina Garifzianova

23 The Colour Revolutions in the Former Soviet Republics
Successes and failures
Edited by Donnacha Ó Beacháin and Abel Polese

24 Russian Mass Media and Changing Values
Edited by Arja Rosenholm, Kaarle Nordenstreng and Elena Trubina

25 The Heritage of Soviet Oriental Studies
Edited by Michael Kemper and Stephan Conermann

26 Religion and Language in Post-Soviet Russia
Brian P. Bennett

27 Jewish Women Writers in the Soviet Union
Rina Lapidus

28 Chinese Migrants in Russia, Central Asia and Eastern Europe
Edited by Felix B. Chang and Sunnie T. Rucker-Chang

29 Poland's EU Accession
Sergiusz Trzeciak

30 The Russian Armed Forces in Transition
Economic, geopolitical and institutional uncertainties
Edited by Roger N. McDermott, Bertil Nygren and Carolina Vendil Pallin

31 The Religious Factor in Russia's Foreign Policy
Alicja Curanović

32 Postcommunist Film – Russia, Eastern Europe and World Culture
Moving images of postcommunism
Edited by Lars Kristensen

33 Russian Multinationals
From regional supremacy to global lead
Andrei Panibratov

Russian Multinationals

From regional supremacy to global lead

Andrei Panibratov

Routledge
Taylor & Francis Group
LONDON AND NEW YORK

First published 2012
by Routledge
2 Park Square, Milton Park, Abingdon, Oxon, OX14 4RN

Simultaneously published in the USA and Canada
by Routledge
711 Third Avenue, New York, NY 10017

Routledge is an imprint of the Taylor & Francis Group, an informa business

British Library Cataloguing in Publication Data
A catalogue record for this book is available from the British Library

Library of Congress Cataloging-in-Publication Data
Panibratov, A. IU. (Andrei IUr'evich)
Russian multinationals: from regional supremacy to global lead/Andrei Panibratov. – 1st ed.
p. cm. – (Routledge contemporary Russia and Eastern Europe series; 33)
Includes bibliographical references and index.
1. International business enterprises–Russia (Federation) 2. Russia (Federation)–Economic policy. 3. Banks and banking–Russia (Federation) 4. Finance, Public–Russia (Federation) 5. Fiscal policy–Russia (Federation) 6. Russia (Federation)–Politics and government. 7. Russia (Federation)–Foreign economic relations. I. Title.
HD2755.5.P356 2012
338.8'8947–dc23
2011032646

ISBN: 978-0-415-61588-4 (hbk)
ISBN: 978-0-203-13037-7 (ebk)

Typeset in Times New Roman by
Sunrise Setting Ltd

MIX
Paper from responsible sources
FSC www.fsc.org FSC® C004839

Printed and bound in Great Britain by the MPG Books Group

To my son Yuri and my daughter Maria

Contents

Tables

Foreword

Traditionally, multinational enterprises headquartered in the developed countries have been the principal actors in the world foreign direct investment market; until not so long ago, they accounted for some 90 per cent of outflows of such investments. They certainly continue to hold the leadership role. But firms headquartered in other parts of the world increasingly challenge multinational enterprises from these countries, as the former invest more and more abroad as well (Sauvant *et al.* 2010). In fact, with an average of over US$300 billion of outflows during 2008–2009, the amount that over 20,000 emerging market multinational enterprises invested abroad on average during those years was six times the *world* average of foreign direct investment flows during the first half of the 1980s. The stock of this investment, located in host countries throughout the world, had risen to a staggering US$3 trillion by 2009 and continues to grow. In other words, multinational enterprises from emerging markets have become full and important players in the world foreign direct investment market.

Why this development? The basic reason is that firms in emerging markets have acquired a range of ownership advantages that allow them to be successful in international markets not only through trade but also through foreign direct investment, often, in fact, following their trade routes. What is more, in a world in which competition is everywhere – through imports, inward foreign direct investment, licensing, franchising and various other forms of transborder engagement – it becomes increasingly necessary, if not imperative, for firms to assemble a portfolio of locational assets. This allows firms to have better access to markets and various tangible and intangible assets (such as technology, know-how, brand-names). This portfolio of locational assets, in turn, becomes a source of the international competitiveness of the firms engaged in outward foreign direct investment.

One of the most important new emerging home countries is the Russian Federation. Starting virtually from scratch only some 20 years ago, the stock of Russia's outward foreign direct investment had reached US$250 billion in 2009, with flows averaging US$50 billion during 2008–2009. While most of this investment is in natural resources – and certainly while most of the country's leading multinational enterprises are in this sector – a growing number of Russian firms in other sectors also seek to establish themselves abroad. Like their competitors headquartered in developed countries, they have to overcome a range of issues related to the 'liability of foreignness' (foreigners operating in a foreign country), ranging from how to enter foreign markets (with understanding how to execute mergers and acquisitions successfully being a particular challenge), to managing integrated international production networks, to dealing with political and other obstacles in host countries (including the apparent rise of foreign direct investment protectionism).

Another issue, often not receiving sufficient attention in countries whose firms are newly internationalising through foreign direct investment, concerns the importance of home country policies. This is an important issue as all developed countries have a range of policy instruments in place to support the internationalisation process of 'their' multinational enterprises – ranging from providing insurance for outward foreign direct investment projects to the conclusion of bilateral investment treaties to protect the assets of 'their' firms abroad and facilitating their operations. The government of Russia will need to review its own policy in this respect to ensure that Russian multinational enterprises are not at a competitive disadvantage vis-à-vis firms headquartered in other countries.

The present volume is a valuable addition to the literature as it examines in detail the rise of Russia's multinational enterprises. It will be of interest to everyone who is interested in understanding the salient features of the international expansion of this country's firms and the forces driving and shaping this process.

Karl P. Sauvant
Executive Director, Vale Columbia Center on
Sustainable International Investment,
Columbia University, New York

Preface

This book, the first attempt to engage with the theme of the internationalisation of Russian firms, is the culmination of a five-year period of research by the author on the track records of Russian firms' international results, in which the international activity of these companies was investigated in multiple studies under the supervision of the author, whose own increasing interest in the topic of emerging multinationals naturally focused on Russian firms.

The outward move of Russian multinational enterprises is an increasingly important phenomenon. Despite recent setbacks in the world economy the growth of multinationals from emerging economies continues and Russia is one of the leading countries in this regard, with its companies continuing to spread across the globe.

This book shows that these firms are just beginning to grow internationally and discusses the issues that affect the rise of Russia's business in foreign markets. It is aimed at those readers who are interested in why Russian firms go abroad, how they internationalise and what their prospects are. Hence, the first important purpose of this book is to enhance the readers' understanding of the real motives of Russian firms' internationalisation; the second is to show the spectrum of strategies and explain the choice of entry modes and post-entry operations by Russian firms in foreign markets; and the third is to discuss the boundaries and consider the future of Russian multinationals.

Acknowledgements

Apart from the efforts of the author, the success of any book depends largely on the encouragement and guidelines of many others. I take this opportunity to express my gratitude to the people who made valuable contributions to the successful completion of this project.

I would like to show my greatest appreciation to Karl P. Sauvant and Vishwas Govitrikar, who were the first to arouse my interest in the topic and in the in-depth study of Russian MNEs and Russia's OFDI. Without their encouragement and guidance in previous projects the present book would not have been possible.

Words are inadequate in offering my very special, warm and heartfelt thanks to my friend and colleague Marina Latuha for her tremendous support, help, motivation and encouragement. She was the most important person in inspiring me to get down to work and finish this book, for which I am profoundly grateful.

Much of what I have learned over the previous ten years and more came as the result of being a part of the Graduate School of Management at St Petersburg State University, Russia. My colleagues and students inspired me in their own ways and have thus indirectly contributed a tremendous amount to the content of this book. A little part of each of them will be found here.

Many thanks are due to my old partner and friend Pertti Naulapää, for his willingness to provide me with his materials on the development of Russia's economy in the twentieth century.

My appreciation also goes to Peter Sowden for his patience and assistance during the writing of this book.

I wish to express my love and gratitude to my beloved parents, Yuri and Tamara, for their understanding and love. And, not least, I would like to thank my wife, Marina Panibratova, for her patience and forbearance during the hundreds of hours I have spent working on this book.

Introduction

Russian multinationals – where are they from?

This book is about the emergence of Russian multinational companies. These are firms that have shown the ability and the ambition to play a role on the global scene. Most of them have done so with dispatch and now enjoy international recognition and ranking among their kind. Proof of their multinational status can be found in the significant scope of their operations, their employment of large multinational work forces, their big-league profits and their globalised custom on world-wide markets. Some of them are relatively mature and can be compared with the multinational enterprises (MNEs hereafter) from developed economies; others are of lesser size, younger and have only recently started to internationalise.

There are three main reasons for singling out Russia for examination. To start with, Russia is the second-largest country in outward foreign direct investment, with affiliates almost all over the world. Second, Russian firms pursue an unusually wide range of strategies in internationalising and thus invite examination on that score alone. Third, Russia is one of the least examined economies in business literature and therefore research can but increase the existing pool of knowledge.

While most Russian MNEs are well-known leaders in their home market, only a few of them have been accepted onto the world stage as equal players. This is not surprising as in many cases their internationalisation became possible only as of 1991: that is to say, with the appearance and consequent increase of private business in the post-communist period. Hence, most Russian multinationals are younger, less experienced and weaker than their western counterparts. Yet they possess sufficient ambition to compete on foreign markets, have just enough money to make some significant foreign investments and have shown a competitiveness that has international mettle.

The origins of Russian multinationals

Prototypes of Russian MNEs go back to the time of the Soviet Union (the so-called 'red multinationals'), and were both owned and controlled by the government. A majority of these firms were involved in supporting Russian exports abroad (raw resource marketing, infrastructure support, banking, insurance, etc.). After the decline of the Soviet Union toward the end of the 1980s, these companies were mostly involved in restructuring and consolidation of assets inside Russia; only after having orientated themselves to post-communist politics, new ways of conducting business under a new type of economy, a new financial order and a new foreign policy did they gird themselves to seek their fortune abroad.

Their first toe-dip took the form of cross-border mergers and acquisitions. Finance was still only incipiently organised so that money was short, sufficing only for modest greenfield investments. Even so, there was no lack of courage in taking risks, attesting to the rebirth of the previously familiar habit of gambling on a quick return in the face of a lack of experience.

The mainstream research in the field of Russian MNEs has traditionally focused on the amount of outward foreign direct investment (OFDI), a measure often taken as indicative of international expansion. In the immediate post-communist period Russian investment abroad was often seen as frivolous, nothing but a method of escape from the doldrums at home, an understandable view because the country's way of doing business was absolutely unpractised. But, somewhat curiously, there existed government incentives to internationalise. These certainly helped to persuade Russian capital to venture abroad.

Until recently, Russian OFDI remained more of a quantitative binge than a well-considered qualitative strategy. The changeover occurred as experience with free-market foreign countries accumulated, and with the relatively recent emergence of a more serious and considered strain of Russian MNE the internationalisation of our firms may now be studied as a qualitative phenomenon rather than as a mere social curiosity.

The Russian multinationals that enjoy a global star rating operate in oil and gas, electricity, metallurgy and banking. An orientation towards the energy and commodities sectors is not the only similarity with other emerging MNEs. Companies servicing mass clients (in electronics, telecommunications, retail and hardware) confront the challenge of serving low-income consumers after initial efforts with more affluent ones in Moscow and St Petersburg, regions with the highest income per capita. Only when these markets become saturated and competitive pressure intensifies do companies explore markets in other regions and adapt their strategies to serve low-income consumers. During expansion in their domestic regional markets, Russian MNEs encountered problems of underdeveloped infrastructure and distribution networks; thus exposed to these challenges, and having grown in an unstable economic environment (that is, the financial crises of the 1990s), these companies have become resilient to shock and quick in their reactions.

Knowing their country better than potential foreign competitors, Russian firms know where to find attractive market niches – namely, underdeveloped parts of the country. Generating free cash flow from those 'backwaters' enables Russian companies to invest abroad. In segments where foreigners wish to invest Russian firms have needed to mount defensive tactics, and this sometimes provides them with innovative ways to retaliate – by expanding into foreign lands.

The organisation of the book

The phenomenon of Russian MNEs cannot be treated holistically. Historical background, scale of operations, the role of the government, investment approaches, managerial attitudes and innovation: these various features in different combinations make the behaviour of MNEs too varied to be analysed and discussed as a whole, as the total picture that results is too blurred. Hence, this book, which consists of ten chapters, is organised in the following manner.

Chapters 1 and 2 present the main issues of the development of the Russian economy, focusing on the internationalisation of industries and the rise of Russian MNEs. The first chapter explains how the Russian economy adjusted to the globalisation of markets or, to put it another way, how enterprises responded to change and evolutionary forces and processes in the external and internal environments, and which factors affected the adjustment process. The place of Russia within the BRIC group of powerful 'next-gen' countries is also discussed in this chapter. In the second chapter the OFDI from Russia is considered as the impulse that led to the genesis of Russian multinationals. Different industries' perspectives of internationalisation are presented, rendering a preparatory sketch of the more in-depth analysis that follows of the most salient and interesting sectors of Russia's globalising economy.

Chapters 3 to 7 present the main approaches of Russian MNEs to foreign market entry and the development of post-entry strategy. Case studies will be employed here. Each chapter contains an overview of the industry and then a few (usually two) case studies, chosen to illustrate the dynamics of Russian internationalisation.

Chapter 3 considers Russian MNEs in the oil and gas sector. Export dominates here, as does government control. Three cases used here are Gazprom, which is not fully state-owned yet at the same time is probably one of the Russian multinationals most influenced by the state; Rosneft, which is fully state-owned but is not as state-controlled as Gazprom; and Lukoil, which is a private company, less politically and more economically motivated to do business abroad than the other two.

Chapter 4 deals with the internationalisation of Russian high-tech companies. The nature of the sector allows it to be less investment-focused and more partnership-orientated, showing that alliances and networks provide Russian firms with the best kind of internationalism for their purposes. Case studies here are Kaspersky Labs (software) and Sitronics (the leading Russian company in electronics and IT).

Chapter 5 tells the story of the international expansion of Russian banks. The two biggest and most active players are Alfa Bank and VTB Group, which are both exemplars of internationalisation via subsidiaries, and that mostly in the Commonwealth of Independent States (CIS) countries. In this sector, where the acquisition of smaller foreign banks is one of the most efficient modes of entry, Russian banks' post-entry strategy is focused on the attraction of new customers in the host market and on servicing domestic customers who go abroad.

Chapter 6 describes the international strategies of Russian firms in ferrous and non-ferrous metallurgy. Case studies here focus on Rusal (one of the largest manufacturers of aluminium in the world) and, in the steel industry, Severstal and Evraz. While the former seeks resources, explaining its interest in Africa, the second and third are more focused on customers in developed economies.

Chapter 7 continues the theme of market-seeking and customer-following firms, using as examples MTS and VimpelCom, both in the telecommunication sector. While the developed markets are extremely competitive, customers are loyal to already established brands, and internationalisation can turn out to be expensive. Russian companies are interested mainly in the markets of CIS countries, where they can relatively easily and cheaply acquire smaller local players.

Finally, Chapters 8 to 10 discuss 'special' issues relating to the genesis of Russian MNEs. Chapter 8 examines companies that are global by nature, but totally different from one another in the sense of their historical development paths, scales of operation, industry and strategic importance. One such company, Inter RAO UES, was established as a division of a national monopoly that exports Russian electricity to the West, while another, Yandex, was originally an Internet company that had internationalised through the web.

Chapter 9 presents two extremes of the footholds of Russian MNEs: government involvement and marketing. While two case study companies (Rosenergoatom and Rosoboronexport) benefit from government support, two others (Wimm-Bill-Dann and Russian Standard) rely on their own capability to explore markets and develop brands.

Chapter 10 discusses the boundaries of Russian firms' international expansion. One case study, that of Sberbank, deals with that company's attempt to take over a leading western firm, Opel. A second study deals with efforts to internationalise on the part of small Russian firms in high-tech and fast food.

Taken together, the ten chapters attempt to provide the main pieces of the mosaic that in its finality portrays Russian business internationalisation. A story of successes, dashed hopes and ongoing forays – proof that Russia is recapturing its rightful position in world business.

1 The internationalisation of the Russian economy

Russia transforms – economy and enterprise

In Russia the transition from a planned economy to one based on free enterprise began in the mid-1980s but progressed notably slower than in some other parts of the Soviet bloc. The reasons for this have been widely studied at the macro level. At the micro level economists found it harder to move ahead.

Why? The short answer is that a tradition of secrecy shrouded the working parts of the economy. Statistics were 'doped' to accommodate a system of command. Companies were obliged to withhold financial information from system outsiders. The 'near abroad' of the economy's dirigiste heartland – barter trade, cash transactions, government subsidy of inefficient enterprises, as well as other sweetheart practices, carried over from Communism. In sum, that made for a fuzzy terrain, difficult and even perilous to investigate. Researchers often needed to dare to expose data rather than just find it.

It had been easier before the advent of Communism. The progress of Russian enterprise was then well documented. Before World War I there was a brisk development of the country's economy, despite the presence in it of some statism. The country developed a strong industrial base. Then, during the period of the Revolution of 1917, a regime of so-called War Communism was imposed. Large enterprises were nationalised and thus bereft of their profit motivation. This was replaced by the motivation of political correctness. What transpired can only be described as a demoralised economy.

The New economic policy of the 1920s aimed to fix this by dismantling the War Communism system. As the 1920s waned, a centrally planned economy was launched. It created monster industries and monstrous agriculture, but sufficed to win the mother of all wars. In this titanic effort it became stiff in joint and short of breath, failing altogether in 1991. Shortly before that happened, however, a transition process from the spirit of communism began to materialise. It varied in different industries and different regions in Russia, but, as it developed, it brought considerable change in the country's industrial structure, its product and its entrepreneurial way. This entire process is shown in Table 1.1.

Table 1.1 Different phases of Russian enterprise development in the twentieth and the twenty-first centuries

Year	*Phase*
	The onset of industrialisation
1900–1916	Fast industrialisation
	Shaping essentials of planned economy
1917–1920	Nationalisation and War Communism
1921–1928	New economic policy
	The life cycle of the planned economy
1929–1941	Foundation of centrally planned economy
1941–1945	War economy
1946–1954	Recovery
1955–1964	Economic growth
1965–1984	Stability and stagnation
	Transition to market economy
1985–1991	*Perestroika*
1991–1994	Mass privatisation
1995–1998	Restructuring and adjustment
1998	National economic crisis (NEC)
1999–2000	Post-NEC recovery
	Integration to global economy
2001–2007	FDI-based growth of economy
2008–2009	World financial crisis (WFC)
2010–	Post-WFC development of companies

The stages of transition are highlighted in more detail below.

Stage 1: onset of industrialisation

In 1913, foreign investment accounted for about a quarter of the capital of industrial enterprise in Russia. It is estimated that national income (GDP) in that same year was about level with that of the United Kingdom. It was slightly below that of Germany and 21 per cent of that of the United States. On a per-capita basis, however, Russian income was only about one-third of Germany's.[1]

Small manufacturing enterprises played a major role in the progress made in the first two decades of the 1900s. In 1915, such firms employed about 67 per cent of those engaged in manufacturing, or 5.2 million persons. They logged 33 per cent of the total industrial output. But productivity was low: the output per individual was only a quarter of that of workers in large-scale manufacturing.[2]

Stage 2: shaping the planned economy

Immediately after the Revolution of 1917, strong administrative oversight was applied to the running of the national economy. Workers' control over factories was imposed; land and banks were nationalised. In mid-1918, all large factories were nationalised. War Communism, in addition to nationalising large enterprises, also banned private trade. It restricted the movement of industrial workers, appropriated by force peasants' surplus production and set about creating a moneyless society.[3]

One result of this was runaway inflation. In the years between 1917 and 1921 prices rose yearly, on average, by 1,000 per cent. Combined with the famine of 1921, this led to a collapse of industrial output. Attempting to countervail this, the government thought up the New economic policy (NEP).

The NEP did not lack élan. It attempted to combine planning and market forces by returning agriculture to the hand of the peasant and largely decentralising the management of industry. Private trade was legalised again, pricing partly freed from planning, leeway granted to the regulation of employment. Using these as its principal tools, it eventually managed to stabilise the rouble.

Yet heavy industry, transport, foreign trade and banks remained nationalised and the ones rated as strategic continued to be shackled to the centralised planning system. To be sure, the bulk of nationalised firms were freed from government control and, instead, instructed to operate commercially. They formed themselves into large trusts, growing later into syndicates, which soon became the dominant form of industrial organisation. They were, one could say, the Soviet counterparts to the capitalist cartel.

According to the official statistics, the NEP seemed to be leading to a recovery of the economy. The figures for 1928 showed national income as well as industrial and agricultural output as rising more than 10 per cent above their 1913 levels. It seems curious, therefore, that it was in that same year that the New economic policy was abandoned. National security and policy were cited as grounds, but the main reason given – and never mind the story told by the official statistics – was that industrial capacity had developed unsatisfactorily.[4]

The fact was that, after eight years of Soviet management, investment and military commodities accounted for the same proportion of industrial output as they had before the Revolution. In 1924, steel output had dropped almost a quarter (23 per cent) over 1913.

Stage 3: the life cycle of the planned economy

When the failure of the NEP finally had to be officially conceded, a debate at several levels within command and control decided on a programme which strongly favoured crash development of the manufacturing industry. It did so at dire cost to agriculture as well as to the private sector. The result was famine in Russia's breadbasket, but also a glut of muscular new manufacturing.

During the 1930s there was a shift from general manufacturing to manufacturing of the heaviest kind. The economy's excellent growth rates recorded for 1934–36 were in large part due to the completion of big plants begun during the early 1930s. A particularly large success was claimed for the construction industry, but productivity elsewhere was also impressive, doubling from 1932 to 1937.[5]

Toward the end of the 1930s economic growth slowed, especially in metallurgy and construction. One reason for this was a national policy-dictated shift into the military sector owing to the increasing likelihood of war with Germany. It was the most important thing the planners got right, for Germany did indeed attack, in June 1941.

As the foe advanced, the Soviet government spared no effort to dismantle and relocate enterprises. It shipped workers eastwards. By November 1941, some 1,500 industrial enterprises were thus evacuated. Heavy industry, built in the 1930s in western Russia, now produced armaments in the Urals. It was in good part due to this emergency relocation that the share of national income devoted to the war effort increased from about 10 per cent in 1940 to just below 50 per cent in 1943. And, by 1945, over half of the country's metallurgical output came from the Urals.[6]

Upon cessation of hostilities, a reconversion of war factories to civilian production was begun. The number of ministries, the main function of which consisted of planning and controlling the development of various sectors of the country's economy, expanded quickly, totalling 33 in 1947.[7]

In the 1950s the Soviet government turned its attention to agriculture. Foreign trade and the economic cooperation between the Soviet bloc countries expanded sharply, and between 1950 and 1958 the volume of Soviet foreign trade almost tripled.[8]

In 1965, a new development programme was adopted which sought to shift operative decision-making from the syndicates and trusts to newly created industrial ministries. These, in turn, were expected to find ways to implement the government's industrial policies. But while the reform was intended to help industry managers act on their own initiative, the way in which it was handled helped the bureaucrats instead. To cut a long story short, the bureaucrats won.

During the 1970s there was a move to merge enterprises into larger corporations, or associations, within the ministries. Deprived of the power to change matters, these bodies were ineffectual. Many of the products selected by the corporations or associations had components supplied from within different ministries. The bureaucratic jungle thickened.

From the late 1960s, industrial growth in the Soviet Union plummeted. The period beginning in 1970 and extending through the first half of the 1980s became known as 'Zastoy', meaning stagnation with no hope of surcease. In 1980 only the oil and the passenger car industries attained their production targets. From 1981 to 1985 the rate of growth of machinery and equipment production, as well as the rate of investment, substantially declined. Technological progress slowed and imbalances flourished throughout the economy.

Stage 4: transition to a market economy

Yet another comprehensive reform in the economic system, the so-called '*perestroika*', is generally considered to have started in 1985, though some piecemeal changes had preceded it in 1983. A programme concerning industrial enterprises came into force in 1987. Legislation followed, obliging enterprises to finance all their activities from internally generated funds. Failure to do so meant the state could declare the enterprise bankrupt and liquidate its assets.

In practice, though, the government continued to subsidise unprofitable enterprises. But *perestroika* did unclog the economy by permitting limited private ownership of assets and land.

A large-scale transfer of assets into non-state hands began in 1989. Joint ventures with foreign firms were allowed from January 1987. The purpose of the Joint Venture Decree was to encourage closer cooperation between Western and Soviet enterprises. In 1991, there were 1,145 joint ventures.[9] In May 1991 the Law on Foreign Investments enabled foreign firms to set up wholly owned companies. But joint ventures in manufacturing lagged behind those in other sectors and their volume of output remained low.[10]

In 1990, the legislative framework for small enterprises (private or state enterprises with fewer than 200 employees) was established, allowing SMEs to develop faster. This new legal status granted tax advantages. Systematic privatisation, which can be broadly understood as all measures contributing to the de-statisation of economic activity, began in 1991. Its legislative framework was laid down in 1992.

The core 'technology' of privatisation in Russia was the 'corporatisation' of large and medium-sized enterprises by converting them into joint stock companies prior to their restructuring.[11] The aims were to make enterprise independent of state administration, delimit the size of its ownership and separate shareholders from management.[12] In the privatisation programme large and medium-sized enterprises (those with workforces of between 1,000 and 10,000, and 200 and 1,000, respectively) have played the main roles.[13]

The 1992 privatisation programme divided lines of business into several groups. Natural resources, television and radio were barred from privatisation. Mining and energy, transport companies and very large enterprises, city transport networks and pharmacies, among others, required special permission to privatise. The last group consisted of enterprises whose privatisation was made obligatory, including retail and wholesale trade, construction and light industry, unprofitable enterprises and unfinished construction.

Privatisation accelerated quickly. By the end of 1992, only 18 large and medium-sized enterprises had been privatised and 3,485 industrial enterprises were leased.[14] By the end of 1993, 8,509 large and medium-sized enterprises had been privatised, and one year later the figure stood at 16,462. The pace slowed down during 1995, but by the end of that year 17,937 large and medium-sized enterprises stood privatised. They accounted for 88.3 per cent of Russia's total industrial output.[15]

In late 1996 there followed a clean-up. It lasted a few years, mainly targeting large enterprises. In that year the World Bank published a survey of 439 industrial enterprises in Russia.[16] Of this sample (which was ranked by both industrial sector and region), over 60 per cent had been privatised, 25 per cent were still state-owned and 10 per cent were start-ups.

By 1995 most industrial enterprise had been privatised, but it all still needed restructuring. Access to capital for the development of existing companies and for new investments remained tight. This steered restructuring into crisis.

Interruption: national economic crisis (NEC)

The Russian financial crisis, also called 'Rouble Crisis', hit Russia in August 1998. It was caused mainly by the Asian financial crisis, which started in July 1997. Given the ensuing decline in world commodity prices, countries heavily dependent on the export of raw materials, such as oil, were affected. Oil, natural gas, metals and timber accounted for more than 80 per cent of Russian exports, leaving the country vulnerable to swings in world prices. Oil posed a special problem. The sharp decline in its price meant a shortfall of taxes paid by energy and manufacturing industries to the state. This helped to bring about Russia's default on its debt obligations in August 1998. A loss of investor confidence followed, leading to the devaluation of the rouble.[17]

The weakening of global demand and the unprecedented fall in prices caused a sharp fall in export earnings (by some 11 per cent year-on-year in the first half of 1998). This had a major impact on Russia's external and fiscal balances. The tightening of fiscal policy squeezed the economy further and in the second quarter of 1998 recession set in.

We now find ourselves in the first half of 1998. At this point, according to Rosstat, the consolidated budget deficit stood at 4.8 per cent of GDP, but the overall position was made considerably worse by extra-budgetary problems. The strain was palpable, though hard to analyse; however, it sapped confidence in the ability of the government to correct the situation and led to increasing difficulty in placing new debt. This was visible in July 1998, when Sberbank decided not to roll over and renew its portfolio of GKOs (short-term treasury bills). The economy understood this as a meaningful indicator of the fragility of the situation.[18]

In reply to the crisis the Russian government proclaimed a moratorium on new debt and converted short-term GKOs into longer-term debt instruments. This followed the previous (unsuccessful) attempt to exchange GKO holdings for longer-term debt issued in dollars. Despite the small level of international exposure to Russia, there followed a significant decline in prices on international financial markets, as well as substantial downward revisions in forecast levels of capital inflows to developing and transition economies. Noted also were unfavourable shifts in indicators of such economies' creditworthiness. One such concern was yield spreads on external bonds in secondary markets along with the tax shortfall from the important energy sector.[19]

Here the popular perception in the West is that the unwillingness of Russia's oil and gas companies to pay taxes is what required correction. Critics should remember that the Russian government insisted on uninterrupted provision of service (that is, no disconnection for non-paying customers). These effective cash loans to customers burdened oil enterprises with double taxation. In time, such pressure can cause a demonetisation of the economic system. Its impact then tends to impede the payment of wages and pensions. To deal with this highly political issue there usually follows sporadic efforts to pay off wage and pension arrears and this, in turn, grows into a systemic problem.[20]

Inadequacy of information and lack of transparency will generally not suffice as excuses for lag in a government's response. Many of Russia's troubles stemmed from times when the weaknesses in national macro-economic policies, the banking system and the underdeveloped legal and corporate governance frameworks were well documented. Despite these factors, capital flow was abundant – perhaps because the country was implementing the International Monetary Fund (IMF) stabilisation programmes.

Thus the presence of transparency, not the lack of it, may be seen as the cause of the 'Russian experience'. After all, it was transparency that influenced the behaviour of international lenders and investors. And it was transparency that alerted foreign investors to danger and impelled them to withdraw from the Russian economy. They doubtless discerned that a crisis loomed that was rooted in Russia's economic structure, Russia's institutional environment and Russia's political process. Yet the character of the crisis had much in common with others in the series of recent financial crunches in emerging markets. As elsewhere, the Russian crisis must be seen in the context of policy failure and abortive reform during the 1990s. Its unfolding reflected mismanagement of the opening of the country's financial markets to foreign lenders and investors. This foreign link left Russia vulnerable to the risk that domestic financial difficulties (such as those of the management of the market for government debt instruments) could develop into a full-blown currency crisis. And when it struck it served to highlight the interaction of weaknesses in external and internal economic policy attending the Russian government's efforts to transform a centrally planned economy into a market economy. For this the Russian public was fated to suffer.[21]

The consequences of the crisis notably included a lapse of confidence among external and internal investors. But there also obtained the tendency of FDI to escape from some national industries and the disappearance of external and internal sources of central-government budget-deficit financing, as well as the rise of inflation, the crisis in banking, the enfeebling of the Russian share market, the decrease in the national standard of living and the rise of social discontent: or, in two words, political instability.

In time, countervailing measures were taken. Imports were restricted and export stimulated; remonetisation was spurred with measures aimed at curbing cash transactions and barter; banking underwent yet another restructuring. Possibly as a result, the bank sector began to pay much closer attention to the real sector.[22] This sort of regime was familiar in regions outside Russia (excepting the EU), and it was in the former Soviet bloc, and particularly in post-Soviet Asia and Eastern Europe, that what was happening in Russia had the greatest effect.[23]

In the event, the recovery of Russia itself did not take long. As 1999 began, international interest in the Russian stock market remained low and trading sluggish. In fact, though, the low turnover was soon seen to undervalue Russia's natural wealth. When that was appreciated, speculative investment took off. Growth approached almost 200 per cent by the end of 1999, making the Russian commodity market the fastest growing in the world.[24] The ensuing year saw another doubling. The main reasons for the rapid recovery were a sharp increase in oil prices, which raised the value of exports, and a shift in the composition of imports that greatly helped to improve the trade balance.

Indeed, the precipitous rise in world oil prices in 1999–2000 contributed massively to large trade surpluses in those years. Also of help was the devaluation of the rouble. It allowed pricing of Russian goods that attracted foreign importers while, at the same time, raising prices of imported goods, discouraging Russian purchase of them. Almost incredibly, recovery was also spurred by the fact that, while still in a slump, the Russian economy operated to such a large extent on barter and other non-monetary instruments of exchange that the financial crash impacted many producers far less than it would have had the economy been more dependent on the banking system. Finally, the economy was helped by the burgeoning cash flow that resulted when enterprises became able to pay off back wages and taxes. This, in turn, allowed increased consumer spending on the goods and services of Russian industry. For the first time in many years, unemployment fell in 2000 as enterprises added workers. Since the 1998 crisis, the Russian government has managed to keep social and political pressures under control.

The devaluation fostered substantial import-substitution and export-promotion, placing Russia in step with global business. It was at this point that Russian business began putting its mind to cutting costs while investing to enhance operational efficiency.[25] This amounted to an incipient globalism of Russian business which has by now reached considerable depth. The presence of independent directors on corporate boards was a novelty that has taken firm root; the publication of financial statements and the increased availability of company charters are becoming more routine; dividends are being paid; and some companies now offer shareholder protection that is patterned on the best in the West.

Stage 5: integration into the global economy

As we have seen, rapid economic recovery after the NEC in 1998 was primarily due to the severe depreciation of the rouble. It provided Russian exporters with price competitiveness and also prompted import-substitution. As a result, since 2001 the Russian economy has been expanding briskly. GDP in the period 1999–2004 has grown at an average of almost 7 per cent per year in real terms. In 2003 and 2004 GDP grew by more than 7 per cent; in 2005 it was about 6.5 per cent; it returned to 7 per cent in 2006; and growth of 8.5 per cent followed in 2007.[26]

At the beginning of the 2000s virtually nobody foresaw such solid and rapid growth. When it actually transpired, it fuelled a lot of debate about the phenomenon's causes as well as its future outlook. Two main speculative views on this have since emerged, being noteworthy enough to appear in the works of Goldman, Colton and others.[27] The first mainly attributes the growth of the Russian economy to factors exogenous to pure economics, such as the rouble depreciation, or the surge in prices for oil and other minerals. It foresees an economy that will remain resource-dependent for some time to come. The second attaches more limited importance to exogenous factors, and instead emphasises the positive role played by government. In support it cites the tightening of budget control, improvement in tax enforcement, updating of customs and bankruptcy policies, curbing of the barter economy and deregulation of business. Hanson (2004) attributes the growth to success in the effort to create a general perception of stability and confidence in Russian business.[28]

Regardless of one's view, FDI played a key role. Both kinds, outward and inward, performed wonders, both in reviving the Russian economy and in setting its noteworthy growth pace in the period 2001–2007. In this period Russian outward investment rose via cross-border mergers and acquisitions (M&As). While M&A purchases by Russian MNEs grew healthily between 2001 and 2008, they soared more than tenfold in the subsequent four years, reaching 5,500 deals in the period 2001–2004 and 72,000 in 2005–2008.[29] Most of the acquisitions were in the primary sector (mining and extractive industries), which accounted on average for 60 per cent of investments. As for investments in services by Russian companies, their share of M&As increased to 34 per cent in 2001–2004, but then dropped to 16 per cent in 2005–2008. Within services, telecom was by far the most important industry, with 143 deals in 2005–2008.[30]

The inward FDI to Russia amounted to US$14.3 billion in 2001, rising to a peak of US$121 billion in 2007, the highest level recorded so far. The leading sectors of foreign investments in Russia were wholesale trade and commission trade, manufacturing, mining and quarrying. Top-investing countries during this period included Cyprus, the Netherlands, Luxembourg, Great Britain and Germany.[31]

To sum up, during 2001–2007 inward FDI to Russia from the international market (mostly EU) exceeded Russian outward FDI, whereas the flow between the Russian Federation and the CIS countries ran the other way. The main investors from the CIS in Russia in 2007 were Ukraine, Kazakhstan and Belarus, while OFDI from Russia was mainly concentrated on Belarus, Ukraine and Kazakhstan, in that order.

The recent challenge: world financial crisis

The impact of the world's financial crisis of 2008–2009 has been dramatic. Before its onset, outflow and inflow of the FDI had been favourable to Russia. That enabled increased capital investment and public sector funding, which included significant increases in infrastructure projects. A rapid increase of the gold and currency reserves was observed. As oil income spiked, expansion in the federal budget was possible. But socio-economic development continued to lag and tension zones in it lingered.[32]

The reasons for the crisis in Russia in 2008–2009 were multiple: the overheating of the consumer market, the loss of competitiveness of Russian goods due to the strengthening of the rouble caused by aggressive foreign investment in Russia; the overheating of the housing market; trouble with savings and loans; limited social growth; and the sudden flight of foreign capital as a result of the armed conflict with Georgia, which caused a liquidity and banking crisis in Russia.[33]

In 2008 the crisis passed through three stages: 'escape from overheating' (May to August 2008), 'projection of external shock' (September to October 2008) and 'crisis of internal economic policy' (after November 2008).[34] In the first stage, the main problem was overheated activity in municipal housing. Later on, the sudden outflow of foreign capital, frightened by the conflict with Georgia, resulted in a deep shock to the Russian stock market. In the second stage, this outflow quickly led to increased pressure on the balance of payments and the stability of the banking system. Simultaneously, a crisis in the real estate sector began to develop, in which the contraction of the raw materials market and the slump in prices for raw materials quickly brought on a crisis in export-orientated branches. The volume of investment in fixed capital began to plunge. In the third stage of the crisis we encounter contradictory monetary policy. There had been a turn to 'expensive money', while at the same time the rouble was gradually made to devalue. The inflationary effect of this was successfully curbed in late 2008 and early 2009. The exchange rate steadied and savings recovered.

As for the consequences of the world financial crisis for Russia, the positive ones were a renewal of the economy, the revival of entrepreneurial initiative, the increase in purchase of domestic goods and the development of competitive enterprise. Market competition picked up, resulting in lower prices for some goods, notably petrol and real estate. On the negative side were shrinkage of incomes, the devaluation of the rouble, the substitution of a considerable amount of private capital by public capital, a reduction in public infrastructure as well as construction, investment and mortgage programmes, plus aggravation of all this by a rise in interest rates for loans.[35]

Curiously, despite the global crisis, large multinational corporations did not shun investment in Russia. These included Coca-Cola, which planned to invest US$1.2 billion in the following few years; McDonalds, which announced plans to invest US$120 million in 40 new restaurants; and Wal-Mart, which continued to invest in expansion. The World Bank advised the Russian government on a large stimulus package and foresaw a gradual recovery of oil prices as well as a slowing of inflation, leading to modest economic growth in 2010. The World Bank also advised Russia to implement reforms aimed at raising productivity and improving its competitiveness.[36]

Metamorphosis: from state-owned to market economy

In the second half of the 1990s most of the largest companies in Russia were outsider-owned and had a large number of controlling shareholders holding more than 5 per cent. Foreigners held about 15 per cent.[37] Managers assumed firm control of their enterprises from the very beginning of transition processes. As the central planning system disappeared, interim control rights passed from the state to enterprise directors who had previously managed on the state's behalf. These same directors thus remained in control, but in their own right.

Reformers in the Russian government expected that, by introducing hard budget constraints, by exposing enterprises to the market and by chivvying state-owned enterprises to competition, they could bring about structural change (more private ownership) along with organisational change (better and more efficient management).[38] In the event, instead of this, the system and its structuring survived. Within enterprises networking and the sway of the director shaped management. It has been said that in Russia the bureaucratic way is seductive.

In the late 1990s, most of the enterprise in Russia was insider-owned and firmly controlled by managers, which has raised several questions concerning the performance of the enterprises during and after restructuring. Three major problems of insider ownership eventually surfaced: the difficulty in managing the supply chain; the difficulty of managing financing; and decision-making and corporate governance. Regarding finance, foreign investors typically require some control, or, if denied this, higher rates of return: or, if denied both, they refrain from investing. How to cope? As for decision-making, the diverse preferences of a heterogeneous workforce may lead to policies that are not value-maximising.[39] On the other hand, there may be benefits in the form of higher motivation and productivity, reduction of social conflict and augmented flexibility. How to decide?

In the transition economy managers owed employment to their effectiveness in lobbying the government for credits and investments and for their ability to create networks to ensure supply. Often, managers trained to the ways of a command economy and then appointed to manage newly privatised enterprises proved unable to oversee restructuring programmes.[40] The problem of the entrenchment of unqualified managers was exacerbated by the weakness of other corporate governance mechanisms. Boards of directors were usually dominated by old school managers or by government officials linked to them. General managers were also usually active politically and more willing to develop government support than to develop market-orientated efficiency.[41]

Though enterprises in Russia started restructuring only during the mid-1990s, general directors wanted to expand immediately and, in doing so, showed a strong bias toward increasing production. Only in few cases were restructuring plans based on objective analysis. Overarching it all was shortage of cash and high taxes.

In the first phases of transition the companies were generally preoccupied with de-politicisation, internal power struggles and shareholder control issues. They responded enthusiastically to the opportunities that novel legislation offered. The general pattern that evolved had management inventing means of securing the future of the enterprise: it looked for state support, consolidated monopoly positions, leased or sold off assets, engaged in parallel commercial and financial activities and looked for outside finance or outside partners, or alliances.[42]

Most Russian industrial enterprises were survival-orientated, a posture in which it is typical to sacrifice long-term profit for short-term survival. More emphasis is placed on current cash flow than on the long-run value of assets. The survival instinct of Russian enterprises was closely linked to the deterioration of network capital.[43] This should be seen as a residual effect of central planning, with its high degree of vertical linkage between enterprises.

Three elements in the strategies of post-Soviet enterprises were observed in different proportions in different firms and at different stages of their development.[44] The first element was the need to survive (survival-seeking), to which end primacy was given to devoting the enterprise's resources to securing the short-term survival of the enterprise as a unit of productive labour.

The second element was rent-seeking, in which senior managers were preoccupied with their personal interests. This often involved the diversification of enterprises, usually into financial and commercial lines. Links with subsidiary or associate companies figured in this, with managers milking these to their own profit. Such activity – such as, for example, selling the enterprise's products or assets to themselves at a discount price – often crossed the border of legality. The third element was market-orientated profit-seeking, targeted to the long-term profitability of the enterprise in the rising market economy.

In the reorganisation of enterprise, the first step usually consisted of expanding the commercial and financial branches of management, which play the leading role in adjustments to changing market conditions. Restructuring was typically associated with a dualistic management structure. The day-to-day management of the enterprise remained in the hands of the chief engineer and of production supervisors. They stood for the preservation and reinforcement of traditional authoritarian management and organisational structures. Management of the controlling or shareholding company was orientated toward the economic and financial direction and tended to favour a rent-seeking strategy.[45]

Enterprises in Russia operated in various types of networks, of which the two most typical ones were survival networks and entrepreneurial networks.[46] In the former, the enterprise manager oversaw a large survival structure in which political and market power were paramount. In the latter, the main interest of the enterprise manager was to improve market performance and profit. In Russia, survival networks compete with entrepreneurial ones, each prevailing or failing depending on whether they operated during the pre-, post-, or in-crisis periods of the national economy.

The economic system which has emerged in Russia as the first result of the transition process was a kind of virtual economy.[47] It was based on an illusion about almost every important parameter: prices, sales, wages, taxes and budgets. At its heart was the pretence that the economy was much larger than it really was.

In a Russian business priority is given to the development of a spirit of enterprise. Entrepreneurs need the ability to adjust to the market situation. Russian entrepreneurship, as a phenomenon, is not radically different from that in other countries. Entrepreneurs are mainly young and well-educated. Russia did have one big difference, however: would-be entrepreneurs still dwelt under the thrall of the country's historic heritage, the communist ideology and the absence of suitable business laws.[48]

Privatisation in Russia has created a system of insider-owned and controlled enterprises, mainly resource-based or defence-related to a larger degree than is seen in any other economy in the world. The nature of the Russian privatisation programme meant that pre-1991 insiders generally became significant equity owners, having played important roles in restructuring. These reflective attitudes resonate in the positions managers take on major issues, such as foreign investment, different forms of market entry open to foreign investors, acquisitions, or strategic alliances and/or joint ventures.[49]

Generally there were three basic forms of privatisation in Russia: leased buyouts, voucher privatisation and direct purchase by insiders. Only after business entrepreneurs ceased to be made owners by government appointment did mutual trust between free agents begin playing a significant role. It has been noted that the element of trust has greatly increased in importance in the new non-hierarchical model composed of self-made entrepreneurs.

To be sure, it did prove hard for the individual entrepreneur to gain privilege and success. Under the market system one's strivings could be contested by other players. Collective action, on the other hand, became seen as not only less costly but also more effective. Consequently, a bureaucratic regime began shaping up in the late 1990s and early 2000s. It led to both stronger concentration of market power and the vertical integration of enterprises in the form of conglomerates that possessed sufficient power to go nose-to-nose with crucial governmental bodies. The reason for this, of course, is that in the inter-conglomerate competition for power and resources such a course gets results.

Russia also has oligarchic enterprises. These emerged mostly from informal arrangements with the authorities. Every company maintained its own contacts with representatives of the state. The practice represented a kind of 'capitalisation' of such contacts. The routine of seeking proximity to representatives of authority, and the protection it offered, explains the opportunistic behaviour of oligarchic enterprise.[50]

In whatever guise, big business combined to ensure the protection of property rights by maximising the corporate value of share issues – and by securing additional protection by selling large blocks to foreign investors. In 1999, for example, foreign investment increased by 4.5 per cent, the first such growth since 1990. Investment growth has continued at a high rate from a very low base, with an almost 30 per cent increase in total foreign investments in 2001 compared with the previous year. As for FDI, which includes contributions to starting capital and credits, and which was extended by foreign co-owners of enterprise, this rose slightly in 1999 and 2000, but decreased again in 2001 by about 10 per cent. Foreign portfolio investment, which includes shares and securities, decreased dramatically in 1999, but has experienced slight growth since then.

As the spirit of enterprise gained hold, a certain degree of mutual distrust and a conflict of interest between business and state arose. There was never more than a precarious balance between the largest companies and the government. The trend now is toward governmental assertiveness. This has become especially clear in the area of natural resources and rent. Laws imposing taxes on mining and on product-sharing agreements betoken that. On the one hand, the authorities' imposition of a natural-resource rent was a way of angling for popular support; but, on the other, big business determined not to yield freely such value. Resistance proved strong enough to transgress legality.

While in the late 1990s there was an obvious dominance of big business over the state, by the summer of 2004 there had been a swing to absolute state domination, which is maintained by keeping the 'rules of the game' fuzzy – especially so in such fields as tax legislation and privatisation law.[51] When operating in such foggy conditions, every enterprise is bound to break some rules and is consequently condemned to dwell in the shadow of prosecution. Only when behaviour is 'correct' in the opinion of the government body concerned is transgression passed over.

Whether this situation can persist has come into question. Times are changing, and the social atmosphere in Russia is changing with them. This change is partly attributable to the mistakes made on the way to privatisation and to large-scale corruption within the system. It is so despite the fact that economic freedom in the 2000s improved on that of the 1990s, and that upward social mobility has increased. There has been a shift in the air from a 'state capture' model to a 'business capture' model, and a resultant increase in the importance of private businesses.[52]

The 2000–2007 period was characterised by the relaxation of business regulation, the development of the domestic market in Russia and a rapid process of transnationalisation. A number of laws concerning tax legislation were enacted, reducing the tax load on business from 34–35 per cent to 27.5 per cent. There was a tax load redistribution in oil. Thus the tax load on business has actually lightened slightly. It was also a period marked by high investment activity, including inflow of foreign investments. Average income and average consumption grew quickly, thereby stimulating demand and production. As a result, not only did Russia's energy sector prosper but so did manufacturing as a whole. As regards Russia's increasing globalisation, the main propulsive force here was the activity of MNEs, mainly giants such as Gazprom and Lukoil, two leading Russian oil and gas companies. During this period Russian companies began to embark on the transnationalisation of their investments.[53] The export of private direct investments grew consistently in the period 2000–2006, with 2007 following as the most successful year for FDI.

It should be noted here that Russian companies of renown have established themselves abroad as purchasers of assets there. In general, the expansion of Russian firms abroad was confined at first to a handful of companies in oil and gas, metals and mining, and telecoms, but the current trend involves other industries, with domestic telecoms companies such as VimpelCom and MTS and investment holdings such as AFK Sistema and Alfa group leading the way.[54]

The presence of Russian companies abroad has allowed the country to become counted in the company of other globalisers. International indicators now heed these enterprises. Despite this, the main aim of governmental support of Russia's globalisation – as an aid to the diversification of domestic industry – has not greatly succeeded.

Diversification was deemed important because of the country's excessive dependence on oil, gas and mineral resource rents.[55] This dependence was seen as the main cause of the 2008 crisis. But in fact other factors also contributed: the decline of export earnings from resource-based activities, over-leveraged balance sheets, credit and banking failures, a real-estate bubble, an outbreak of mortgage default, mounting capital flight and, of course, the rouble devaluation. The crisis thus produced soon affected the stability of Russian business. Many companies went bankrupt and whole sectors of the economy found themselves in danger of having to close down. As the crisis progressed there were predictions that the Russian economy might lose up to one-third of its SMEs, while the residue would be forced to throttle down production. And, indeed, companies did react by curtailing production, slashing wages and ordering lay-offs. Top companies were reporting a reduction in production for 2009 of approximately 20 to 30 per cent. The Russian government confined itself to supporting sectors such as the airline business, construction and development, oil and other exports, machine building, organisations of the industrial trade complex and agriculture.

The world financial crisis has strongly affected Russian companies. The effect has been negative for operations in both foreign and domestic business. Development in general, notably including internationalisation, has been slowed, especially in companies not active in the extractive sector or telecommunications, as those companies which survived to continue in business after the crisis had only just begun to get involved in the internationalisation process when the crisis struck.

The recovery of the Russian economy began in the third quarter of 2009, mainly in the area of export. In 2010 growth persisted. According to forecasts, the economy is to reach the pre-crisis level in the second half of 2012. Manufacturing sectors, especially that of consumer goods, and the construction industry (which suffered most grievously during the crisis) were likely to grow even slower than GDP. But, on the whole, company activity may be said to have recovered expeditiously. Russian manufacturing finished 2010 well: starting in August, new orders began increasing very fast. Some companies announced successful marketing campaigns conducted during that month. This was corroborated in the index covering the launch of new products and business.

Over time, though, recovery from the world financial crisis was slow and required governmental revitalisation measures. The competitiveness of Russian companies on the global market was seen to be in need of a boost, and work was carried out on the Russian image via changes in the country's institutional environment. Past policies of the Russian government were seen to be in need of repair, and relevant action was taken.

Russia's place in emerging markets

In attempting to decide whether the 'BRIC' group of countries still exists, and whether Russia is still a part of this group (in terms of general trends and value of economic performance and OFDI), one needs to take into consideration differences between the constituent countries. Brazil, China and India have proved to be more resilient in the crisis of 2008–2009 than Russia.

Brazilian, Chinese, Indian and Russian overall economy results

The term BRIC has been used since 2001 to refer to the countries of Brazil, Russia, India and China. They were considered to be at similar stages of economic development and some experts were arguing that, owing to population size, abundance of resources and speed of progress, they would in the next decades become more important power centres than current global leaders, such as members of the G7.[56]

Initially there was no thought of an alliance, but since 2009 the leaders of BRIC countries have converged closely enough to hold annual summits.[57] This has shown the need felt by their countries to put their common interests on international display. Of these interests, the overarching one is conversion of economic power into enhanced geopolitical status.

Outside BRIC there are also some countries which are developing quickly – most notably South Korea, Mexico, Turkey, Nigeria, Indonesia and South Africa. South Korea and Mexico were not included in BRIC because they already belonged to the OECD, while Turkey, Nigeria and Indonesia still had but small economies.

However, South Africa, which had not at that stage even reached the N-11 development stage, was invited to join, turning BRIC into BRICS. Its inclusion, however, is thought to have had more to do with politics than with commerce. Although its economy is much smaller than those of the other participants (under 50 million citizens; thirty-first in global GDP), the country is seen as an important gateway to growth opportunities in Africa, especially for Chinese and Indian companies. Above all, it testifies to an incipient trend toward economical and political bloc building. And it adds the third continent to BRIC geography. (South Africa is not considered here because this section deals with pre- and post-crisis situations – that is, a period in which South Africa was not yet a member of BRIC).

Currently BRIC countries have an 18 per cent share in world equity, which is expected to rise to 31 per cent in 2020 and 41 per cent in 2030.[58] It is predicted that in 2027 China will overtake the US in market capitalisation. In comparison, N-11 share growth is forecast to rise from 5 per cent now to 6 per cent in 2030. The forecast for BRIC is shown in Table 1.2.

Population and area are the most distinctive markings of a BRIC member. But economic heft, expressed in the number of multinationals, also counts. The 2007 Forbes list of 2,000 global companies included 109 Chinese (including Hong Kong), 48 Indian, 34 Brazilian and 29 Russian companies. In 2009, the list had 28 Russian companies with aggregated annual sales of slightly below US$0.5 trillion and assets of over US$1 trillion. However, their aggregated market value was much less – US$235 billion. That can be attributed to the consequences of the global economic crisis. BRIC companies were actively present in the Fortune 500 list and other global rankings.

Table 1.2 BRIC and the global economy

		1991–1994	*2000–2004*	*2005–2009*	*2015 (forecast)*
Population	BRIC	44.7%	43.6%	42.8%	41.8%
	Other EMEs	23.1%	23.2%	23.6%	23.9%
	USA	4.8%	4.7%	4.6%	4.5%
	Euro area	5.6%	5.1%	4.9%	4.6%
GDP	BRIC	5.8%	8.5%	13.1%	21.6%
	Other EMEs	10.6%	10.8%	13.3%	15.4%
	USA	26.2%	30.6%	25.6%	22.0%
	Euro area	24.8%	21.3%	22.0%	16.6%
Exports	BRIC	4.2%	7.9%	12.4%	20.1%
	Other EMEs	13.0%	15.8%	18.6%	18.3%
	USA	13.3%	12.0%	9.7%	9.6%
	Euro area	34.7%	30.9%	29.1%	23.0%
Imports	BRIC	4.0%	7.0%	10.5%	18.8%
	Other EMEs	14.4%	14.8%	17.2%	18.0%
	USA	14.6%	17.1%	14.1%	12.3%
	Euro area	34.0%	29.5%	28.5%	21.9%

Source: Goldman Sachs; Rosstat.

Notes: Values are averages for each period; EME: emerging market economy.

Table 1.3 displays the 18 largest economies of the world ranked by their GDP. All of the BRIC countries rank within the world's 20 largest economies. Nevertheless, their size differs substantially. The GDPs of India and the Russian Federation differ only slightly, whereas Brazil has a higher GDP. China's GDP is approximately four times as big as Russia's and India's.

In comparison with previous years, emerging economies (including BRIC) have grown substantially. Moreover, projected growth rates far exceed the forecasts for developed economies. According some of these forecasts, BRIC countries will be among the largest economies in the world by 2050, China being the largest of the world and India the third largest after the United States. Even though Russian and Brazilian growth forecasts are substantially lower, they will nevertheless rank as fourth and fifth largest economies.

The BRIC group has been pushing for reforms since the global financial crisis of 2008, arguing that the current system is unfairly dominated by advanced economies such as the United States, Japan and Europe.

According a study by Goldman Sachs, between 2000 and 2005 BRIC countries contributed roughly 28 per cent of global growth in US dollar terms and 55 per cent in Purchasing Power Parity (PPP) terms. Their share of global trade continued to climb at a rapid rate during the crisis.[59]

Trade among the BRIC countries has also accelerated, with intra-BRIC trade representing nearly 8 per cent of their total trade compared with 5 per cent in 2000. There have been numerous signs of developing trade relationships, including the sharp increase in Brazilian trade with China and Chinese investment in

Table 1.3 Top 18 largest economies ranked by GDP

Rank	*Country*	*(US$ billions)*
1	United States	14,256
2	Japan	5,068
3	China	4,909
4	Germany	3,347
5	France	2,649
6	United Kingdom	2,175
7	Italy	2,113
8	Brazil	1,572
9	Spain	1,460
10	Canada	1,336
11	India	1,296
12	Russian Federation	1,231
13	Australia	925
14	Mexico	875
15	Korea, Rep.	833
16	Netherlands	792
17	Turkey	617
18	Indonesia	540

Source: World Bank.

Brazil. India (in intellectual property) and Brazil (in agriculture) have also demonstrated their policymaking lead among developing countries by successfully developing links with the WTO.

BRIC members have played an important role in global financial development. Goldman Sachs estimates suggest that BRIC now holds more than 30 per cent of world fiscal reserves. China is the dominant holder, but Russia, India and Brazil have all accumulated substantial reserves. It remains to be observed that, despite this, the real exchange rate in each of these countries appreciated over the 2000s.

On an individual country basis, all of the BRICs and seven of the N-11 (Bangladesh, Egypt, Indonesia, Iran, Nigeria, the Philippines and Vietnam) contributed more to world growth in 2007–2008 than in 2000–2006.[60]

Between 2007 and 2009 Mexico, Russia and Turkey saw the deepest downturns in the two groups. These three countries had their economies shrink in 2009. China, India, Indonesia and Bangladesh experienced only relatively mild slowdowns.[61]

Goldman Sachs uses the so-called Growth Environment Score (GES) to measure the strength of a country's sustainable growth. In this regard the major mover within BRIC at the end of 2000s was Brazil. Not only was it one of the 35 best performers globally, but also it is now the highest-placed BRIC in the GES ranking. This gain was broad-based across sectors, with particularly strong advances in technology (mainly mobile telephony), as well as macro-economic and political conditions. This improved GES for Brazil is reflected in the widening acceptance of Brazil as deserving of BRIC status.[62] China's GES also improved, albeit mildly. It gained mainly on the technology and political condition fronts, but made no progress on human capital. A higher government deficit, higher inflation and a lower degree of openness partially blemished its overall performance.[63] India's GES declined modestly, which is noteworthy because it started as the weakest of the BRICs. The decline was largely due to the rising government deficit and inflation.[64] Russia's GES fell by the same amount as India's, although the causes for it differed. Most of the deterioration was attributable to a wobble in macro-economic stability, where all three components (technology and macro-economic and political conditions) deteriorated.[65]

In 2010 China's GDP rose by 10.3 per cent, India's by 8.9 per cent. Brazil had the highest growth rate at 11.3 per cent. Even at a relatively lower rate, the Russian economy grew faster than those of the United States (3.2 per cent), Japan (1.9 per cent), Germany (3.7 per cent) and France (1.7 per cent). Many developed countries are still struggling to recover growth rates after the recession. In contrast, Brazil's GDP growth rate increased dramatically to 11.3 per cent in 2010 after a recession in 2009 which was attended by a loss of 7.9 per cent.[66]

With regard to the GDP growth rate, comparative data from 2005 to 2010 from BRIC countries shows that China attained the highest sustained growth rate, with an average of 10.5 per cent annually, followed by India at 8.4 per cent. Russia posted the slowest growth, at only 5.2 per cent in the last quarter. (According to the Russian statistical agency Rosstat, gross domestic product rose in the second quarter of 2010 at a rate of only 5.2 per cent per year.)[67]

The industries absorbing the largest OFDI from BRIC are listed in Table 1.4.

Table 1.4 The largest industry recipients of investments from BRIC, 2005–2010

Country	*Sectors*
Brazil	Energy, mining, services
Russia	Oil, gas, metal, manufacturing, telecommunication
India	Pharmaceuticals, agriculture, software, IT, broadcasting
China	Trade, services, manufacturing, IT, extractive (oil, gas, minerals)

Source: Goldman Sachs; Rosstat.

BRIC countries invest abroad: recent trends

An overview of the recent OFDI development in BRIC countries, compared with OFDI from USA, is given in last three columns of Table 1.5. Although the 2008 financial crisis did not spare outward FDI in some countries, the statistics of the table testify to steady growth of OFDI in BRIC countries. Ten-fold jumps over the period 1995–2005 are not uncommon.

The largest sector for OFDI from BRIC economies was services, where companies from emerging economies became visible players in a wide range of fields, including financial services, hospitality (hotels, restaurants), telecoms and trading activities. The aggressive push of firms from China, India, Russia, Argentina, Malaysia, Chile and Turkey into natural resources (oil and gas, mining, metallurgy, electricity) was mostly motivated by a perceived need to secure current and future requirements. The OFDI from the manufacturing sector was mostly attributable to firms in the food and beverages, machinery and textiles sectors.

By 2005–2007 the global OFDI share of developing countries had increased significantly across a broad range of industries, reflecting a shift in the relative position of emerging market firms in global production processes. The global OFDI share of the developing region stood at 1.5 per cent in services, 7 per cent in manufacturing and 8 per cent in primary activities in 2005–2007.[68] There were 14 industries where developing economies' OFDI accounted for at least a 5 per cent global share and 6 where they commanded at least a 10 per cent share.

Table 1.5 Outward FDI stock of selected economies, various years (US$ billion)

	1995	*2000*	*2005*	*2007*	*2008*
United States	1,363.8	2,694.0	3,638.0	5,228.0	3,071.2
Hong Kong	78.8	388.4	471.3	1,011.2	775.9
Russian Federation	3.3	20.1	146.7	370.2	202.8
Brazil	44.5	51.9	79.3	136.1	162.2
China	17.8	27.8	57.2	95.8	147.9
India	0.5	1.9	10.0	44.1	61.8

Source: Panibratov and Kalotay 2009.

The broad trends described above appear to confirm the increasing internationalisation of emerging country firms as a genuinely long-term structural feature. However, ongoing research on individual emerging market OFDI from China, India, Brazil and Russia indicates wide diversity in internationalisation among the MNEs.

Russian multinationals started to invest abroad more recently than firms from India and China. With the important exception of a few companies, Russian OFDI is dominated by privately owned firms in natural-resource-based sectors and is narrowly focused on the neighbouring CIS countries.[69] Although the global economic and financial crisis did not lead to an absolute contraction in Russian OFDI flow between 2007 and 2008 – as happened for India – its growth rate, nonetheless, was reported to have fallen during 2009.

A good picture of the dynamics of BRIC OFDI can be gained by comparing three investment periods: before, during and after the financial crisis.

BRIC OFDI before financial crisis

On the whole, OFDI flows in BRIC countries were on the increase in the period preceding the crisis. Tendency varied by region. As of 2007, China and India both started challenging the dominance of Asia's traditional tigers (Hong Kong, South Korea, Singapore and Taiwan). Since 2004, China and India developed their share of the total outflow from the Asian region as a whole from 10 per cent to 25 per cent.[70]

Looking at each BRIC country in particular, China's OFDI was minimal during the first two decades of economic reform from 1978 to 2000. At the turn of the century, government policy switched from mildly permissive to strongly encouraging. By 2006 Chinese outward FDI stock reached US$73 billion, the sixth largest in the developing world. Some of this overseas expansion involved other developing and transition economies. For example, the first group of eight overseas economic and trade cooperation zones includes countries in Africa (Nigeria, Mauritius and Zambia), Asia (Mongolia, Pakistan and Thailand) and Eastern Europe (Kazakhstan and the Russian Federation). In 2007 China also established a government investment company to manage a US$200 billion fund tapped from the huge foreign currency reserve.

Although Indian OFDI pre-dates Chinese efforts (1960), India's restrictive OFDI regime limited them to private company efforts in small, minority joint ventures in developing economies. After 1991, several factors accelerated matters: intense domestic economic competition, the growing global competitiveness of Indian firms and liberalisations in OFDI and capital market policy. The sectors holding greatest appeal were IT, pharmaceuticals, telecoms, automotive, metal and services. In most of these, Indian companies have sought to become global leaders.

Three major structural shifts occurred in Indian OFDI during the past decade.[71] First, annual OFDI flows rose 50-fold, from US$340 million in 2000 to an average of US$18 billion in 2007–2008. India has become the world's twenty-first-largest outward investor. Its average annual OFDI flows are now higher than those of many developed market economies. Second, manufacturing has displaced services as the principal OFDI sector. It dominated Indian OFDI flows at the turn of the decade and now its share is the one that is growing quickest. While pharmaceuticals, consumer electronics and automotive accounted for the bulk of manufacturing OFDI in the first half of the decade, the second half has seen a concentration on metallurgy, energy and natural resource investments, as well as increasing activity in consumer goods as well as food and beverages. Third, over a half of India's total 2002–2009 OFDI flows went into developed economies, most of them in the form of M&As. In fact, since 2000, Indian firms have tended to use cross-border M&As as the main mode of entry into developed economies. For entry to emerging markets, they use greenfield investments. In other words, it is a double-barrelled strategy, via which Indian companies have systematically acquired leading developed-country firms. Such acquisitions capture domain expertise, technological competitiveness, market size and brand recognition.

Some of these acquisitions were undertaken to attain global size and status, and to build new competitive advantage by combining international technology or know-how with lower-cost Indian labour. Energy and mineral security have driven large greenfield investments in developing countries. Other areas (for example, telecoms, consumer goods, food, IT, metal and energy) are now also using M&A deals to build market presence.[72]

India's FDI outflows have thus boomed, with 2006 levels almost four times higher than those of 2005. Whereas Chinese FDI outflows used to be driven by state-owned enterprises and encouraged by proactive government policies, recent Indian investments have been made by private conglomerates, such as the Tata Group. As an example, Tata invested US$11 billion to acquire Corus Group (United Kingdom and the Netherlands) in early 2007, creating Tata-Corus, the world's fifth-largest steel maker by revenue.

The new FDI flows from Asia to developed countries are caused by the emergence of China and India as investors, coupled with active M&A activities by investors based in the Asian newly industrialised economies (NIEs) (particularly Singapore). During 2006, Asian investors became a driving force in the M&A boom in Europe. According to UNCTAD's *World Investment Prospects Survey*, South, East and South-East Asia were the regions most favoured by MNEs, followed by North America and the EU.[73]

In 2007, FDI outflows from Latin America and the Caribbean, excluding offshore financial centres, surged by 125 per cent to US$43 billion. The natural-resource-based sector was the main target of outward FDI, followed by manufacturing and telecommunications. Brazil was the region's principal source country, with US$28 billion in FDI outflows: the country's highest level ever with, for the first time, its outflows climbing higher than its inflows. The US$17 billion purchase of Inco (a Canadian nickel producer) by the country's mining company, CVRD, was responsible for a significant share of the increase. It was the largest acquisition ever undertaken by a Latin American company, and reflects CVRD's strategy of diversification away from Brazil and iron ore.

It is only recently that Brazilian companies started venturing abroad. From 2000 to 2003 OFDI averaged US$0.7 billion annually. From 2004 to 2008, this annual average jumped to nearly US$14 billion. During the financial crisis of 2008, when global FDI inflows fell by roughly 15 per cent, Brazil almost tripled its foreign investments; they exploded from just over US$7 billion in 2007 to nearly US$21 billion in 2008. Central Bank data puts the current stock of Brazilian OFDI at US$104 billion, an increase of 89 per cent over 2003.[74]

In addition, a series of other acquisitions and investments by Brazilian companies, such as Itaú (banking), Petrobras (oil and gas), Votorantim (cement, pulp and paper, steel and mining), Gerdau (steel), Odebrecht (construction services, petrochemicals) Camargo Corrêa (cement), Weg (motors and generators) and Marcopolo (buses), also contributed to the country's outward FDI. Apparently large Brazilian companies are pursuing a strategy of internationalisation through FDI. Much of Brazilian FDI traditionally flowed to offshore financial centres in the 2000s, but the trend over recent years has been for FDI to target developed countries rather than financial centres: their share in Brazil's total outward FDI stock jumped from 13 per cent in 2001 to 35 per cent in 2005, while that of developing and transition economies other than financial centres fell from 13 per cent to 8 per cent.[75]

In 2007 FDI from Eastern Europe countries increased for a fifth consecutive year, amounting to US$18.7 billion. Russia dominates here, accounting for 96 per cent of the total. Moreover, this was a significant increase (41 per cent) over 2005. The Russian FDI was largely commodities-based, although Russian banks also contributed their part. FDI outflows from other countries in the region remained modest in 2006 – less than US$1 billion.[76]

Russian FDI displays deeper and healthier drivers than during the pre-transition period of the 'red multinationals', when trading relations rather than productive facilities were OFDI drivers. Since a good part of the Russian OFDI derives from foreign takeovers by Russian companies, the dynamics of Russian OFDI can be followed using data on cross-border M&As. In the period January 2005–June 2008, M&As exploded more than ten-fold compared with 2001–2004, from US$5.5 billion to US$56.8 billion. Cross-border purchases were mostly in the primary sector (59 per cent of deals January 1997–June 2008), followed by manufacturing (23 per cent) and then services (18 per cent), where telecoms dominated.

Russian firms have generally targeted developed country investments, especially in Europe and North America. Of course, Russian investment has flowed bountifully to neighbouring CIS countries Belarus and Ukraine, followed at some considerable distance by fellow CIS members Kazakhstan and Armenia. For some of these countries, Russia is a major source of inward FDI.[77]

BRIC OFDI during the crisis

Global foreign direct investment had overcome a rough patch by 2000. In 2007, the value of such transactions amounted to US$1,637 billion, 21 per cent higher than the previous record in 2000. Cross-border M&As contributed substantially to the global surge in FDI, and this trend will continue as global companies consolidate. The sub-prime mortgage crisis in the United States did not have a visible dampening effect on global cross-border M&As. Large multinationals are the stable actors and wealthy sovereign funds the new on the FDI scene.

The global financial crisis began to bite into FDI flows in 2008. Most national policy changes continued to encourage FDI, although terms became less attractive. In South, East and South-East Asia and Oceania, both inward and outward FDI flows rose to their highest levels ever.[78]

By 2009, even though the global financial and economic crisis began fading, FDI flows were expected to fall to US$900–1,200 billion in 2009. The mix of FDI was shifting to the benefit of developing and transition economies (43 per cent in 2008). However, FDI flows to developing countries proved to be more resilient in 2008 and 2009 than other capital flows, such as portfolio investments and bank lending. The main reason for this was that FDI has more of a long-term nature than purely financial capital flows.[79]

China's OFDI stock reached US$246 billion by the end of 2009, well over eight times the US$28 billion recorded in 2000 and far above the negligible US$4 billion of 1990. In recent years, the spectral distribution of China's OFDI has remained stable. The bulk of China's investments goes to Asia, accounting for US$186 billion (76 per cent) of total OFDI stock in 2009. However, most (89 per cent) of that stock actually went just to one destination, Hong Kong (SAR China). Media attention worldwide, however, has focused on Chinese investments in Africa, which has risen sharply but was still less than 4 per cent of the country's global total OFDI in 2009.[80]

With a relatively small exposure to the US sub-prime market, China was less affected by the sub-prime crisis and its aftermath than the developed economies. GDP growth slowed as the country's export markets suffered, but remained strong owing to an early, large and fast-acting government stimulus package. With high cash reserves and ample support available from the government, China's MNEs continued to expand their overseas acquisitions. In 2008, when global OFDI flows fell by 15 per cent, Chinese OFDI flows more than doubled. But for the failure of one large M&A transaction (the Chinalco–Rio Tinto deal, with an expected value of US$19.5 billion), the result would have been an increase in China's total OFDI of 36 per cent.[81]

The global economic crisis jarred the outbound dynamism of the Russia economy. From 2007 to 2008 FDI growth still continued, but only by about 15 per cent (from US$46 billion to US$53 billion). In the first quarter of 2009, however, OFDI fell by 15 per cent (from US$16 billion to US$13 billion) on a year-to-year basis.

It seems that, despite mounting difficulty, the financial crisis has not stopped Russian companies from seeking to expand internationally. The going has been tough, since commodity prices fluctuated disturbingly and market capitalisation shrank. In 2009 there were no signs of the repatriation of Russian financial assets from abroad, notably from international financial centres such as Cyprus, the Netherlands, the British Virgin Islands and Gibraltar, which partly serve as tax havens for Russian firms. These locations still figured prominently in the OFDI flows of Russia in the first quarter of 2009.[82]

BRIC OFDI after financial crisis

Global FDI flows began to bottom out in the second half of 2009. The modest recovery in the first half of 2010 sparked some cautious optimism for FDI prospects.

In the longer term, the recovery in FDI flows is seen to be gathering momentum, with an expected US$1.6–2 trillion by 2012. However, these FDI prospects are fraught with risk linked to the fragility of the global economic recovery. Some major changes in global FDI patterns will probably gain momentum in the short and medium term. Firstly, developing economies will capture greater shares as both destinations and sources of global FDI. Secondly, the decline in manufacturing FDI, relative to that in the services and primary sectors, is likely to proceed. Thirdly, in spite of its serious impact on FDI, the crisis has not halted the growing internationalisation of production.[83]

After eight years of growth, FDI inflows to South-East Europe and the CIS shrank to US$69.9 billion in 2009, a 43 per cent decline from 2008. FDI inflows to both subregions dropped in 2009, although flows to the CIS were hit harder than those to South-East Europe. FDI flows to the Russian Federation almost halved owing to sluggish local demand, declining expected returns in projects related to natural resources and the drying-up of round-tripping FDI. Despite this bleakness, the Russian Federation still ranked sixth in the global ranking of top locations in 2009. Although cross-border M&As collapsed as a result of sluggish acquisitions by EU firms, investments from developing countries, China in particular, were on the rise. The contraction of FDI outflows from the region (–16 per cent) was not as severe as the decline in inflows.[84]

In 2009 the Russian Federation became a net outward investor, thanks to stronger commodity prices, a new round of privatisation and economic recovery in large commodity-exporting countries (Kazakhstan, the Russian Federation and Ukraine).

Before the crisis all four BRIC economies were becoming important sources of OFDI. BRICs firms were making direct investments abroad in developed countries as well as in emerging markets (developing economies and economies in transition). Brazil and Russia mainly invested in natural resources, while Chinese and Indian OFDI mainly focused on services. Indian companies were especially interested in knowledge-intensive industries such as automotive and pharmaceuticals. The performance of these ‘emerging outward investor countries’ was uneven, but perhaps suggested that they were revving up in preparation for take-off. For there had, in fact, been acquisition activity by BRICs in a number of developed countries, some of which succeeded while others failed (such as the attempted acquisition of Opel by Sberbank).

The globalised world economy is characterised by the liberalisation of trade and investment regimes. Companies can no longer withdraw into home markets as a relatively secure source of profits. Rather, competition from foreign firms has penetrated everywhere – through imports, inward FDI, non-equity forms of participation and so on. Emerging markets are beginning to recognise the importance of OFDI for their firms’ competitiveness and their economies’ performance. Some two-thirds of the OFDI stock of emerging economies is subsumed in five economies. A substantial share of this investment is in other developing countries, including countries in the same region.[85]

Owing to the need that is felt to strengthen corporate competitiveness, the motives for OFDI often begin with the desire to support trade – by buying nitty-gritty in the form of warehousing assembly plants, distribution networks and financial services (banking, insurance) – or to break into new markets. In the services sector, in particular, new markets can typically be opened only through investment (given the limited biodegradability of most services). Access to natural resources and cheap labour also plays a role for a number of firms, as does the desire to diversify risk.

Global OFDI rose from US$50 billion per year at the beginning of 1980s to an impressive US$2.1 trillion in 2007. Owing to the financial crisis, it fell by 10 per cent in 2008, to US$1.9 trillion. BRIC countries accounted for US$142 billion in 2008. By keeping pace with, and even outstripping, global growth, emerging market MNEs became important investors not only in developing countries but also in developed ones.

So, the main crisis factors and consequences for outward FDI from BRIC were the following:

- economic growth decline (which influenced the demand on home and target markets);
- FDI supply side problems (even if there was *where* to invest, there was not always *in what*);
- credit crunch (a large share of greenfield and M&A investments was supported by credit);
- tightening FDI policies worldwide (protectionism);
- outward FDI from BRIC countries significantly rose before the crisis, and substantially declined during it; now the flows and stocks are increasing.

The main outward FDI targets for BRIC countries were services (including trade support services) and natural resources companies.

While all four BRIC countries had strict restrictions on inward FDI, China and India have now developed programmes supporting their companies in the 'go global' policy (including OFDI). Russia and Brazil have not done this but instead are now less rigorous in their enforcement of the restrictions.

During the crisis some enterprises had to divest themselves of foreign subsidiaries and affiliates. But BRIC countries have comparably large proportions of state-owned companies, and their huge foreign currency reserves allow them use of long-term planning, thus leaving opportunities for OFDI.

Economic growth in host countries is what determines the scale of emerging MNEs' investment effort abroad. Outward FDI from BRIC decreased at a substantially lower pace than that of developed countries, and it also has recovered faster.

2 Multinational genesis

Russian multinationals grow and expand

In a mere flash of history, Russia has become a major outward-investing country on the global stage. The volume of its registered OFDI increased from US$2 billion in 1993 to US$203 billion in 2008, making it the second-largest among emerging economies behind Hong Kong (US$776 billion in 2008). Russian MNEs hold more assets abroad than Brazil (US$162 billion), China (US$148 billion) and India (US$62 billion) (see Table 1.5).

A number of Russian firms, such as Gazprom, Lukoil, Rusal and Severstal, have already attained global status. Others, such as Alfa Bank, Sitronics, Wimm-Bill-Dann and Yandex, are incipient MNEs.

Despite the fact that such Russian firms represent different industries and display divergent motivations and strategies, they do share at least two key characteristics. One is that they mostly deal in natural resources. The other is that they are strongly linked to the Russian government and thereby profit from the growing supportive role of the Russian State.

Understanding the phenomenon of Russian MNEs

While the theory of internationalisation was originally seen to apply only to developed countries (mostly European ones and the US), there have been several attempts to test its applicability to less-developed markets. Outward FDI and emerging economies' MNEs were investigated in pioneering studies by Heenan and Keegan (1979), Lall (1983) and Wells (1983), and more recently in Benito and Narula (2007), Globerman and Shapiro (2006), Goldstein and Shaw (2007) and Luo and Tung (2007).

Similarly, various international organisations (OECD, UNCTAD, World Bank) have kept track of the internationalisation of firms from emerging economies over the span of the last decade. World Investment Reports, EIU Country reports, UNCTAD papers and publications of Columbia University and Bank of Finland illustrate the increasing spread of interest in the emerging-market MNE (EMNE) phenomenon.

MNEs from developed economies concentrate on advanced technology and marketing skills to lend distinction to their products[1] and to buttress their struggle for competitive advantage. They strive to expand their palette of assets as well as integrate operations across national boundaries.[2] EMNEs, in contrast, rely mostly on tweaking technologies originally developed in Western countries. EMNEs appear to attain a competitive edge by application of appropriate managerial skill.[3]

According to Luo and Tung, EMNEs use international expansion as a springboard to: 1) become more competitive; 2) overcome a latecomer handicap; 3) counteract rival MNEs' activity in their home market; 4) bypass tight trade barriers; 5) alleviate domestic institutional constraints; 6) secure preferential treatment offered by emerging-market governments; and 7) exploit competitive advantage in other emerging or developing markets.[4]

FDI flows towards less developed countries have not always produced the sort of long-term growth that should be expected, however.[5] Russia, along with other transition economies, has a fundamental problem: it has few alternatives to FDI in the quest for outside capital, know-how and networking. Countries in transition, in many respects, appear to be closer to developing, rather than developed, economies when it comes to their particular experiences with hosting FDI.[6]

To be sure, FDI is not a cure-all. It is questionable, for example, whether firms in transition countries benefit much from the technological superiority lent by foreign investors – though this usually does hold true for developed host countries.[7] Both pioneering and established EMNEs gain from their natural-resource vertical integrator status. Controlling upstream and downstream industrial activities gives these EMNEs market strength. Russia's Gazprom and Lukoil, and Brazil's Vale, exemplify this.[8]

Most research in the field of EMNEs has focused on their outward FDI. Such outflows from emerging economies are different in terms of motives, goals, preparation of deals and results obtained from the investments that established MNEs in developed markets make in emerging markets.[9]

The study of emerging multinationals covers a great deal of ground. Generally, though, the focus has been on Chinese, Indian and Brazilian EMNEs, rather than on those of Russia. Studies of Russian EMNEs began to appear at the end of the 1990s, but there have not been enough of them to cover the field satisfactorily.[10]

Outward FDI from Russia started to grow in the second half of the twentieth century. Its progress, however, was slow and its depth modest. At the end of 1983, Soviet firms had about 320 affiliates in foreign countries,[11] a tiny figure considering the large size of Russia's economy. These affiliates were often registered as joint ventures and were mostly situated in neighbouring Council for Mutual Economic Assistance (CMEA) countries. There were about 115 affiliates in OECD countries and 30 in developing countries. In 1990, the value of Soviet OFDI abroad amounted to less than US$1 billion.

Prototypes of today's multinationals date back to the time of the Soviet Union. In China, too, the beginnings hark back to Communist days, long before these same multinationals came to be partially or wholly privatised.[12] In his 1986 study of foreign operations of Soviet firms (which were all state-owned), Geoffrey Hamilton refers to these companies as 'red multinationals'. His observations showed that in most cases these companies carried out only marketing and sales operations. A few of the 'red multinationals' eventually adopted the practices of Western multinationals.[13]

The USSR exercised strict control of its multinationals, and usually owned them.[14] It had them engage in supporting Russian exports (raw-resource marketing, infrastructure support, banking, insurance and so on). These first-generation Russian MNEs conducted their activities very intensively, selling more than 50 per cent of total Soviet exports.

One of the pioneers in the research of this field, Detelin Elenkov, investigated the role played by the military in the internationalisation of the Russian economy. Concerning the non-military sector, he noted its bumbling and bungling resulting from bureaucratisation, corruption and just plain inefficiency. The military sector's mark was its practice of financing organisations rather than projects.[15] This created a tendency to allocate budget according to the size of an organisation, while technological viability and profitability were allotted secondary importance. The non-military sector operated with obsolete technology, owing to the lack of strong technical staff and the limited access to advanced R&D. The military did not have such problems.

The crash of the Soviet Union brought about disruption in Russia's economic activity. Recovery from this shock and adaptation to what followed took almost ten years. During this period, Russian companies cleaned up the shambles of the Soviet enterprises, mostly engaged in restructuring, privatisation notably included, and consolidation of assets inside the country. Only after having done that did they set forth to explore foreign markets.[16]

Kuznetsov points out that inward FDI from MNEs enabled Russian companies to reinforce their own investment activities via that foreign capital participation.[17] It took until the eve of the 1990s for Russia's FDI to pick up pace. Or, as a British periodical chose to see it, 'until 2000, Gazprom and Lukoil accounted for around 90 per cent of Russian assets abroad'.[18] When change did come, it mainly took the form of cross-border mergers and acquisitions. Greenfield investments also played a role, but on a much smaller scale. These actions reflected the habit of Russian investors to go for the quick return and their impatience with the sort of enterprise based on solidly acquired experience.

Kalotay suggests that oligarchic structuring, incorporating the strain of statism prevalent in Russia, may have something to do with Russia's perky OFDI flow. He observes that the oligarchic investing pattern also happens to be the one followed by countries at a higher stage of development than attends Russia's fellow members of BRIC.[19] There are also stimuli for Russian capital to venture abroad, partly because of the government's inhospitality toward domestic business and the incentives it offers business to internationalise.[20] Even though Russia now has the largest OFDI among BRIC countries, the performance of its multinationals has been largely overshadowed by the emergence of Indian and Chinese MNEs, and as a result it is not sufficiently addressed in the literature.

Trying to determine whether Russia really fits into BRIC obliges one to consider the differences between its members. When that is done it at least comes clear that the economies of Brazil, China and India did better in protecting their MNEs from the downturn of 2008–2009 than did Russia. Nevertheless, all the MNEs of the four members of BRIC continue to evolve from regional multinationals into global multinationals.[21]

Nowadays emerging markets show very lively activity in the field of internationalisation. The Russian market, for example, is considered by most potential entrants as offering great opportunities, and the ways in which Western MNEs entered the Russian market have become the subject of wide study. Inward FDI from Western MNEs was principally based on the following models: a foreign company with money to invest seeking transparent projects; a foreign investor entering the Russian market with its own project and own management but then going into business networking with local firm(s); a company studying the optimal entry mode to Russian market via a marketing office, sales subsidiary or modest export before more FDI-intensive projects; and, quite frequently, a Western company choosing a local partner to help in preparing to manufacture in Russia.

MNEs that entered the Russian market at the beginning of the transition processes are now the leaders in their segments. All the risks and difficulties which these firms faced during the initial stages have been overcome. The surviving companies – for some departed after failing – have attained profitability. MNEs that succeeded in taking hold in Russia managed to do so only after conducting purposeful and persistent marketing. At the heart of the chosen entry strategies to the Russian market were: orientating to high quality; adapting marketing policies tailored for Russia; and fostering local partnerships.[22]

Regarding international springboarding, Luo and Tung advise inward investment before undertaking outward FDI; leapfrogging; and co-opetition (i.e. competitive cooperation) with global players.[23] Companies in emerging economies wishing to enter foreign markets should introduce new marketing, practice locally acceptable human-resource management, select appropriate technologies and develop unique projects.

Outward FDI from Russia: motives and destinations

Russian multinationals like to invest abroad. Many studies have covered this topic, and most of the research has focused on the interest of these MNEs in diversifying their holdings through international investment. Most of the companies analysed are in select industries (oil and gas, metallurgy and telecoms).

OFDI from Russia is often compared to an 'escape valve', whereby firms invest abroad owing to the negative characteristics of the Russian business environment. Business conditions are not the only cause, however; OFDI also appeals to profitable Russian firms (with free cash flow and retained earnings) that invest abroad to enjoy higher expected rates of returns.[24]

Starting from a relatively low base, the strong FDI inflows into Russia in the period 2006–2008, were equal to, or even outpaced, those of other BRIC countries. According to the Economist Intelligence Unit, by 2009 the estimated inward FDI-share-of-GDP in Russia was similar those of to Brazil and China. Russia also had the highest FDI per capita among the BRICs.[25] As outward FDI from Russia reached US$52 billion in 2008, the dominance of Russia in the CIS region became internationally orientated; only India dominated in the South Asia region to a comparable degree (Table 2.1).

Recent data on Russian outward FDI is even more impressive. OFDI flow reached US$10.3 billion in the first quarter of 2010, according to the Russian Central Bank (Table 2.2), having amounted to US$46.1 billion in 2009, showing that the dynamics of OFDI remained stable in 2010 in spite of the crisis. At the same time, over a half of outward FDI by non-banking corporations went offshore (Cyprus, the Netherlands, Gibraltar, Luxemburg, Switzerland and the British Virgin Islands), lending this aspect of foreign investments a pseudo-FDI quality. This demonstrates that capital flow need not be synonymous with capital flight.

Table 2.1 FDI flows, by region and economy, 2006–2008 (US$ million)

Region/economy	*FDI inflows*			*FDI outflows*		
	2006	*2007*	*2008*	*2006*	*2007*	*2008*
World	1,461,074	1,978,838	1,697,353	1,396,916	2,146,522	1,857,734
Developed economies	972,762	1,358,628	962,259	1,157,910	1,809,531	1,506,528
European Union	590,305	842,311	503,453	697,193	1,192,141	837,033
USA	237,136	271,176	316,112	224,220	378,362	311,796
Developing economies	433,764	529,344	620,733	215,282	285,486	292,710
CIS	44,657	78,074	103,481	23,328	50,125	57,862
Russia	29,701	55,073	70,320	23,151	45,916	52,390
South and Central America	69,014	105,996	121,418	45,101	26,266	37,255
Brazil	18,822	34,585	45,058	28,202	7,067	20,457
East Asia	131,769	150,353	186,982	82,301	111,176	136,156
China	72,715	83,521	108,312	21,160	22,469	52,150
Hong Kong, China	45,054	54,365	63,003	44,979	61,119	59,920
South Asia	27,758	33,982	50,669	14,871	17,758	18,182
India	20,336	25,127	41,554	14,344	17,281	17,685
South-East Asia	54,967	69,482	59,923	23,298	45,805	32,117
Singapore	27,680	31,550	22,725	13,298	24,458	8,928

Source: UNCTAD 2009.

Table 2.2 Foreign direct investment flows from Russia (US$ billion)

	2009					*2010*
	1 Qtr	*2 Qtr*	*3 Qtr*	*4 Qtr*	*Year*	*1 Qtr*
Inward	9.4	10.1	12.4	7.0	38.7	9.9
Outward	13.6	11.6	9.8	11.0	46.1	10.3

Source: Russian Central Bank.

The motives of Russian outward investment vary significantly. It is not surprising that the most typical investment motives of Russian MNEs are the search for markets and resources. In addition, some investments are of the strategic-assets-seeking kind, and are rarely efficiency-seeking. Sometimes, OFDI from Russia is driven by image-building concerns or domestic political risk prevention.[26]

The variety of OFDI is demonstrated by top Russian deals (Table 2.3). Keeping in mind John Dunning's 'OLI' paradigm, which identifies ownership, location and internalisation as the three important drivers of internationalisation,[27] it can be clearly seen that Norilsk Nickel and Evraz rely on ownership advantage, Lukoil and Alfa Group on their location advantage, and Basic Element and Yandex on the internalisation of knowledge (when importing technologies from foreign markets into Russia).

While some Russian MNEs have affiliates almost throughout the world, overall historical and cultural ties as well as geography significantly affect outward investments. It is tempting to thus explain the concentration of Russia's OFDI in the CIS region. Moreover, the pull of other continents on Russian investors is flimsy. Latin America is seen as a far-away underdeveloped region, with institutional barriers such as the lack of bilateral double-taxation and investment treaties. African countries are *terra incognita* to Russian companies.[28] India and China, however, are more familiar and therefore attract more investment.

The scale and the sectoral distribution of Russian investors are functions of the longevity of companies' presence in an economy. As a rule, the longer a Russian firms has been in operation the better its international experience and results. On the other hand, recently established firms do also internationalise, and thus established successors of Soviet multinationals can nowadays be seen working side by side with companies which began internationalising only recently.

The prominent outward investment activity of Russian companies in oil and gas and metallurgy (who control the bulk of their country's foreign assets) meant that these companies represented areas of Russian specialisation in the world economy.[29] Only belatedly have companies specialising in electricity, food, defence, telecoms, electronics and the Internet started expanding internationally, but they can now be found amongst the most prominent Russian investors abroad. (Such companies are considered in following chapters of this book.)

Classic MNEs still dominate the Russian multinational scene, but important foreign assets are also held by some companies outside this classification, such as those that exploit transnational economic ties within the former Soviet area, like Gazprom or Inter RAO UES (a subsidiary of Russia's energy giant RAO UES that was established specifically to manage the international operations of the firm). The steel firms Severstal and Rusal invest in the most developed markets, but it is unclear whether their intention is to facilitate transfer of foreign technologies into Russia or to help capital flight.

Fluctuations in the geographical priorities of Russian multinationals have also been studied (Table 2.4). According to Kuznetsov, these firms evolve from intra-regional multinationals (which operate within the CIS area) or bi-regional multinationals (the CIS plus the European Union) into global multinationals.[30]

Table 2.3 Ten largest M&A deals by Russian MNEs, 2005–2008[1]

Year	*Acquiring Russian company*	*Target company*	*Target industry*	*Target country*	*Shares acquired (%)*	*Estimated/announced value (US$ million)*
2007	Norilsk Nickel	LionOre Mining	Gold ores	Canada	100	6,287
2008	Evraz Group	IPSCO	Steel pipe and tubes	Canada	100	4,025
2007	Gazprom	Beltransgaz	Natural gas distribution	Belarus	50	2,500
2008	Evraz Group	Sukhaya Balka GOK	Iron ores	Ukraine	99	2,189
2008	Lukoil	ERG SpA – ISAB Refinery	Oil and natural gas	Italy	100	2,098
2007	Evraz Group	Oregon Steel Mills	Steel works	United States	90	2,088
2005	Lukoil	Nelson Resources	Gold ores	United Kingdom	100	2,000
2007	Basic Element	Bauholding Strabag	Industrial buildings	Austria	30	1,637
2005	Alfa Group	Turkcell	Telecommunication	Turkey	13	1,602
2007	Basic Element	Magna International	Motor vehicles	Canada	18	1,537

Source: UNCTAD, cross-border M&A database, http://stats.unctad.org/fdi/.

1 Panibratov and Kalotay 2009.

Table 2.4 Russian OFDI to 'Western' and 'Eastern' economies (US$ million)

	2007		*2008*		*2009*	
Destination	*Value*	*%*	*Value*	*%*	*Value*	*%*
World-wide	45,211	100	54,202	100	44,868	100
Non-CIS countries	41,967	93	51,789	96	41,760	93
CIS countries	3,244	7	2,413	4	3,109	7

Source: Bank of Russia data, 2010.

Overall, the appearance of non-European countries (such as Canada, India, the United Arab Emirates and the USA) among the most important destinations of Russian OFDI testifies to the spread of Russian companies' internationalisation (see Chapter 3).

Industrial perspectives of internationalisation in Russia

Starting in the early 1990s, Russia changed from a rigid centralised economy into an emerging-market one. This entailed a change in management styles from Eastern to Western trim and an adoption of international management standards. Some laissez-faire creep resulted. As a result, the grizzled successors of Soviet multinationals may now be doing business side by side with newbie private companies that began internationalising only yesterday, comparatively speaking. While the energy- and natural-resource-based companies own the bulk of Russian assets abroad, many other Russian industries, as noted above, have begun investing there. Companies in machinery, electricity supply, food, transport, telecoms, pharmaceuticals, electrical equipment and financial services are now to be found on the list of top Russian investors abroad.

In this section we will deal with the variety of internationalisation in Russia. The selection of industries to be treated is confined to those with clear relevance to the topic, but which are not treated in the subsequent chapters; and, in the interests of clarity, discussion is confined to three groups of industries, all of which enjoy a high degree of internationalisation. The first group is manufacturing (automotive and pulp and paper); the second is services (air transport and logistics); and the third a 'virtual' group (media and education) – so termed because it covers enterprise without kickable assets.

Of these, airlines, carmakers and media tend to be highly outward-drawn, while paper companies, supply chain companies and universities tend to be stay-at-homes.

Special attention, moreover, will be paid to the construction industry, which is unique in that it likes to wander as well as stay at home. Significantly, it both manufactures and services. Putting it dramatically, construction is a rare *omnium gatherum* that cries out to be covered.

Automotive industry

In 2007, Russian automotive sales grew 35 per cent, to 2.8 million cars, compared with the previous year. Russia is thus the second-largest market in Europe after Germany. Over the five years prior to the world financial crisis, the demand for cars increased five-fold in value, from US$10 billion in 2002 to more than US$53 billion in 2007. The main reasons for such rapid growth include steady increases in personal disposable income, better access to car financing and expansion of sales outlets and dealership chains across the country.

Government forecasts indicate that the Russian car park, currently around 28 million vehicles, will grow to between 55 and 75 million vehicles by 2020. This growth is accompanied by a transformation of the market's structure. Russian car manufacturers are losing market share to foreign brands, which either import or assemble locally. These foreign brands accounted for 78 per cent of the market by transaction value in 2007. This is not surprising, considering that the government offers tax breaks to companies that start major assembly lines in Russia. Global brands such as Ford, General Motors, Hyundai, KIA, Mitsubishi, Nissan, PSA Peugeot, Renault, Suzuki, Toyota and Volkswagen are already assembling in Russia, or are building plants that will be doing so. Unless something unexpectedly harmful happens, in the next decade domestic production of light vehicles could double, and the greater part of them will be Western-branded.

The Russian new-car market shrank by 45–47 per cent in 2009 but nonetheless posted a value of about US$19.1 billion, representing a compound annual growth rate (CAGR) of 5.9 per cent for the period spanning 2005–2009 and a volume of 1,432,000 units in 2009. Russia accounts for 4.9 per cent of the European new-car market's value. Its carmakers generate 35.3 per cent share of the total new-car market's volume.

Automobile manufacturers

The 'Big Four' Russian auto companies are AvtoVAZ, GAZ, UAZ and Sollers. AvtoVAZ is primarily involved in the production and sale of passenger automobiles and car components internationally and throughout Russia. It is headquartered in the Samara region of Russia, where most of its manufacturing facilities are, and has around 130,000 employees. The VAZ factory is one of the biggest in the world, with over 90 miles (144 km) of production line, and is unique in that most of the components for its cars are made in-house. This is a far cry from the Toyota model of independent partner-suppliers.

AvtoVAZ operates two divisions: automobile and financing. The automobile segment produces and sells vehicles, assembly kits and components, both of their own make and for other producers. The financing segment operates a subsidiary bank, AVB.

AvtoVAZ was one of the first Russian carmakers to compete with Western ones. Having gone into production in 2001, it still turns out Chevrolet-branded cars through its joint venture with General Motors. A main aim of the sale to Renault of a 25 per cent stake in AvtoVAZ in 2008 was to revive the flagging Lada brand.

GAZ, another large automaker, has about 110,000 employees and is headquartered in Nizhny Novgorod. The company manufactures passenger cars and other vehicles (vans, buses, trucks, jeeps, armoured cars, tanks and station wagons) as well as combustion engines for the automobile industry. The GAZ Group comprises 18 enterprises in Russia, as well as the LDV Group in the UK.

UAZ is an off-road vehicle manufacturer. The company produces mainly SUVs, buses and trucks for the Russian market, as well as for markets in various developing countries. The company employs some 25,000 persons and is headquartered in Ulyanovsk. Severstal, the largest Russian steel maker, controls UAZ via its subsidiary Severstal-AvtoTatarstan. Around 20 per cent of UAZ vehicles are exported.

Sollers is a Russia-based company that manufactures off-road and sports utility vehicles, light trucks and minibuses. The company also manufactures agricultural equipment, special-purpose vehicles and engines for off-road vehicles. It provides a finance service through its subsidiary, Sollers-Finance. Its other subsidiary, Trade House Sollers, runs its own dealership network. The company primarily operates in Russia and is headquartered in Moscow.

Russian cars sell very poorly abroad. Noteworthy exceptions include an order for 3,000 of UAZ's basic Hunter jeeps for the Afghan police force and a large order of GAZ's Volga-brand vehicles for Baghdad's burgeoning taxi fleet. However, Russia better internationalises in trucks.

Trucks and tractors

The Russian truck market shrank by 51.2 per cent in 2009 to a value of about US$2.5 billion. It accounts for 3.9 per cent of the European trucks market in value. In comparison, French trucks account for 22.7 per cent. Russia accounts for 4.3 per cent of European light trucks and 3.5 per cent of European medium and heavy trucks.

KamAZ is a Russian manufacturer located in Tatarstan, Russian Federation, employing about 48,000 people. KamAZ Inc. ranked eleventh among the world's heavy-truck manufacturers and eighth in the world in the production of diesel engines. As an eight-time winner of the Dakar Rally in the truck category, KamAZ is well known worldwide. Every second truck produced in Russia or the CIS is a KamAZ. Its biggest customers in Russia are the Russian Ministry of Defence, Gazprom, Lukoil, SUEK and TNK.

KamAZ is active in partnerships with foreign companies, the aim being to share technology and expertise. Sales of KamAZ vehicles and spare parts are expanding throughout the world. Some of its newer markets are Saudi Arabia, India, Chile and Nicaragua. The company has been increasing its activity in Iran, Sudan, Afghanistan and Angola. Following a hiatus, it has now resumed selling to Venezuela and Panama. In 2007 it exported 13,500 vehicles (25.5 per cent of its total production). The company exports every fourth truck made.

Among the partners of KamAZ are the German company Knorr-Bremse AG, which produces electronic brake systems (in 2007 the joint venture Knorr-Bremse–Kama was established), the transmissions manufacturer Zahnrad Fabrik (in 2005 the joint venture ZF Kama was launched) and American Federal Mogul Corporation, which makes engine parts for KamAZ. In addition, America's Cummins Inc. went into production in Naberezhnye Chelny, making diesel engines for KamAZ trucks.

KamAZ has assembly plants in Vietnam, Iran, Kazakhstan, Pakistan, North Korea and India. It plans to open new facilities in China, Sudan and Venezuela. In its assembly plants only self-made components are used. In its foreign ventures the company agrees with its partners on the degree of local production and assembly. The key future markets are India, Kazakhstan, Pakistan and China.

In 2008 KamAZ established a joint venture with an Indian partner, Tata Vectra Motors, covering the assembly, sale and service maintenance of cars, with 74 per cent of the joint venture belonging to KamAZ. The joint venture is sited in the city of Hosur on ground belonging to Tata Vectra Motors. The new enterprise aims to become the flagship of Russia's truck production abroad. It is expected that the production cost of KamAZ vehicles in India will undercut Western competition.

Also in 2008 KamAZ officially announced another new joint project: assembly of KamAZ trucks and buses in Karachi (Pakistan). The planned maximum capacity is 500 vehicles a year. The plant was created with the assistance of Bibojee Services Limited, one of the oldest automobile holdings in Pakistan, which manufactures cars, trucks, bus chassis and tyres.

KamAZ also has a long history of sales in China. Trucks and special equipment were sold there during the Soviet period. To 1992 it had sold China over 50,000 cars,[31] after which year things changed. Rapid growth of the Chinese car industry, combined with problems at home starting in the mid-1990s, led to a loss of market share, and since 1996 sales in China have practically ceased.

KamAZ regained interest in China in 2002 as matters improved domestically, and as the Chinese automobile market (including its truck segment) suddenly opened to growth. After some negotiating two joint ventures were created (Tangshan–KamAZ and Mu-dantszjan–KamAZ). But difficulties then arose which led KamAZ to withdraw. KamAZ complained that Chinese requirements, as well as restrictions on its management role, had become unacceptable. The Russians balked at Chinese insistence on the preponderant use of Chinese parts, along with the demand of a controlling stake in the partnership.

KamAZ's most recent international projects of significance are joint ventures with Germany's Daimler and Italy's Case New Holland. The agreement with the German company Daimler AG foresees the creation of two joint truck-assembly ventures under the brand names of Mercedes-Benz and Fuso. An investment of almost 20 million was agreed on.[32] The deal contains a provision whereby Daimler promised to purchase 15 per cent of KamAZ shares from Troika Dialog, owner of 44 per cent of KamAZ shares.

Daimler thus gains access to the Russian market through the extensive KamAZ dealer network. The Russian company, in turn, gets access to technologies and competences in niches of freight motor transport in which KamAZ lags. One joint venture will specialise in the manufacture and sale of light trucks. Here the brand name is to be Fuso Canter, and product will be niched in the 3–7.5 tonne range. The second joint venture will engage in the assembly of heavy trucks,

Mercedes-Benz Actros and Mercedes-Benz Axor. Daimler seems to have gone for the deal because development of its own manufacturing facilities would have required too large an investment. In addition, there was urgency to get started because Daimler's competitors already had Russian assembly projects going.

In the autumn of 2009 KamAZ signed a partnership agreement with machine-builder Case New Holland (CNH), a part of the Fiat Group,[33] to manufacture agricultural and construction machinery. This would allow KamAZ to enter what is, for it, a new line, while splitting investment and risk with its foreign partner. The new 50–50 joint venture will make some models under the CNH brand, including agricultural tractors T9040 and T805, combine harvester CX7080 and dredge-loader LB115B. Assembly is to be sited at KamAZ's Naberezhnye Chelny facility. CNH will bring to the joint venture technology and know-how, an existing distribution network, access to an extensive base of suppliers and its established brand.

Pulp and paper industry (PPI)

The global pulp and paper industry is dominated by North American (United States, Canada), northern European (Finland, Sweden) and East Asian countries (mostly China and Japan). Australasia and Latin America also have significant pulp and paper industries. India and China are expected to play key roles in the industry's growth in the near future.

Papermaking is a large, capital-intensive industry, characterised by machines which operate at close tolerances and high speed. A complex and costly system of control is therefore required in the manufacture of products for education, administration, communications, marketing, packaging and construction. The industry's global annual revenue exceeds US$500 billion in value and over 300 million tonnes in production volume.

The pulp and paper industry is highly capital-intensive. Firms in it participate in a significant number of M&As, presumably with the objective of consolidating their position in the market as well as achieving economies of scale and scope. To stay in touch with industry developments, firms must continually invest to modernise, innovate and implement changes in the supply chain and in organisational structuring.

Russia has no lack of raw material: forests cover about 40 per cent of its territory (about 720 million hectares). Yet it produces only 3 per cent of world's pulp and paper products – eight times less than the USA, six times less than China and 2.5 times less than Japan. Total 2008 PPI production in Russia was 9,962,400 tonnes.[34] The main part of Russian export of pulp, paper and paperboard in the 2000s went to China, Germany, India, Ukraine, Belarus and the UK.

The Russian pulp and paper industry is experiencing a period of strong growth. Much of its expansion is financed by inward FDI. At the end of the 2000s there were about 160 pulp and paper mills in Russia. Ten major ones furnished more than two-thirds of total output, and all were increasing production. Russia's output growth was mainly focused on foreign export markets, with 28 per cent of pulp production and 45 per cent of paper and board exported.

Export of PPI products holds a dominant position in the total Russian export of forest-based products. Although the tonnage of Russian paper and paperboard export greatly exceeds the tonnage of imports, the trade balance in value has continued to deteriorate, as Russia increasingly imports higher-value, relatively expensive paper products such as high-quality materials for containers and packaging, coated paper and tissue, whereas it exports less valuable products such as newsprint and kraft linerboard.

Multinational PPI companies would do well to consider doing business in Russia, however. An abundant natural resource and growing domestic markets provide opportunities that are not readily available elsewhere.

Main PPI companies in Russia

The main Russian companies in the pulp and paper industry are located in Arkhangelsk, Syktyvkar, Kondopoga, Solikamsk, Svetogorsk and Segezha. Ilim Pulp dominates the industry, with three mills in its subsidiary in Kotlas (Arkhangelsk region in the north-west) and in Bratsk and Ust-Ilimsk (in the Irkutsk region of south-central Siberia). They produce over 2.2 million tonnes of chemical pulp, representing around 40 per cent of total industry output. Ilim Pulp is Russia's largest producer of containerboard, cartonboard, kraft paper and uncoated wood frees, the lot totalling over 1 million tonnes. Ilim's paper production facilities include the St Petersburg Cartonboard & Printing Mill. Including pulp operation, sawmills, panel board mills and logging, Ilim Pulp is the largest and most broadly based and vertically integrated forest-products business in Russia. Inclusive of its subsidiaries in Kotlas and in Bratsk it is the leading producer of containerboard, with an annual output of around 500,000 tonnes, equivalent to around 25 per cent of domestic production. Its St Petersburg mill is the largest producer of cartonboard, with an annual output of over 200,000 tonnes. This is equivalent to around one-third of domestic cartonboard production. The Ilim group exports to Europe, North America, China and South-East Asian countries.

Kondopoga PPM, based in Karelia, adjacent to Finland, produces newsprint and is the market leader in that line, with a share of up to 40 per cent. Over 75 per cent of the company's output is exported.

Volga Pulp and Paper Mill (VPPM) and Arkhangelsk PPM (APPM) are also major players. VPPM is owned by the Ost-West Group, an investment fund. It is located in the Nizhegorodskaya region (Volga Federal District) and concentrates on newsprint. APPM is affiliated with the Titan Group and Pulp Mill Holding and ranks second to Ilim in corrugated case materials. Between them these two top players control around 45 per cent of the corrugated case materials market.

Segezha PPM is an integrated producer based in Karelia, manufacturing sack kraft paper and kraft liner. The company has invested in growth, both in quantity and quality, and received media coverage when it acquired Korsnas Packaging of Sweden in 2006 for a reported €74 million. The transaction propelled Segezha PPM into a clear second position globally in sack kraft and industrial sacks. It also represented the first foreign acquisition by a Russian forest-products manufacturer.

Because foreign investors love this sector, inward FDI in the industry is significant. Exemplifying this is the acquisition of Syktyvkarsky LPK (Syktyvkar Forest Industry Complex) by Mondi. Located in the Komi Republic, 1,200 kilometres north-east of Moscow, this facility is now operated by the Anglo-American Mondi Business Paper division. Since acquisition, Mondi has invested to upgrade its facility, undertook construction to expand, made grade switches (types and qualities of products manufactured) and invested in environmental improvement. Concurrently, it divested itself of non-core operations such as the tissue and plywood mill.

A potential new inward FDI is Norway's Larvik Cell, which has announced plans for a €400 million high-yield pulp mill in the Pskov region of north-west Russia. Anglo-American, Mondi's parent, announced it was considering a US$1.5 billion pulp mill at its Syktyvkar site. Stora Enso and Metsa-Botnia were also known to harbour ambitions to produce pulp in Russia.

Finally, China is seen as an important future investment partner as a result of the severe fibre deficit in that country. Accordingly, rumours have flown relating to greenfield pulp mills involving either Chinese partners or ones that otherwise aim at the China market.

Air transport

The Russian airline industry enjoyed reasonable growth from 2005 to 2007. In 2008 it showed a decline, but since 2009 it has grown again. Industry volume increased, with a CAGR of 5.3 per cent over 2004–2008, to reach a total of 29.9 million passengers in 2008. Volume is expected to rise to about 37 million passengers by the end of 2013, representing a CAGR of more than 4 per cent for 2008–2013.

The domestic segment proved pre-eminent in 2008, with a total of 21.1 million passengers and 77.7 per cent of the industry's total volume. In comparison, the international segment counted 8.8 million passengers in 2008 and generated the remaining 29.3 per cent of the industry's aggregate volume at the end of 2009. Russia accounted for 7.6 per cent of the European airlines industry value. In comparison, Germany accounted for 19.2 per cent of the European value.[35]

There were about 235 Russian airlines at the end of 2009. Five years before, only 24 airline companies provided 85 per cent of all air transportation. Russian airlines operate against tough international competition, which may explain the extreme price sensitivity of the Russian airline industry. It operates in a buyer's market, with price wars being the norm. Other modes of transport, such as trains, are expensive and slow alternatives, but it is possible that proliferating technologies such as videoconferencing may, in the future, turn out to affect business air travel. In response, airlines could adjust the services they offer, by, for example, increasing share of cargo with the aim of rendering themselves less reliant on passenger fares.

Brand loyalty is low in this industry, since switching costs for customers are negligible. In an effort to increase repeat sales, airlines have introduced loyalty schemes to snare and keep customers.

In these times of global crisis many sectors are pushing cost reduction. Costs targeted here include jet fuel, the price of aircraft and labour. Staffing cost is a major item. Flight activity entails ground personnel such as mechanics and reservation and ticket agents. Fuel is not taxed in many countries, but rising fuel prices present a problem. Another challenge lies in the contracts for purchasing or leasing aircraft from suppliers. Breaking these contracts when business lags can result in onerous expense.

The Russian airline industry comprises a large number of companies but is dominated by Aeroflot. The main growth in recent years, however, has been in budget airlines. As elsewhere in the world, some Russian airlines bet on superior equipment and high-class service to entice custom. For the present, however, high price sensitivity is paramount.

The first decade of the 2000s proved difficult for many carriers, with mergers and acquisitions becoming hard to ignore. A deficit of money has led to the rise in fares and additional fees. This, in turn, exacerbated the problem by reducing customer demand and loyalty. Exit barriers are high in this industry, as it entails the divestment of bulky assets: it's hard to sell large aircraft. High fixed costs, such those for salaries and maintenance, are also factors in industry-wide competition.

Main companies

The three leading domestic companies are Aeroflot, S7 Airlines and Rossiya. All three operate internationally, covering hundreds of destinations in dozens of countries all over the world.

Aeroflot flies to over 93 destinations in some 45 countries, and maintains representative offices worldwide. The company provides multiple services, including hybrid transportation of cargo via air, road and rail, completion of customs formalities and transport of international cargo.

S7 Airlines offers flights to every major city in Russia and the rest of the CIS. It also operates scheduled flights to Europe and countries in the Asia-Pacific region, as well as charter flights to 20 countries around the world. It operates around 60 aircraft.

Rossiya has routes to 35 cities within Russia and around 90 destinations worldwide. It operates VIP flights on behalf of the Russian government, including its president.

While M&A is the favoured model for internationalisation in the airline industry, international joint venture has managed to stay in the running by building strength via expertise in the handling of government regulation, access to knowledge and marketing channels (for example, reservation systems). One example is Aeroflot Russian International Airlines, which is highly active in alliances. It is a member of the SkyTeam alliance and participates in marketing alliances with Air France, Delta Air Lines and KLM. It has also collaborated with British Airways to create new routes (code-shares) exploiting new links from Europe to the Orient. In addition, it operates a joint venture with the Turkish airline which allows Aeroflot to operate in their shared markets as if the two companies formed a single airline. Another joint venture with a US partner has permitted it to extend its international cargo operation into an area formerly barred to it.

Aeroflot's outward investment has helped the company grow, enhance its position in the domestic market and cope, as well as collaborate, with global competition. It has facilitated its access to new and more advanced technologies and has even helped to reinvigorate company management.

Aeroflot's international reputation has risen over time. The company ranks fourth in business and fifth in economy class, and has made progress in general customer satisfaction with its on-board customer service on long-distance flights – a distinction that sells tickets. Moreover, it has maintained its lead in the 'Best Airline' category of National Brand ratings. It holds an OISA Certificate (in 2008 Rossiya also got the award) certifying that it observes the kind of advanced safety stipulated for the international aviation industry. It thus allows itself to claim superior attention to safety among its domestic rivals.

Despite a financial pinch, smaller Russian airlines also persevere in attempting to penetrate foreign markets. In doing so, they hope to gain additional trade and advanced technology, and to obtain a better run at financing opportunities abroad.

The Russian government has traditionally considered air transportation a strategically important sector of the national economy and erects protectionist barriers to aircraft import and investment. At the same time, however, it lacks resources to support the industry, provide subsidies, finance big orders and promote national air carriers abroad.

Logistics

The demand for transport services rose considerably in Russia in the 2000s. In the second half of the decade, the market volume for logistics totalled about US$120 billion, with an average growth rate of 15–18 per cent being forecast.

The Russian logistics market in the 1990s was characterised by lack of competition, poor transparency and limited know-how. Many companies complained of excessive storage and transport costs, and started to rely on supply chain outsourcing to solve the problems. As a consequence, demand has increased for more and more sector-specific and innovative logistics. However, bureaucratic problems and poor infrastructure continue to bedevil logistics in Russia, along with unruly competition and insufficient transparency. And this at a time when Russia – instead of Finland – could become a future hub between Asia and Europe!

The long-term prospects for supply chain companies in Russia are sweetened by the fast growth of the automotive market, one of the main drivers of supply chain growth. Vehicle production entails the application of logistics. Most of the global car-makers have plants in Russia and these require logistical services to ship in components and to export their finished goods. Logistics is also a primary management tool in the energy sector (oil and gas) and for metallurgy. No wonder the government is making efforts to reassess and re-invest in the national road infrastructure.

Time was when two basic logistics functions, transportation and storage, were run in parallel as two virtually distinct services. Similarly, transportation, customs procedures and insurance were also handled as distinct operations. In the 2000s companies came to realise that the time had come to mesh logistics and services. That brought in its train all sort of change. Transport companies began renting or building their own distribution centres. Warehouse operators added transportation to their core competency. Customs brokers and freight forwarders began offering delivery services.

The best customers for logistics services are energy producers and large retailers handling consumer goods (FMCG) and perishables. Large-scale retailers, especially the foreign ones, use 3PL (third party logistic) services. When entering the Russian market, they expect the same level of service as in Europe, and preferably from the same providers. Quality is somewhat more important than the price it commands.

In the world today there are about 100 global 3PL providers, of which Russia hosts about 20.[36] In Russia foreign 3PL operators outnumber the domestic ones, and outclass them in terms of the quality of services offered. However, major Russian transport companies and distribution centres have started providing 3PL. As a consequence, the Russian market poses extraordinary problems for foreigners as Russian competition gears up.

Main foreign competitors

Provision of 3PL in Russia is a recent development. From 2004 to 2006 the leading Western logistics operators in Russia increased their revenues more than two-fold. Even so, the volume of foreign 3PL activity in Russia remains relatively small, failing to exceed 3 per cent of activity in the global market.

A notable exception is the French company FM Logistic, which earns 25 per cent of its revenue from Russia. FM Logistic Vostok is owned by the holding company FM Logistic, which was founded in France in 1968. DSV, founded in Denmark in 1976, has been working in Russia since the early 1990s. In 2008 this company merged with an international logistics operator, ABX Logistic. In Russia, international logistics operators pursued the major food and FMCG manufacturers and their distributors for their market entry. Established links in home countries helped the new foreign entrants.

Among foreign companies, German 3PL operators have been the most active. More than 25 German companies operate in the fields of freight transportation, freight forwarding, warehousing and express services.

The quality and reliability of service of foreign 3PL providers still outmatch those of the domestic ones. Hence, most suppliers of 3PL outsourcing in Russia are capitalised from abroad.

Development of Russian logistics companies

During the crisis, many 3PL providers saw business drop and demand for 3PL services decrease. Among measures taken by the logistics companies in view of the crisis two stood out: optimisation of existing business procedure and a review of relations with suppliers.

But whatever Russian logistic companies have tried, they have not succeeded in competing successfully with their international rivals. The fact is that Russia's national transport system is dominated by domestic market demand, and not the ins and outs of international trade flows.

Struggling, as they is, on their home market, Russian logistics companies are not in any rush to go abroad. To be sure, there are companies that do brave it, and dabble abroad. But, even here, such effort is confined to big companies.

Russian logistic companies have succeeded in penetrating the closest markets (Baltic and CIS countries). Here conditions resemble those in Russia: namely, the lagging infrastructure. While countries in Western and Central Europe have strong competition and saturated markets partly due to highly developed logistics, Russian supply chain firms have not attained that standard. They make do by establishing themselves in the CIS and Eastern Europe and leave it at that.

The common model for Russian logistic firms is to start by gaining know-how on the home market. Only then will they gradually and carefully go into the nearest foreign countries, such as Ukraine, Belarus and Kazakhstan. 'Carefully' means that Russia's leading domestic players look for partners not only in Russia but also abroad, to share the risk. One recent example is the announcement in 2009 of the joint venture by Russian Southern, a river port, and one of Europe's largest container carriers, Rhenus.

Russian 3PL companies are of two sorts: one with the characteristics of transport and logistics companies (STS/RLS Logistics and Interterminal), and another with the characteristics of the transport and logistics divisions of large holding companies (Energy, Alidi, Meridian Logistics, RDB). For example, Fogel was originally established within the holding company TRUCK 2001, while Petrovizard began as a St Petersburg freight forwarding company that only later began offering its customers a full range of logistics services. The international activity of many major Russian logistic firms is currently handled by their services areas.

The group of companies calling itself Russian Logistic Service has its own network of regional companies in 20 cities of Russia and Kazakhstan, and provides a full range of 3PL services in them. The group Eurosib is a network consisting of ten or more logistics terminals, all close to the Chinese border or the near-abroad. ABX Logistics operates in Russia and the CIS, with offices in Moscow, St Petersburg, Minsk and Kiev. It provides transport services, customs clearance, storage and logistics.

In the 2000s the share of the top 20 companies constituted about 9 per cent of the total transportation and logistics market in Russia. The list of top 20 players includes 8 Western 3PL providers.

Russian companies go international in proximate countries (mostly of the CIS), where they can rely on market knowledge dating back to the days of the Soviet Union. Ukraine, Kazakhstan and Belarus have logistics requirements approximately at the level of maturity of Russia. They share Russia's problems, such as lag in IT, obsolescence of infrastructure, delayed industrial development, out-of-date structuring and so on.

Internationalised logistics is an area of endeavour to which Russian companies must still adapt. They need to acquire linkage to the global state of the art and a surer instinct for trends. Integration into international logistics entails plugging in to a complex of processes. In inclusive terms this would involve grooming Russian companies to international standards and introducing them to modern techniques of supply chain management – or to put it another way, matching the level of the West's functional, organisational and institutional configuration.

Media

Media here refers to print, broadcast and online media. According to the Russian Ministry of Press, the country has around 37,000 media outlets, including over 2,200 newspapers and around 12,000 periodicals. 90 per cent of these are privately operated. There are over 3,000 television channels and 2,000 radio stations. The Russian government owns two of 14 national newspapers, 60 per cent of lesser newspapers and, in whole or in part, all six national television networks.

With the passage of time the concept of media as something 'informative' has become a thing of the past, with TV and newspapers coming to play the role of tools used to 'form' and entertain the popular mind.

Borrowing from European and American media legislation, as well as from recommendations of the Council of Europe, the European Union and other authoritative organisations, media laws in Russia are now officially claimed to accord with the global standard. This is belied by TV broadcasting in Russia, which follows not global practice but, instead, is mainly run by the state or owned by companies with close links to the government. The government controls *Channel One* and *Russia One* – two of the three main federal channels – while the government-linked energy giant Gazprom owns the third, *NTV*. Not surprisingly, some Western critics contend that independent reporting has suffered as a result.

Print publishing

Russia's print publishing is currently one of the most attractive markets in the world. As markets elsewhere wane, Russia offers great growth opportunity for publishers and their suppliers. This is coming to be recognised by some percipient publishing companies. As an example, Swedish-based Metro International announced in 2009 that it was leaving the US newspaper market and, instead, intended to focus on Russia, where the advertising prospects were better.

Internationalisation of the media differs from that in other business sectors, perhaps because media operations have an inbuilt international aspect to them. Part of their function is the transfer of information from its place of origin to the place where it is required – abroad notably included.

Newspapers published in English, but sited at locations that are not Anglophone, are the most evident examples of this. The *Moscow Times* (an English-language daily) and the *Moscow News* (an English-language weekly) were initially intended to serve foreigners resident in Russia. More recently, both papers have trimmed themselves to address, as well, Russians conversant with English.

Until 2005 the *Moscow Times* was owned by Independent Media, a Moscow-registered publisher that also prints Russian-language versions of popular glossy magazines such as *FHM*, *Men's Health* and *Cosmopolitan*. Subsequently, Independent Media was acquired by the Finnish publishing group Sanoma.

The Russian newspaper *Komsomolskaya Pravda*, published in regional editions within Russia, has other editions in CIS countries such as *Komsomolskaya Pravda v Ukrainye* (Ukraine), *Komsomolskaya Pravda v Belorussii* (Belarus) and *Komsomolskaya Pravda v Moldove* (Moldova).

The Russian-language business daily *Vedomosty* was established as a joint venture by Dow Jones, the *Financial Times* and Sanoma, publisher of the *Moscow Times*. Being the offspring of inward investment, *Vedomosty* has gained a following for the validity and accuracy of its reporting among Russian and foreign readers and critics.

Television and radio

Among audiovisual media, *Channel One* is a company in which the Russian government controls 51 per cent of shares. The company broadcasts worldwide thanks to a network called Channel One Worldwide. *Russia One* is a state-owned Russian television channel founded in 1991. It belongs to the All-Russia State Television and Radio Company (VGTRK). The channel's audience is more than 117 million and its remit covers CIS countries, Western Europe and the Middle East. An English-language satellite channel, *Russia Today*, was launched in late 2005. Its accent is on news and its stated aim is to convey 'global news from a Russian perspective'.

Radio stations in Russia are mainly controlled by the government. The most popular stations are *Radio Russia*, *Radio Mayak*, *Russkoye Radio* and *Voice of Russia* (a state-run external service that broadcasts in English and other foreign languages). The most popular independent station is *Echo of Moscow*, which some Western observers describe as 'the last bastion of the free media in Russia'. Based in the capital, *Echo of Moscow* broadcasts from many Russian cities, as well as from some in the near-abroad (through partnerships with local radio stations), and via the Internet. Most of the content is news and talk that focuses on social and political issues, which the station attempts to present from different viewpoints. The remit of *Echo of Moscow* covers Russia, the USA, and Baltic and CIS countries.

There are around 30 sizable information and news agencies in Russia. Some of them specialise in financial or economic news, but the majority offer broad coverage of ongoing issues. The best known are Interfax, ITAR-TASS, RIA Novosti, RBC (RosBusinessConsulting) and RBN (Russian Bureau of News). Almost all the news agencies run well-developed online versions.

Over the course of the 2000s Russian media organisations made great progress. They did so by internationalising their practices – both domestically (by, among things, partnering with international media organisations in Russia, forming ventures and being acquired by Western companies) and abroad.

Education

The present education system in Russia developed during the 1990s. With the country's transition to a market economy it split into two segments, public and private.

The public sector remains a government fief, while the private sector may be seen as a market. Education in Moscow and St Petersburg has evolved in contrast to that in the rest of Russia. Partly this is due to these cities' long-existent contacts with foreign education, and it should not surprise, therefore, that Moscow and St Petersburg responded more quickly to post-Communism's new ways. Here new institutions offering educational services of high quality at a market price materialised on short order. But, as was to be expected, so did low-grade kinds.

The cost of higher education in Russia varies from 20,000 to 300,000 roubles (US$700–10,000) per year or even more. The cost of higher educational services depends on the prestige of the educational institution and on the demand for its graduates in the labour market.

Russian education contrasts sharply with other European systems. In 2003 Russia committed itself to adopting a two-step system of education (undergraduate and graduate) by the year 2010 and to introduce accreditation of educational institutions, as well as official definitions of disciplines and credits following established European practice. Only the large Russian universities reacted negatively to the idea of the adoption of this Bologna system, believing that their graduates would be able to find good employment without it.

Non-state (i.e. private) educational institutions do not have it easy. Unlike state institutions, they are saddled with high rents for their premises and high taxation on their profits. In addition, private educational institutions have to invest heavily in promotion because state institutions receive government subsidy to help them compete with the private sector. Private schools also must contend with poorly prepared legislation on registering and examinations. In sum, conditions created by the State for private education adversely affect the growth of competitiveness within the market.

What the two strands of education – state and private – have shared is permeation by the ways of the wider world. Indeed, this has affected all endeavours. Modern technology and the rapid development of education via mail or the Internet have opened national borders to forms of teaching immune to the strictures of the Russian government, as is demonstrated by the international MBA fairs held in Moscow and other big cities, for example, and the financial support given by major European business schools to Russian students. Another exemplar is the educational programmes offered by many American, English and European universities and business schools in Moscow and some other Russian cities.

The most popular form of internationalisation of higher education is student mobility or, put another way, Russian students studying abroad. Globalisation and employment opportunities offered by MNEs also stimulate the mobility of students. Although the mobility of teaching staff is not as pronounced, it can be considered the second most important form of internationalisation of higher education.

Traditionally, the international mobility of teachers has been motivated by the desire to continue studies and research in more promising conditions than the home country was able to confer. Some regions and certain areas of education, such as management and business administration, offer specialised training to young researchers and professionals that may not be available in Russia, even in Moscow or St Petersburg. In such cases there is no choice but to study abroad. One may view this happenstance as a form of education internationalisation.

The role of global institutions such as the Global Alliance in Management Education (CEMS), the Association of MBAs and others is linked to internationalisation of education all over the world. These bodies help educational institutions to strive to meet the demand for and the requirements of educational services of higher quality globally.

Russia's integration into the world system of higher education has taken place over the course of the last two decades (1990–2010). The preceding period, however, saw a drastic reduction in the state's ability to pay to make this happen, while the transition to the market economic system that resulted engendered the wish that the state now start paying its way. In the event, the outset of this transition shook the economy to an extent that Russia found itself degraded from its former prominence in the world market of education: 10.8 per cent of all foreign exchange students, the world over, studied in Russia before the collapse of the USSR, while only 3.8 per cent studied in Russia in its aftermath, at the end of the 2000s.

Successful international activity by some Russian universities, and their experience in creating new forms of cooperation with their counterparts abroad, seeded a trend. It was a trend that is even now continuing to internationalise state educational policy. The internationalisation of education in Russia has three sources: a surge in academic mobility, the build-up of international educational programmes (including double degree diplomas), and the proliferation of institutional partnerships in the form of networks and alliances.

The development of an export of Russian educational services lags because it is obstructed by tradition and old laws. Take the effort to put into practice the international two-level bachelors–masters system. While already legally adopted in Russia, it simultaneously conflicts with the Soviet era's 'specialist' degree. More important in practice is the fact that many Russian employers show a reluctance to recognise the bachelor's degree because it does not correlate with the old qualification system accepted in the Russian labour market.

Underdevelopment of infrastructure and non-conformity of educational conditions in Russia with Western norms are serious obstacles for the expansion of Russia's participation in the international educational services market. This is why academic mobility with developed countries remains a 'one-way street': Russian students stream to the USA, France and Japan for education, but unsatisfactory living conditions in Russia discourage foreign students from studying here.

To improve the competitive stance of its national educational system, Russia must fulfil some requisites, including satisfactory computer facilities, state-of-the-art laboratories, sufficient classroom space and acceptable dormitories. This would take large investments that are beyond the financial means of most universities. International education can develop only in concert with an international exchange of ideas. To achieve this requires Russia to draw foreign teachers to its national institutions. However, at this stage it is too costly for most Russian universities to invite highly qualified professors. Unfortunately, nothing is being done to overcome this problem.

To conclude, several of the analysed sectors behave in various different ways in striving for internationalisation – both of the inward and the outward kinds. In some branches and regions activity of international investors is low owing to the poor development of institutions and/or the infrastructure.

It can be hard for a Russian firm to decide whether it is best to avoid internationalisation in order to avoid competition from abroad, or whether it should opt for internationalisation in order to enhance its competitiveness. If it decides to go for internationalisation, then it must decide to do so only at arm's length, for instance via collaboration with foreign firms (as most media companies or nano players do), or wholeheartedly, including acquisitions, brand wars and so on (as some technology-intensive companies or food manufacturers do).

Russian industry that is attractive to foreign investment can react to foreign firms' intention to take over Russian ones in two ways. One is to deliberately focus on the home market in an attempt to defend its operations (as in pulp and paper, logistics or food). The other way is to deliberately expand abroad, calculating that the best defence of the home market is an attack on the would-be intruders (as in air transport, autos or banking).

Inward and outward investment: the case of construction

In this section two modes of internationalisation will be discussed – inward and outward – as reciprocals in one of the most conservative industries, namely construction.

Though this book does not claim a primary interest in internationalisation theorising, a look at the application of its key approaches to the management of Russia's construction sector seems appropriate, in which the process of international construction's entry into Russian market can be evaluated and an overview of the internationalisation within Russian enterprise presented. It is worth illuminating how international construction enterprises have entered the Russian market and then contrived to adjust to it; identifying the factors affecting and explaining their results; and considering how Russian firms have responded to the activity of international players.

Why construction?

Construction is one of the major Russian economy sectors in hard, entrepreneurial terms. But it is also of great importance to Russia's civilisation, as it furnishes its shelter and domestic milieux. It also invites study because it encompasses contracting, building materials and construction machinery, each one of which is important to the Russian economy in its own right.

The Russian construction industry generated total revenues of US$51.5 billion in 2007, representing a CAGR of 10.6 per cent for the period spanning 2003–2007. In comparison, the Polish and Hungarian industries grew with CAGRs of 7.8 per cent and 8.2 per cent, respectively, over the same period, to reach respective values of US$35.4 billion and US$9.8 billion in 2007. The non-residential segment was the most lucrative for the Russian construction and engineering industry in 2007, generating total revenues of US$29.5 billion, equivalent to 57.3 per cent of the industry's overall value. In comparison, the civil engineering segment generated revenues of US$22 billion in 2007 – that is, 42.7 per cent of the industry's aggregate revenues. Overall, Russia accounted for a 7.5 per cent share of European construction/engineering value. In 2012, the Russian construction and engineering industry is forecast to attain a value of US$80.3 billion, an increase of 56 per cent over 2007.

The construction industry of the Russian Federation comprises more than 130,000 organisations and enterprises, including 114,000 construction companies and 9,000 producers of building materials. Approximately 90 per cent of all organisations operating in the sector are small businesses (up to 50 employees). At the end of the 2000s the Russian construction sector employed over 5 million people, representing almost 10 per cent of Russia's total workforce.

There is much room for growth for Russian construction. To illustrate, its largest westward neighbour, Poland, has 38 million inhabitants and approximately 345,000 construction firms. That is three times the number of construction companies for a population about one-quarter the size of Russia's! In Russia, the 130,000 enterprises noted above attend to the building needs of over 143 million citizens.

This is the reason why large foreign companies such as Bouygues, Hochtief, Strabag and Vinci have moved into the Russian market. The volume of foreign investment in the Russian construction sector soared before the financial crisis of 2008. According to Rosstat data, the industry attracted US$183 million in foreign funds between January and June of 2006 – that is 80 per cent of the FDI inflow posted in 2005, of which US$90 million represented FDI and US$93 million was in the form of other investments, mostly loans. According to press reports, foreign investment funds pumped US$1.5 billion into Russian real estate projects in 2006, nearly twice as much as in 2005. This should come as no surprise, as real estate investors saw, and continue to see, returns of over 10 per cent in Russia, when Western Europe and the US yielded no more than 4–5 per cent.

Developing relations between the European Union and Russia have affected the construction industry. During the 1990s unruly competition was sorting itself out and entrepreneurial culture, in general, was maturing. One could say that management was becoming more professional, which would certainly serve to underpin a conclusion offered by 'Emerging Trends in Real Estate Europe', a piece of research by PricewaterhouseCoopers which argued that the Russian market has become one of the major destinations for international investment.[37]

Inward perspective

European companies in the Russian construction industry deal mostly in construction materials and construction instruments. Some companies export the goods they produce; others sell them on Russia's domestic market. German firms are among the most active foreign investors in the Russian economy. For example, Knauf, which started up by acquiring a single Russian firm at the beginning of the 1990s, kept raising its bet so that by the mid-2000s it had become a major investor in the Russian construction industry.[38]

In addition, producers of windows (Rehau, Veka), finishing materials (Caparol, Bau-Color), glues (Henkel Bautechnik), sanitary fixtures (Grohe, Villeroy&Boch) and construction instruments (Bosch, Hilti, Kress) have successfully operated in the Russia for several years.

American and European MNEs operating in construction-related industries (elevators, earth-moving equipment, tyres, cranes, construction materials and so on) mainly based their entry strategies on the following models:

- company invests money in a project that it investigates and finds transparently viable;
- company enters Russian market having a project in mind and then organises a network of local contractors to help carry it out;
- company with money to invest comes to Russia to explore how, or why, to enter the market.

Often, Western companies use the services of a Russian partner to help them get into business and then operate in Russia. An example is Skanska (a Swedish contractor), which was contracted to build facilities for Philip Morris, Rothmans and Gillette when they decided to come to Russia.

Western companies have worked hard on standardising construction and management procedures. Dom Lemkon (a subsidiary of the Finnish construction company Lemminkainen) uses 'the model of project management Lemkon', according to which the whole construction process is divided into separate packages which the primary Russian contractor then assigns to sub-contractors with relevant expertise. The contractor operates on behalf of the customer by supervising his network of subcontractors. The advantage of this system resides in the achievement of economy of time in starting construction and, subsequently, on proceeding from there. In the latter stages the contractor, on behalf of the customer, encourages competition between his subcontractors and their suppliers in order to keep costs down. The contractor is also pledged to keep the customer informed of costs incurred along the line so as to maintain transparency.

Consider now the example of another construction company from Finland, YIT. It chose to penetrate the Russian market via a subsidiary. From January to September 2008, a time when the world financial crisis was spiking, this subsidiary began construction of 3,622 residential units in Russia (it had around 2,800 under construction in Finland at the same time). At the end of September 2008 YIT had a total of 11,768 units under construction.[39]

According to YIT, it takes two years to build a housing project in Russia because of the larger size of residential complexes there, whereas on Finland's scale it takes only a year. In Russia, apartments come unequipped and unfurnished (which is unacceptable to Finns). It was the Finnish way that YIT decided to do it in Russia.

In-depth study of construction-related companies (among them Konecranes and Nokian Tires from Finland, Knauf and Henkel from Germany and Caterpillar and Otis from the US) has helped to identify factors that brought these firms success. The companies investigated were selected for their overall high degree of competence as well as for maturity in international activity. All of them were industry leaders in their sector (construction, engineering, building systems, development, elevators for commercial and residential housing, construction materials, rubber and tyres for construction machinery).

The investigation showed that outstanding factors for success in Russia are (Panibratov 2009):

- the right choice of mode and time of entry to the Russian market;
- quality of production (including perceived quality conveyed by the brand of the MNE's country of origin);
- marketing activity, with a strong focus on communication with customers;
- the right local partnership.

Basic investment-related factors included owning manufacturing facilities, adaptation to the local market conditions and early entry to the Russian market (early birds found themselves advantaged). Late-comers favoured the creation of wholly owned greenfield subsidiaries more than had the early birds. This had to do with diminished availability of promising acquisitions, an increase of the investment attractiveness of the Russian market and the rise of competition.

MNEs that entered the Russian market at the beginning of the transition process in the national economy (late 1980s–early 1990s) became industry leaders in their segments during a span of a decade or two. All the risks and difficulties which these firms faced along the way were then overcome and they duly attained profitability toward the end of the 2000s at the latest.

Outward perspective

At the turn of the century the competition in Russian construction increased for both international and local firms. A period now dawned in which investors were well advised to heed Porter's five-forces doctrine, which teaches that, before investing, the following rules of thumb be observed: weigh the risk of challenge by other entrants; the bargaining power of buyers where you plan to sell; the threat posed by substitute products or services; the bargaining power of suppliers; and the rivalry between existing firms.[40]

In Russia the most significant driver of competition in the construction industry is rivalry among existing firms. Buyer-power is less of a problem, because a pent-up and unsatisfied demand for housing persists. The threat from other potential entrants is not great because entry barriers into this industry remain daunting. There is no substitute for housing, so this threat does not obtain. And the bargaining power of suppliers is sometimes handled by bribery, which is one of the problems in Russian construction.

The Russian construction industry's outward internationalisation is hampered by a lack of experience. Russian construction firms simply are not in the habit of exporting, of setting up abroad, of selling abroad, and do not build manufacturing facilities abroad. Because foreign construction firms have quality and well-organised procedures to offer, it follows that anywhere that they can establish themselves in Russia means hard luck for existing Russian firms.

Russian business's most effective defence of its home market is achieved by attacking foreign invaders after they have established themselves on Russian soil. Since Russian firms are not able to match in effectiveness contractors from the USA, France, the UK, Germany and Finland, they resort to making life as miserable as they can for the foreigners.

So, when Western MNEs think of doing business on the Russian construction market, they should realise that they have less chance of succeeding than they would have in other branches of business. Russian construction must fight for its life on the home soil, because it doesn't operate on foreign soil. This may partly explain the high rate of withdrawal of many foreign construction firms from Russia – totally in some cases (for example, Skanska and Polar) or partially in others (for example, Knauf).

Obviously, the degree of an outfit's know-how will weigh in the balance between success and failure. According to interviews with experts and CEOs of large construction firms, the most efficient strategies for survival have to do with four factors: product, pricing, marketing and capacity (the examples given in Table 2.5). Illustrate the methods and motives of large Russian construction companies in their recent international ventures, be it for export projects or for inward FDI.

Those exceptional Russian construction companies that have attempted to internationalise have done so on the following grounds: a change of business strategy; a shift of geographical targeting owing to lack of building plots in Russian cities; a search for new sales opportunity; and image improvement.[41]

In 2008, with the onset of the global financial crisis, property developers began encountering problems in financing their projects. Banks became more stringent and selective in lending to both corporations and individuals. In Russia, the impact has been less significant than in other CIS countries and this was reflected by healthy growth in the value of such construction as was completed in 2007 and the first half of 2008.

Table 2.5 Competitive action types as motives of internationalisation in construction

Action Type	*Description*	*Implementation by Russian contractor*	*Internationalisation*
Product action	Investment in new product development or key technology breakthroughs	LEK introduced studio flats. After a few years this offer became very popular in the real estate market in Russia	Not suitable for internationalisation; already available abroad
Pricing action	Price cuts, rebates and discounts	LenSpecSMU proposed significant discounts to buyers who were prepared to make up-front partial payments	No internationalisation potential
Marketing action	Marketing campaigns, advertisement investments, brand management	Stroimontazh created new brand (Mirax) when establishing the Moscow partnering company, investing into this brand when moving in the markets of former CIS countries. Important marketing budget	Possible first step in the internationalisation process
Capacity/ output action	Changes in company's capacity or output	M-Industria established its subsidiary in Germany; its activity focused on training and educating the company's employees and also on attracting foreign specialists to work on the company's projects in Russia; Etalon-LenSpecSMU when planning entry to Portuguese and Spanish markets had seek plots in these countries	In most cases led to the internationalisation of the Russian construction firms

Source: Panibratov 2009.

This occurred because Russian developers have not had to rely on loans, financing instead from internal funding. Another reason was that infrastructure development projects (for example, transport, energy, hospitals), for which the state provided the financing, dominated the construction portfolio. As a result, in 2007 the year-on-year increase in construction output matched the 2006 figure of 18.2 per cent, and reached €94.1 billion. This was followed by an even higher increase of over 22 per cent in the first half of 2008, when output reached €48.9 billion.

As a result of this, the internationalisation process in Russian construction industry has proceeded slowly and unevenly in respect of both the state of the business environment and opportunities to expand.

This study of the business environment indicates that industry performance was sensitive to the share of the market available to its competitive segment, meaning the part that practised competitive pricing, bidding and tendering; or, put it another way, that part of the market which practised free competition. Increasing the competitive share of the market is therefore found to be necessary in order to increase market activity as a whole. Enforcement of public tendering is required, as are new quality standards and norms which reflect present and future customer requirements. Adoption of such standards will have the beneficial side effect of increasing competition.

The aspects of this research relating to enterprise reveal the importance of marketing and partnership in the success of MNEs in Russia. Marketing seems to be in satisfactory shape in many of the Russian companies. Their weaknesses reside in pricing, effectiveness of bidding systems, internal sharing of information and a lack of customer feedback. These are all matters that should be heeded by those MNEs that face the problem of developing partnerships with a Russian firm.

Despite the dramatic impact of the 2008 financial crisis on all sectors of the world economy, it also provided opportunities for those 'bottom-fishing' firms (both Russian and foreign) that bought up the plots and the projects frozen by other players.

It is usually easier for big and well-known construction companies to develop internationally. At the same time, their complicated organisational structure leads to slower decision-making. Therefore, despite pitfalls and risk, it behoves emerging-economy construction companies to keep in mind expansion into foreign markets as a hedge, in a time fraught with crisis, against political and economic risk in their home countries and, with the luck of the astute, as a means to increase profitability.

3 Exporting from Russia

The oil and gas industry

Strategies in oil and gas on international markets

The global integrated oil and gas sector is basically composed of companies engaged in exploration for and production, refining, distribution and retailing of oil and gas. At the periphery it also includes specialised work in chemicals. In 'petrospeak' the exploration and production activities are termed 'upstream', whereas the refining, distribution and retailing are 'downstream'. The sector, as a whole, experienced fluctuating growth in 2003–2007. It generated total worldwide revenues of US$3.6 trillion in 2007, representing a CAGR of 16.7 per cent for 2003–2007.[1]

Because oil and gas are such enormous revenue sources, their production is often tightly controlled by the governments of the countries holding reserves. Many countries – Saudi Arabia, Abu Dhabi, Venezuela, Norway and Mexico are but a few examples – have completely nationalised oil and gas sectors. Other countries, such as the USA, the UK and France, are completely private. Some countries have mixtures. That is the case in Russia, where state-owned and private giants co-habit, sometimes on uneasy terms.

The integrated oil and gas sector is dominated by large MNEs such as British Petroleum, ExxonMobil, Royal Dutch Shell, Total and many others. These MNEs are typically active in all businesses, both upstream and downstream. Oil and gas products are commodities with limited product differentiation, which encourages a high level of rivalry within the sector. The large capital outlays, stringent environmental regulations and cut-throat competition present daunting barriers to entry.

Buyer power within the integrated oil and gas sector is moderate. The major oil and gas companies, those having highly vertically integrated operations that cover oil exploration, production, refining, transportation and marketing, have the clout, and new entrants on a smaller scale, who are less vertically integrated and therefore need to make acquisitions to improve this aspect of their business, have none.

Supplier power within this industry is also moderate. Major suppliers are oil and gas equipment and services companies such as Baker Hughes, Technip, Schlumberger and Halliburton. But some power is wielded by a small number of equipment and services companies who are large enough to provide some shelter from the strategies of the majors. But as they tend to be backward-integrated and use third-party services to supplement their own potential, they lack the punch of the majors, who, in turn, need to be supplied by the furnishers of crude, a group that is largely cartelised and thus able to regulate the supply of the majors.

The threat of new entrants into the integrated oil and gas sector is weak. Oil and gas companies are among the largest companies in the world and are usually highly vertically integrated multinationals that leverage the scale of their production and distribution networks to generate substantial profits. The substantial capital outlay and fixed costs of the apparatus required for large-scale drilling and production operations present a high barrier to entry, especially for companies running offshore operations. The oil and gas industry is tightly regulated, which makes entry difficult, in particular as regards obtaining permission from national governments to explore and exploit new fields. This is a lengthy and complex process, with no guarantee that efforts will pay off, albeit the winner takes all.

Substitution is also difficult in this sector, although it varies from one country to another. That goes not only for persons but also for processes. In the field of power generation it is hard to substitute for coal and nuclear power. Hydroelectric generation may be highly significant in certain countries, such as Brazil and Norway. An important use for natural gas, other than power generation, is heating, and electricity can substitute here. Fossil fuels have few significant substitutes as vehicle fuels until the technology relating to electric vehicles becomes more viable. Some plant-based alternatives are beginning to attract interest. But, overall, switching costs for substitutes are generally high.

Russian market overview

The oil and gas market in Russia generated total revenues of US$270 billion in 2008, representing a CAGR of 20.7 per cent for the period spanning 2004–2008. Natural gas represents the bulk of the segment in 2008, with total revenues of US$168 billion, almost two-thirds of the market's overall value.[2]

The performance of the market is forecast to decelerate, with an anticipated CAGR of 5.1 per cent for the five-year period 2008–2013, which is expected to drive the market to a value of US$347 billion by the end of 2013.[3]

The export of oil and natural gas is critical to Russia's economy. In 2007 it generated 64 per cent of Russia's export revenues and 30 per cent of all FDI in the country.[4] The financial crisis and the severe drop in crude prices in 2008 led to a 10.1 per cent drop in the GDP in the first half of 2009, causing some turmoil in Russia's financial sector.[5] Russia nonetheless managed to become the world's largest exporter of both oil and natural gas in 2009.[6] At the same time Russia accounts for 26.4 per cent of the European oil and gas market's value.

Although Russian oil production has surged, many of the oil fields are old gushers, and are now depleting. There remain, of course, many potential new fields to discover and exploit. Deposits in the Arctic and in the Caspian Sea are noteworthy, with reserves in the north-western Russian Arctic estimated to hold well over four billion barrels of oil (bbl). Russia's proven natural gas reserves at the end of 2000s amounted to 47 trillion cubic metres, 26 per cent of the world's total.

The bulk of Russian gas production comes from a few giant fields that are depleting at a rate of 20 billion cubic meters a year. The growth of this sector has been impaired by Russia's state-run natural gas monopoly Gazprom's domination, by state regulation and by insufficient pipeline capacity. By the end of the 2000s Gazprom held more than a quarter of the world's natural gas reserves, produced nearly 90 per cent of Russia's natural gas and operated the country's natural gas pipeline network. The company's tax payments accounted for approximately 25 percent of Russian federal tax revenues. Gazprom is heavily regulated, and by law must supply the natural gas used to heat and power Russia's domestic market at government-regulated, sub-market prices.[7]

Energy issues are at the heart of Russia's uneasy relations with its neighbours, including the Baltic countries, Poland, Ukraine and Georgia. The government is heavily involved in oil and gas companies, and has influenced the sector in several ways. Foreign ownership is limited to less than a 50 per cent stake. Contractual enforcement as a result of pressure from local authorities, where political rather than economic factors dominate, remains a salient risk for participants. Given the unstable political environment, the possibility that government involvement may change discourages the long-term investment required for such large projects.

The performance of other Russian energy companies also reflects the impact of large-scale government participation. Take the example of Lukoil, the privately held company in which ConocoPhillips holds a 20 per cent stake. The company has thrived by maintaining a low political profile and as a result of ConocoPhillips' technological and managerial expertise. Lukoil is increasingly turning its sights abroad, despite attractive opportunities at home. Whether this reflects the desires of its foreign investor or the uncertainty about being able to continue competing in the long-term with the likes of government-supported Rosneft is unclear.[8]

Like Gazprom, Rosneft takes advantage of the stability associated with government ownership. Analysts forecast that Rosneft production will expand at a healthy CAGR of 12 per cent, compared to Lukoil's 10 per cent and the sector's 3 per cent average.[9] With government support for Rosneft's consolidation efforts, the company is likely to continue to receive tax breaks and access to new exploration or production licenses.

Russian government policy in the energy sector is clear enough. It can be defined in two words: effective control. Take Gazprom – though its charter is private, the state, supported by contrived legislation, actually controls it. At the same time government spending draws on gas and oil revenue, so that Gazprom's heft leverages the government to help keep oil prices high. The pampering of Gazprom contrasts with the government hostility toward foreign investors. Decision-making in today's Russian oil and gas industry is opaque and beset by rumour. What is clear is that the government tends to call the shots.[10]

The potential growth in both oil and natural gas in Russia is hampered by the lack of modern Western oil-exploration technology and techniques of development and production, as well as by government intervention. The government has repeatedly tried to prevent exports and protect the industry from foreign ownership. Yet it has failed to follow up by providing encouragement to update obsolete technology for the production and export of high-quality refined products. Russia's need for technology is more acute here than it is in other sectors. Only 35 per cent of the sector's 50 top-seeded technology items have come into use here.[11] On top of that, there is insufficient capital to help expand Russian oil and gas production and pipeline capacity.

The pipeline problem affects export. Potential investors complain that the investment climate in Russia is inhospitable. Protection of intellectual property is poor, tax laws are burdensome and the government bureaucracy inefficient. Also inhibiting investment is the reputation enjoyed by some Russian players for corruption and even extortion. Foreign investors, whether in upstream or downstream activities, hesitate to enter a market with an uneven playing field.

Competitive landscape

The Russian oil and gas market is characterised by the presence of large, diversified and powerful international companies with vertically integrated operations reaching from oil exploration to production, refining, transportation and marketing. These companies are buyers and players within the entire value chain. The presence of such powerful operators acts as a significant barrier to entry. In addition, given the need for substantial initial investment, to get such equipment as drilling rigs operating makes foreign investors hesitate to proceed in the seemingly unfair regulatory environment.

Because state-owned companies can call for government intercession the industry operates as an oligopoly. As a result, and because of the importance of oil and gas products, there is a waiting line of investors, primarily domestic, wanting to buy in. This in itself weakens buyer power. However, some institutional buyers, such as independent retailers, overcome the barriers via their ability to make large purchases; losing such customers would plainly impact negatively upon the revenues of the sellers, making the sellers keen to court them.

The prices for commodities such as crude oil or natural gas are set by world markets, and imply limited or even non-existent buyer power. Branding is non-existent, and brand loyalty is not a factor within the industry, as individual buyers incur low switching costs. Institutional buyers may encounter spot market price spikes for quick delivery. Overall, buyer power within the Russian oil and gas market is seen as being moderate.

Oil and gas operations are highly energy and labour intensive, with high fixed costs. The market is difficult to exit, with potentially difficult asset divestment. The main companies usually have geographically and vertically integrated operations based on similar business models. Moreover, the major players in the Russian energy industry operate in the same market segments and target similar customers. The main rivals in the market are Gazprom, Lukoil, Rosneft, TNK-BP, Surgutneftegas and Tatneft. Among the world's top 50 oil and gas companies (ranked by 2007 oil-equivalent reserves), Gazprom is number 11 (it is also the world's largest extractor of natural gas and the largest company in Russia), Rosneft number 12 and privately owned Lukoil number 15. TNK-BP, Surgutneftegas and Tatneft are the best known of the other important players.

This chapter will present three case studies: Gazprom, Rosneft and Lukoil. These three are cogently illustrative of the style and mode of operation of the sector as a whole. For all that, each of 'big three' is one of a kind – the first being a privateer but one that the west pigeon-holes as 'a hand of the Kremlin'; the second being the only state-owned firm which behaves like a private one; and the third being really independent and having the most diversified international exposure. As for the rest of the Russian oil and gas industry, its involvement is limited and episodic.

Gazprom: where is the state hidden?

Gazprom and Rosneft are both fully impacted and supported by the government. The paradox is that Gazprom, though formally privately owned, nonetheless is somehow run by the state, which sets company strategy, most notably in the company's international dealings. Indeed, Gazprom has been charged, in Western media, as the powerful arm of Russia in foreign affairs and in foreign conflicts.

Rosneft, being self-confessedly state-owned, has accepted a role that complements that of its sister, Gazprom. It plays the role of patriotic businessman, while Gazprom takes care of the politicised tycoon.

In August 1989, what had been the Soviet Ministry of Gas Industry transformed itself into the State Gas Concern, Gazprom. With that, post-Communism had created a curiosity: an ambivalent enterprise. It is ambivalent in the sense that it was de-Communised and not directly owned by the state. Instead, control was exercised through shares of stock, 100 per cent of which had to be owned, under law, by the state.

Gazprom's political influence increased significantly after the new Russian president Boris Yeltsin made the company's chairman, Chernomyrdin, his prime minister (December 1992).[12] As the new government was committed to economic reform, laws were shuffled and Gazprom turned into a joint-stock company. In 1993 the shareholders, meaning the state, then started to distribute shares under the voucher method, where every Russian citizen received vouchers to purchase shares of formerly state-owned companies. By 1994, 33 per cent of Gazprom's shares had been bought by 747,000 members of the public, mostly in exchange for vouchers. 15 per cent of the stock was earmarked for distribution to Gazprom employees. The remainder of 40 per cent of the shares went to the state but this figure was then gradually lowered to 38 per cent.

And so life went on at Gazprom until in 2000 Vladimir Putin, then Russian president, launched a campaign for state control in strategic companies. An official offensive ensued against what he saw as mismanagement and personal pillaging of state assets. This may explain why, in June 2005, Gazprombank, Gazpromivest Holding, Gazfond and Gazprom Finance BV, all subsidiaries of

Gazprom, agreed to sell 10 per cent of their shares to a state-owned company named Rosneftegaz. This tranche, combined with the 38 per cent share of the State Property Committee, gave the Russian government control over Gazprom. After acquiring control, it lifted the 20 per cent restriction on foreign investment in Gazprom, thereby opening the company to outside investment.

With help such as that, Gazprom became one of the largest gas-producing companies in the world by the end of the 2000s, active in exploration for and production, transportation, processing and marketing of natural gas, as well as in production and refining of crude oil and gas condensate. The company is the only supplier of natural gas to the regulated domestic market and sells over 50 per cent of its natural gas in this market. In 2008, the company sold 287 billion cubic metres of gas in Russia, 96.5 billion cubic metres of gas in CIS countries and the Baltic States and 184.4 billion cubic metres of gas in other countries. It sold 11.8 million tonnes of oil and gas condensate in Russia, 3.3 million tonnes in CIS countries and the Baltic States and 16.7 million tonnes in other countries. Finally, it sold 24.5 million tonnes of refined products and petrochemical products in Russia, 2.4 million tonnes in CIS countries and the Baltic States and 16.7 million tonnes in other countries.[13]

Gazprom is now rated as the world's largest company for natural gas reserves. Over 90 per cent of these were concentrated in its 14 largest fields. For 2008, the company had natural gas reserves of 33.1 trillion cubic metres, 1,601.7 million tonnes of oil and 1,287.1 million tonnes of condensate. Moreover, incremental increase in reserves of natural gas owing to intensive geological exploration amounted to 583.4 billion cubic metres, while the oil and gas condensate reserves reached 61.0 million tonnes.

Gazprom owns the world's largest gas transportation system, which includes a vast network of trunk pipelines, compressor stations and underground gas storage facilities and is capable of long-distance transportation of natural gas to consumers in Russia and abroad. The average transportation distance in 2008 stood at 2,901 kilometres for gas supplied to Russian consumers and 3,322 kilometres for export.[14]

Gazprom Neft operates crude oil refining facilities. Its major refinery is at Omsk and has an installed capacity of 19.5 million tonnes per year. Gazprom Neft also controls 33.3 per cent of the shares of Moscow Oil Refinery (with an installed capacity of 12.2 million tonnes per year). It also has a 50 per cent shareholding in both Slavneft-Yaroslavnefteorgsintez and the Yaroslavl Oil Refinery.

Gazprom Neft mostly markets its own crude oil and petroleum products for export through Gazprom Neft Trading, its subsidiary in Austria. The company's petroleum products are distributed within Russia through some 20 subsidiaries. Most of these are wholesalers, catering either to Rosreserv or to gas-station networks. Gazprom Neft Aero, Gazpromneft Smazochnye Materialy and Gazprom Neft Marine Bunker specialise in the petroleum products for any number of specialised sectors.

Gazprom Neft distributes its refined products in central Asia through three subsidiaries: Gazpromneft Asia in Kyrgyzstan, Gazpromneft in Tajikistan and

Gazpromneft in Kazakhstan. In 2008, Gazprom Neft owned a network of 811 gasoline stations in Russia and another of 78 gasoline stations in Central Asia.

International operations

At the end of the 2000s Gazprom had around 130 subsidiaries, 16 of which were situated abroad, in Germany, Switzerland, the UK, Lithuania, Ukraine, Armenia and Belarus. It also had several joint ventures and cooperation agreements. The reasons for such activity were gaining know-how, reconnoitring and attaining experience in new markets and acquiring resources.

Approaching new markets

Gazprom Neft expanded abroad through acquisitions. In April 2009 it acquired the oil- and lubricant-producing facility belonging to Chevron Italia in Bari (Italy) from Chevron Global Energy. The facility's productive capacity was as much as 30,000 tonnes of oils and 6 tonnes of lubricants annually. The production range included 150 types of oil used in cars and commercial transport, as well as oils for industrial use. Products carrying the Gazprom Neft trade mark were intended to put a line of company strategy – diversification of international operations – into practice.

Gazprom Neft expanded its operations in the Serbian market through the acquisition of 51 per cent of Naftna Industrija Srbije (NIS) in January 2009. The purchase agreement stipulated the reconstruction and upgrading of NIS refining facilities by 2012. As part of the upgrade, measures were to be taken to improve the quality of oil products, so that they met European standards (Euro-5). NIS is one of the largest vertically integrated oil companies in Central Europe and, with this acquisition, Gazprom Neft bought itself a chance to expand into the East European market while simultaneously providing the product to sell there.

Acquiring knowledge

Several agreements by Gazprom made in the 2000s testify to the company's striving to attain technology and know-how by forming partnerships. A contract between Sibneft and Halliburton (a large oilfield services company with headquarters in Houston and Dubai) in 2002 foreshadowed the purchase of Sibneft in the mid-2000s by Gazprom, which renamed its acquisition Gazprom Neft, and a subsequent agreement between Gazprom and Halliburton that paved the way for Halliburton to provide a full range of oilfield services to Gazprom Neft.

The subsidiary Gazprom Neft signed a cooperation agreement with the Norwegian oil company Statoil in 2007 to establish a working group charged with the evaluation of joint exploration and production projects in Russia and overseas. Also in this year, the company formed a joint venture called Northern Taiga Neftegas with Chevron Neftegaz to undertake oil field development.

In 2008 Gazprom Neft and Yokogawa Electric Corporation signed a strategic cooperation agreement for joint work in the fields of innovative technology, management systems, measurement instrumentation and IT systems produced by Yokogawa at enterprises belonging to Gazprom Neft.

Access to resources

In September 2008 Gazprom Neft signed a cooperation agreement with KazMunayGaz Razvedka Dobycha covering cooperation on geology projects and resources exploitation in Russia and Kazakhstan. Under the terms of the agreement, the companies were also expected to jointly work on issues regarding marketing and oil production in Europe and Kazakhstan.

The acquisition of NIS placed Gazprom Neft squarely in the markets of Serbia and Angola. NIS owns refineries in Pancevo and Novi Sad with a total capacity of 7.2 million tonnes annually. It has its own chain of crude oil storages and 480 oil and gas retail stations. NIS produces about 85 per cent of all oil products consumed in Serbia.

It is important here to remember that Gazprom's forays into foreign markets have only been icing; the domestic market was the cake. In addition, by far the most important means of gaining entry into the target market is by exporting products. Here, government agreements pave the way.

The influence of the Russian government certainly helped Gazprom to export. In return, Gazprom exports fostered ties with other countries, enabling the Russian government to – shall we say – export its influence there. This makes it understandable that initiatives taken by Gazprom are synchronised to also serve the Russian government. This arrangement may cost Gazprom something but it also costs Gazprom's principal owner, the government, something. Thus appreciated, it reveals itself as a joint venture between a commercialised government and politicised commerce.

One of the hidden problems Gazprom faces is that almost all of Gazprom Neft's production and other operations are located in Russia. Dependence of a company as large as Gazprom Neft on one solitary region exposes it to political vagaries that it might avoid by diversifying its geographic zones of activity.

Another problem is that Gazprom Neft, owing to its quasi-government status, is committed to transporting its crude oil for export use through Russia's state-owned pipeline system, access to which is regulated by the Russian Ministry of Industry and Energy, while some of its competitors operate their own, which are run at a commercial pace and level of efficiency. Russian law and Russian bureaucracy, however, work at a statelier pace from that of private enterprise, and have different aims. Too bad for Gazprom Neft?

Added to that, a substantial part of Gazprom Neft's revenues are derived from export sales of crude oil and refined products, which are denominated in US dollars. On the other hand, Gazprom Neft's operating costs are primarily denominated in Russian roubles. Therefore, the relative movements of rouble inflation and rouble/US dollar exchange rates contribute significantly towards a jittery management ... or towards happy foreign exchange hedging experts in the finance department.

Rosneft: parenthood obliges

Rosneft, which was established in 1993, emerged from the reorganisation and large-scale privatisation of the Russian oil industry following the dissolution of the Soviet Union. Rosneft is one of the last vertically integrated oil companies.

The company rose from the ashes (and assets) of Rosneftegaz, the successor to the USSR Ministry of Oil and Gas. With numerous management changes from 1995 to 1998, Rosneft suffered and was ill-managed. Oil production fell and oil refining collapsed to just one-third of capacity.

Things changed in October 1998, when the Russian government decided to strengthen the company's management and lift Rosneft back to its rightful place as a key player in the Russian energy market. The new management team immediately set itself to planning the programme that ultimately eased the company out of crisis. Rosneft became profitable again by 2000. Strong growth followed, with average annual oil production increases of over 11 per cent.[15]

In 2001, Rosneft became Russia's official representative on projects with Production Sharing Agreements, and from 2002 to 2005 took part in these projects in Algeria and Kazakhstan.

As of December 2007, the Rosneft group comprised 516 subsidiaries and affiliates, with 17 production and 7 major refining facilities, 4 marine terminals and a proprietary network of filling stations throughout Russia.

The company ran exploration projects in Russia's Far East, East Siberia, the shelf of the Caspian, Black and Azov Seas, West Siberia, Middle Volga, the North Caucasus and Timan-Pechora. It also participated in exploration in Algeria, Kazakhstan and Turkmenistan.

Rosneft is involved in the purchasing, sale and transportation of crude oil and petroleum products. The crude oil is sold in Russia and on export markets (including the CIS). Some of the crude is used as feedstock for the company's refineries or is processed at third-party refineries under tolling arrangements.

By the end of the 2000s Rosneft was exporting a wide range of petroleum products, primarily diesel, fuel oil and gasoline. In Russia it engages in wholesale, retail, storage, transportation and transhipment of petroleum products. The company operates a strong network of petroleum product suppliers and filling stations, as noted above. As of December 2007, Rosneft's retail network included 1,695 proprietary and leased filling stations and 71 franchised filling stations operating under the Rosneft brand. It also engaged in various non-core activities, including drilling services, construction services, banking and financial services.

Internationalisation mode

In the 2000s Rosneft turned its gaze on potential new markets, in which it sought resources rather than plants. To operate it shared in projects such as the ones already cited above in Algeria and Kazakhstan. In 2005, for instance, the company helped to develop a large project on the Caspian shelf in Kazakhstan. Using its characteristic *modus operandi*, it is now active abroad in exploration, drilling and seismic surveys, and participates in exploration projects in cooperation with Russian and foreign partners.

Rosneft became a giant via the acquisition of stakes in competitors and the signing of strategic alliances with major rivals such as Gazprom. For its international partners, alliances with Rosneft offered an entry path to the Russian market. For Rosneft, the gain was access to new technologies and to foreign distribution networks for its exports. In this way both sides cooperated, despite remaining formally rivals, both at home and abroad.

In 2006 Rosneft and BP signed shareholder and operating agreements for joint activity on the East Schmidt (Sakhalin-5) and the West Schmidt (Sakhalin-4) license blocks.[16] Here the aim was to join forces in exploring for and then extracting oil from difficult locations. Another alliance between Rosneft and BP covered the Arctic regions.

Throughout the 2000s Rosneft participated in foreign upstream ventures. In 2001 it signed up with Colombia's state oil company, Ecopetrol, and two other Colombian companies to extract oil at a block in southern Colombian jungle. The site was expected to hold reserves of some 100 million barrels. The project also included the building of delivery and refining stations, and an oil pipeline between Columbia and Ecuador. In Algeria, the consortium of Rosneft-Stroytransgaz teamed up with an Algerian state-owned oil and gas company, Sonatrach, to develop an oil block there.

In 2002 Rosneft, together with a Russian gas company, Itera, signed a protocol with the Mining and Industry Ministry of Afghanistan concerning the restructuring and developing of the country's oil and gas industry. A few months later an Afghan–Rosneft partnership was launched for the Russian supply of oil products to Afghanistan. Later the same year Rosneft associated with Marathon Oil, the fourth-largest US oil corporation, to develop production in Russia's north. The venture also foresaw import of Urals crude oil by the US.

In 2009 Rosneft and Carbon Trade & Finance SICAR went into a joint venture with Dresdner Bank and Gazprombank for the purchase of emission reduction units. Under the strictures of the Kyoto protocol, costly equipment must be used to dispose of pollutants. In the venture under discussion the pollutants were those released by Rosneft's Kharampurskoye and Khasyreiskoye oilfields in West Siberia.

In March 2009 the Algerian National Agency for the Valorisation of Hydrocarbons Resources (ALNAFT) approved plans for the development of some state oil fields by an Algerian–Russian alliance, Sonatrach/Rosneft-Stroytransgaz.

Toward the end of the 2000s Rosneft's geo-strategy shifted towards the Asia-Pacific region. The company began entering ventures with Chinese companies such as China National Petroleum and China Petrochemical. In 2007 it went into a joint project to build a refinery in China in company with the state-owned China National Petroleum Corp (CNPC) at the northern Chinese port of Tianjin. The refinery was planned to have an annual refining capacity of 10 million tonnes (200,000 barrels a day) of crude. Rosneft and CNPC also agreed to set up and jointly operate filling stations in China. The project was delayed by slow progress in concluding an agreement for cross-border crude supplies from the East Siberian Pacific Ocean pipeline, but in March 2009 it was revived and capacity raised to 300,000 barrels a day.[17]

The company's refineries are so located as to enable it to market its products both at home and abroad. Oil and petroleum-product transhipment facilities and access to the Transneft pipeline system and loading terminals along the Volga River enable rail, pipeline and marine transportation of petroleum products from the refineries to European markets. The Achinsk and Angarsk refineries in East Siberia and the Komsomolsk refinery in the Russian Far East supply petroleum products not only to Siberia and the Far East but also to Mongolia, China and other countries in Asia.

Rosneft has also been improving the range of value-added services provided at its filling stations. It has installed fast-food areas, convenience stores, kiosks and car washes. As of December 2010, the company's proprietary and leased filling stations operated 124 car washes, 953 stores and 107 cafés.[18] The company's strong retail network gives widespread visibility in the market and signals the start of a true brand. Strong marketing operations enable Rosneft to penetrate into new markets and gain a stronghold there.

Generally, Rosneft is facing the same problems in its internationalisation process as is Gazprom. One could attribute this to the fact that both companies are state-owned. However, the government runs Rosneft with a looser hand, albeit still carefully watching its step. But it must also realise that it owes the degree of independence that it enjoys largely to the fact that is not as dependent as its rivals on the Russian state-owned oil and gas pipelines: Rosneft has its own pipelines and transhipment facilities which lace Russia.

To be sure, Rosneft remains very much beholden to the government. Like Gazprom, and despite its own transport facilities, it transports a significant portion of its crude over Transneft's pipeline network. And, like Gazprom, it is thus hostage to the pipeline's insufficient capacity. And Gazprom, though more closely linked to the government, suffers as greatly as does Rosneft from fluctuations in the supply of crude oil and natural gas prices.

One problem that is specific to Rosneft is that it is exposed to a certain risk linked to the transportation of its gas. The Unified Gas Supply System (UGSS), which transports all gas in Russia, is owned and operated by Gazprom. Under existing regulations, Gazprom must provide producers with access to UGSS on an equal basis. But that still leaves Rosneft with the worry that the hand controlling the switch belongs to Gazprom.

Lukoil: the stepchild grows up

Lukoil is the second-largest Russian private oil company and the twelfth-largest worldwide, according to Platts top 250 Global Energy Company 2009 ranking. It is active in the area of exploration and production of oil and gas and the production of petroleum products and petrochemicals, as well as in the marketing of these goods.

The company was founded in 1991 as the result of the merger of three state-owned western Siberian companies (Langepasneftegaz, Uraineftegaz and Kogalymneftegaz – the first letters composing LUK). It has around 1.1 per cent of global oil reserves, making the company the second largest in terms of proven oil and gas reserves.

In 2008, Lukoil's total crude oil production (including share of production by equity affiliates) was 95,240 million tonnes (1,921 million barrels per day, 2.3 per cent of global oil production) and total gas production (including the share of production by equity affiliates) was 19,437 billion cubic metres.[19]

Unlike other Russian companies, the company is quoted on stock exchanges in Moscow, London, New York and Frankfurt. Top managers control about 25 per cent of Lukoil shares, while about 20 per cent is owned by the American oil major ConocoPhillips; the remainder trade freely.[20] The Russian government has limited power and influence over Lukoil and cannot use the company as a political weapon to support political alliances or even to help apply pressure.

Internationalisation of Lukoil

Compared with its Russian competitors, Lukoil is more market-orientated and profit-minded. As a result, its internationalisation was motivated more by economic and strategic factors than by Russia's political interests.

Lukoil is Russia's leading oil privateer. It clinched the title when its main rival, Yukos, vanished from the market. Since then it has managed to stay at the top. This allowed the company to start its internationalisation process in the mid-2000s. By the end of the decade, Lukoil had a significant international footprint, running operations in more than 30 countries around the world.

Lukoil's internationalisation process took place in all three segments in which the company operates: exploration and production; refining; and marketing and distribution. As a sideline it is also in chemicals and other activities, but these account for less than 2 per cent of total revenues.[21]

International results in exploration and production

Oil and gas production abroad accounts for very little of Lukoil's business. Most ongoing projects abroad are exploration-oriented. The main countries being explored are CIS countries (Kazakhstan, Uzbekistan, Azerbaidjan). The company started projects in Egypt and Colombia, but total proved reserves so far weighed in as sparse. At this stage the risk still lingers that those investments may fail. In Egypt, Lukoil has invested in an oil project called Melelha, and speculation abounds that the potential reserves are hard to reach. If so, the project would require a large investment for an outcome that is still deemed unsure.

In CIS countries Lukoil's projects are further advanced and more promising. Lukoil used various modes of entry into these countries. In Kazakhstan, it exploited the Tengiz field through its subsidiary LukArco, which owns 5 per cent of the Tengizchevroil consortium. This hybrid corporate structure was needed because the Tengiz field required very advanced technological tools (hence the presence of Chevron and ExxonMobil in the consortium), and because the Kazakh government also insisted on holding a stake.

In Uzbekistan in 2008, Lukoil acquired SNG Holdings Ltd, which held 100 per cent of various production sharing agreements in the country. This acquisition looked risky for Lukoil at first sight, which is why payments for SNG were conditional on an independent assessment of the presence of gas and oil reserves: only then did Lukoil start paying up for possession of SNG.

In 2009 Lukoil was also involved in 15 international geological explorations, mainly in the Ivory Coast, Venezuela, Saudi Arabia and Ghana. These projects were often implemented through acquisitions or joint ventures, enabling satisfactory control over the project: examples include the Luksar joint venture with Saudi Aramco for exploration in Saudi Arabia.

Lukoil's internationalisation strategy often bypasses alliances and partnerships, however, and goes for greenfield wholly owned companies. Ordinarily, when Lukoil needs a technology, it buys it from oil services companies such as Schlumberger. Considering Lukoil's unease with ties that bind, it may surprise that it has put up with American oil major ConocoPhillips' 20 per cent ownership. But this can be seen as a tactical convenience since both companies work closely together in joint ventures in Russia (Timan-Pechora region) and elsewhere to make possible such technological transfers as occasion may demand. As long as it makes both parties money, it remains a win-win proposition.

International results in refining, marketing and distribution

The internationalisation of Lukoil has gone farthest in the fields of refining, marketing and distribution. Certainly, it is easier to conduct such activities abroad since they are less politically fraught than extraction; at the same time, however, this set of activities is less profitable.

To the public, Lukoil's image is rooted in its sizable retail network. By the end of the 2000s, it was selling petrol at stations throughout the whole of Russia (59 regions) and in 25 other countries. The company owns a filling station chain carrying its own name in European countries, and it also operates under the brand names Getty (in the US) and Teboil (in the CIS countries). In total, the company had 6,748 filling stations worldwide at the end of 2008.

Lukoil's growth in this segment was by acquisition and very rapid growth (annually more than 10 per cent). During the second half of the 2000s Lukoil embarked on European expansion. Its first target was Italy, where it relatively soon became a major. In mid-2008, and only after some hard bargaining, it was given clearance to acquire a 49 per cent stake in a newly established joint venture company, ERG SpA, that operates the ISAB refinery in Sicily.

The refinery is jointly operated, with separate divisions for crude oil supply and product marketing. Through this joint venture the Russian oil giant achieved significant benefits, notably improved earnings (via improved local networking). The venture also corrected the imbalance in the company's portfolio. With this acquisition the proportion of Lukoil's foreign oil-processing facilities grew to about 35 per cent of its total. It increased overall refining capacity by 13 per cent and its refining capacity abroad by 60 per cent.[22] Such capacity was reckoned to be needed to supply its intended new markets. In the event, it came to supply Lukoil in the Balkans, Turkey and Western European countries. It also vindicated Lukoil's strategy of doing its refining abroad.

This acquisition aimed at product coordination. The refinery was set up to produce oil of a quality compatible with the Urals blend, so that Lukoil could use it to supply the near-abroad from Sicily and the Caspian region in general via the Baku–Tbilisi–Ceyhan pipeline. The strategy at the heart of the Sicilian acquisition aims at expanding in Europe from its present remit, which is limited to Europe's east (Bulgaria, Romania, Ukraine).

The other pincer in Lukoil's movement on Western Europe was the buy-in of 45 per cent of Raffinaderij Nederland (TRN) of the Netherlands for €570 million. This move both satisfied Lukoil's hunger for profits and contributed to its expansion strategy.

The company's core market remains Russia and, to some extent, the oil-producing CIS countries, and the internationalisation of Lukoil remains modest when weighed against that of the international oil majors. However, if the company does not manage to expand its current oil-field holdings it will have no choice but to pick up the pace of its internationalisation process in order to secure new fields. As regards its refining, marketing and distribution, Lukoil is likely to keep on internationalising via cheap retail acquisitions, franchising and strategic partnerships.

One big problem for Lukoil is that its internationalisation is high in refining and retailing, which are less profitable, and low in production and exploitation, where the returns are higher. Thus, the improvement must focus on this imbalance of resource provenance. It may therefore seem that Lukoil must concentrate more on finding new oil fields and production markets than on expanding its refinery and marketing operations.

Or perhaps not. It is noticeable that Lukoil's most profitable activities (production and exploration) are less internationalised, while the less profitable (marketing, refinery) are already highly internationalised. This leads to the conclusion that internationalisation is not an absolute requirement for high profit margins – at least not in the oil and gas industry.

In oil and gas Gazprom and Rosneft, as statists, seem to be content to trust in the bounty of Russia to assure their future. In essence, they are bending the competition towards their inefficient position in the Russian oil and gas industry. However, the methods that they employ for internationalisation and expansion are justified, given their situation. They are protected, while Lukoil, the only company operating like a profit-seeking organisation, is forced to elbow its way forward.

Other players

TNK-BP Holding (TNK-BP) is involved in crude oil production and has major production assets located in West Siberia, East Siberia and the Volga-Urals region. The group is jointly owned by British Petroleum (BP) and Russian investors Alfa Group, Access Industries and Renova (AAR). The shareholders of TNK-BP own a 50 per cent stake in Slavneft. TNK-BP is organised in three segments: exploration and production; refining, marketing and distribution; and oil-field services.

The exploration and production segment explores for, develops and produces crude oil and gas. In 2007 the group's oil and condensate production totalled 70.4 million tonnes (1.5 million barrels per day). TNK-BP is developing some ten major new projects, many of which are located in remote areas, mostly in Siberia.

TNK-BP produces nonassociated and associated gas[23] in the main oil production areas of Western Siberia and in the Volga-Urals basin. In 2007 gas sales from the group's own resources totalled 8.9 billion cubic metres.[24]

In the same year, the group exported 41.8 million tonnes of crude oil. A significant portion of this was transported in Transneft pipelines, while 12 per cent was exported by rail. The group exported 15 million tonnes of refined products in this year.

TNK-BP owns and operates five refineries (four in Russia and one in Ukraine) with a total effective capacity of 23 million tonnes per year. They run continuously at almost full speed.

Tafneft is the sixth-largest oil producer in Russia. It produced 25,766,000 tonnes in 2008. It operates as a vertically integrated group which includes oil and gas production (15 per cent of total revenues), oil and gas refining, petrochemical production (20 per cent), oil services (42.6 per cent), sales of oil and gas products (11 per cent) and service. The company is headquartered in Tatarstan and employs some 100,400 people. The government of Tatarstan holds 33.6 per cent of total shares through Open Joint-Stock Company Central Depositary of the Republic of Tatarstan (OAO CDRT), while ING Bank Eurasia holds 31.4 per cent.[25]

Acquisition of modern technology from foreign companies is at the heart of Tatneft's business strategy, as exemplified by a joint venture with the French major Total. Total has contributed to Tatneft a state-of-the-art way of improving extraction by the injection of chemicals. Another example is afforded by an agreement signed in 2008 between Tatneft and the Preiss-Daimler Group which set up a joint venture for the production of glass fibre. Tatneft's expansion into retail remains limited, but it has been busy in the near-abroad of Ukraine.

Venturing further abroad, Tatneft has three wells in Syria and one in Libya. But at heart it is a homebody and its activity abroad is motivated by the nationalist politics of its investors. It is along this route of internationalisation and joint ventures that the company has brought advanced technology to Tatarstan.

We now leave Tatneft for Transneft, the operator of one of the largest networks of oil pipelines in the world. The company's pipeline network for crude oil covers Eastern Europe and Asia, and was established as a joint-stock company following the break-up of the Soviet Union via a reorganisation of Glavtransneft, the government agency that controlled the Russian oil industry and pipeline system. Transneft now handles assets which include more than 30,000 miles of pipeline, about 390 oil refilling (pumping) stations and more than 830 reservoirs capable of holding more than 15 million cubic metres of petroleum products. It transports about 93 per cent of the oil produced in Russia. The rest, some 300,000 barrels per day of oil, is transported via non-Transneft-controlled sea routes or via rail.

4 Establishing partnerships

The high-tech sector

The internationalisation of Russia's geekdom

Russia's share in the global high-tech industry, with its estimated 0.3 per cent of the global market, is considerably less impressive than its results in energy-based sectors. In contrast, the US and Japan together account for nearly 50 per cent. Yet, even by the end of 2000s, Russia was still spending comparatively little of its GDP on research and development.

The high-tech industries stimulate growth, productivity, competitiveness and the creation of new, well-paid jobs; a lack of it encourages industrial sloth. High-tech's nervy, inbuilt drive informs innovation, new products and new production processes. The sector is characterised by its high proportion of scientists, engineers and technicians, great expense on research and development, short product and technology lifecycles and strong international competition.

Just how the high-tech sector breaks down into its parts is disputed. The view of the Organisation for Economic Co-operation and Development (OECD) recommends itself for being both authoritative and simple. According to the OECD, there are nine main product groups that comprise high technology manufacturing:[1] aerospace; computers and office machines; electronics and telecommunications; pharmaceuticals; scientific instruments; electrical machinery; chemicals; non-electrical machinery; and armaments. Relating to these groups, Russia has internationally competitive products in aerospace, software, nanotechnology, nuclear technology and military equipment.[2]

In the former USSR, software was a relatively neglected field outside of the military sector. In the late 1980s, it comprised only 1.5 to 2 per cent of the total outlay on computer systems, despite the fact that it employed approximately 500,000 programmers. In the 1990s, as Russia began a transition to the market economy, many skilled software engineers left their low-paid jobs in state enterprises, research institutions and universities. Between 1988 and 1994, a massive departure of software developers from Russia to the West occurred, resulting in a deterioration of Russia's intellectual base. Simultaneously there occurred a marked decline in funding for R&D in general.

Many of the professionals who stayed at home simply moved to new Russian start-ups in the software segment that emerged in the late 1990s. That brought growth. From 1994 to 1998 Russian high-tech began to internationalise as software development centres were opened by Motorola, Intel, LG, Sun Microsystems, Boeing and Samsung. The period 1998–2002 saw the consolidation of local firms, which progressively shifted from mere provision of outsourcing to specialised products and services and partnership. There was a drive to improve quality that included certification of skills and encouraged entry into a learning curve. One result of this was an incipient Russian infiltration of the US market.[3]

Many Russian IT companies have science roots. In the early 1990s the Russian IT and software industry experienced incipient growth when a number of start-ups, staffed by refugees from Soviet-style science, started trying their luck in IT. Today, many of these early birds are well known to software users by their company labels. To name a few such Russian brands, there is ABBYY, Kaspersky Labs and Paragon Software, all of which were launched in the early 1990s. They put an imprint on Russian IT that makes it different from that of, say, India or China.

Market size and evolution

All software companies in Russia are privately held, and with Russian statistics being what they are, it remains difficult to estimate the market's size precisely, or even to identify the leaders in particular areas. But what can be gleaned is that there are about a dozen companies with 50 to 300 programmers which are partly or wholly foreign-owned. Most Russian companies in the IT industry do not restrict themselves to selling computers, but also provide system-integration services. When finally the low level of computer penetration in Russia encountered a sudden and explosive surge in demand, Russia pulled up its socks and got with it. It encouraged foreign firms to move in by imposing only light regulation, and since then system integration has become one of the most profitable businesses in the IT market.[4]

Many foreign enterprises in all sectors have by now established operations in Russia and demand the same quality of IT service as they get in their own countries. This has provided an incentive for purely Russian IT enterprises to update in order to become potential service providers for these foreign firms.

Approximately 65 per cent of the overall IT turnover relates to the sale of hardware, 22 per cent to IT services and 13 per cent to software. The market share of software is lower in Russia than in Western countries. Some sectors, such as banking and finance, telecommunication, big industry and the state (e-government), have already invested in the improvement of their IT systems, whereas numerous other branches and SMEs lag behind.

As regards money, Russian IT is hardly a startling success – its revenues in 2008 were a mere US$5.5 billion. Yet it has greatly outpaced the Russian economy as a whole. While the Russian economy grew by about 7 per cent annually, with 7.7 per cent GDP growth in 2007, the IT sector in the same period grew at the much higher rate of 27 per cent. Within IT, the software segment grew by 63 per cent in 2007.

The Russian software market generated total revenues of US$4.5 billion in 2008, representing a CAGR of 18.6 per cent for the period 2004–2008.[5] Moreover, the

Table 4.1 Digital economy indicators for Russia

Indicator	*Description*	*Penetration rate*	
		2005	*2008*
PC penetration	Number of PCs as % of population	12%	21%
Internet penetration	Number of Internet users as % of population	13%	27%
Broadband penetration	Number of broadband accounts as % of total population	0	2%

Source: Datamonitor.

Russian digital economy indicators (PC, Internet, broadband penetration rates) have grown steadily, as seen in Table 4.1. However, the Russian software industry took a severe hit in the 2008 global financial crisis. Demand plummeted. In 2008 exports of software and software development services decreased drastically (from 52 per cent to 21 per cent). The export target of US$3 billion, set by the Russian IT union Russoft, was not attained, its volume only reaching US$2.65 billion.

Services, financial services and industrial customers provide the demand for sophisticated software that has made it possible for a Russian software industry to form up. Even so, a substantial margin of unfulfilled demand remains, and available supply is not entirely capable of providing technology advanced enough to out-compete Western majors. Russia still has room to grow its IT sector, both in size and in competence.

Market segmentation

To understand the segmentation of IT services (including consulting, implementation, support services, training and certification) and software, one needs to consider customer uses and applications.

IT regards government institutions as places to milk for substantial rewards. Like the biggest of businesses, they buy IT products and services ranging from hardware to integration. But the Russian government, unlike big business, buys services only of selected, mainly domestic, companies. Other big clients include industrial giants in the fields of, say, energy, metals and manufacturing. There are also a great number of moderate-sized and small companies that buy a variety of IT services and products. By now the IT market in Russia has become substantial, although not yet saturated. This, of course, has put a brake on innovation, while not removing the incentive to compete.

Big corporate clients continue to make large annual investments in their information technology, and the relationship between the Russian IT firm and the Russian IT customer has by now settled into a pattern in which IT firms benefit greatly from the repeat business provided by long-term customers. Both customers and software companies are becoming interested in forging mutually advantageous partnerships. In general, customers are very loyal in this industry and segment, and it is therefore in their suppliers' interests to both provide them with high-quality products and understand their businesses in order to anticipate and respond to their needs.

Russian companies that now provide software-related IT services fall mainly into two major categories based on their origin. The first consists of large system integrators that started as IT hardware resellers focused on the internal market; it was not until these companies had established stable hardware distribution channels, after many years of doing business in Russia, that they gradually started offering IT services, namely custom software development. These companies engage in R&D mostly through subsidiaries (usually operating under a different brand name) and only as a way of diversifying their business. Primarily they focus on system integration, consulting and hardware distribution. The second category consists of companies that, from the very start, decided to focus on software development services for Western clients. This group includes a number of 'old-timers' dating back to the 1990s: Auriga, EPAM Systems, Mera Networks, Reksoft, Starsoft Development Labs (by now acquired by Exigen Services), VDI (by now part of EPAM) and so on. Such service companies have their eye on the USA and Western Europe, with Germany (and German-speaking countries) and Scandinavia as primary targets.

Role of IT in the economy

The high-tech sector is not a traditional form of industry, at least not compared with oil or to metallurgy. It now directly affects the functioning of both big business and government because of the productivity leaps that it enables. Therefore, it has become a significant factor in the management of the economy and the state. Modernising Russian high-tech, with its increased vitality, does the country good.

Since the state of Russia's economy changed from command to compete, so has the level of opportunity in the high-tech sector switched from doldrums to boom. And as Russia progressively opened up to foreign companies, fair practice seeped in to make for tidier ground rules. Somehow, in the process, the quality of Russian software was also improved. This favourable situation in Russian IT stymied the brain drain, thereby helping to underpin Russian know-how.

Somewhat paradoxically, this situation also helped Russian big business to internationalise. With most Russian institutions and companies using domestic IT, Russian software had the funds to develop technically as well as in repute. That has led to lively export and in its train an increase in internationalisation. It is now Russian managers who have started going abroad, rather than Russian scientists and 'techies'.

As internationalisation takes a grip, Russian industry seems to take heed and turns to its IT providers for systems that will let it compete on the international market. But currently foreign providers still dominate programming for mass-market (packaged) products. It is difficult to compete for the prime desktop icons when foreign providers have had decades to establish their wares.

There is thus a split between domestic and international demand. According to interviews, demand was mostly international in the early days of transition, but now software developers have begun reporting that they serve mainly domestic customers. At the same time, Russian software development is now strongly in demand internationally and showing stable growth in export. Roughly 30 per cent of the total value of software in Russia was exported in 2007, mainly to Europe and the US.

Overall, the demand for IT is steadily increasing in Russia. Indeed, it has reached a stage at which IT companies are finding it advisable to specialise their activity in order to succeed in the marketplace. They are also finding that the demands made of them are becoming steadily more sophisticated. This is a reflection of the increasing pressure on Russian business to innovate and establish market differentiation.

The government has been developing a series of programmes and policies aimed at developing competitive high-tech industries while also firing up innovation. Its strategy consists primarily of selective interventions to promote particular sectors of the economy or geographical areas, including special economic zones, IT parks, state venture funds, a state development bank, tax incentives, training programs, export promotion and direct government participation in some sectors of the economy.

A number of programmes, supported by state financial resources of over US$600 billion, were fielded in recent years. An example is a high-tech parks initiative conceived in 2005. At the time (2006), a federal task force was detailed to plan it; construction began in 2007. The project involves US$1.1 billion of public and an estimated US$7 billion of private funding. Each of these parks was to stretch over 40–100 hectares of land and to contain 100,000–200,000 square metres of office space and 250,000–350,000 square metres of residential space, production facilities and social infrastructure, as well as a major education or R&D centre. It was felt that programmes such as this would be the best way to promote Russia as an outsourcing destination for knowledge-based high-end tasks.

High-tech exports and FDI

From 2002 to 2008, the turnover from software export grew almost tenfold, and in 2008 made up US$2.65 billion, or about of 50 per cent, of the Russian IT industry's total.[6] As a result of the global financial crisis, however, the growth of software export in 2008 clocked in at only 21 per cent – only half of the average annual growth of over 44 per cent from 2002 to 2007.

Software export from Russia falls into three groups (according to Russoft): packaged software; offshore programming (software development services); and captive software development centres. Packaged software consists of commercial software for sale or lease. Kaspersky Lab, the largest Russian software company, is in that line, developing antivirus software. It had revenues in 2008 of US$360 million, of which US$260 million derived from export (see the company overview below).[7] Other Russian software companies with significant sales on the international market are Doctor Web and Agnitum (both also antivirus developers), Transas (navigational systems), ABBYY (linguistic software, data capture), PROMT (automated translation services) and Paralles (virtualisation and automation services).

'Offshore programming' refers to contractual services provided by Russian companies to a foreign company, which hires Russian specialists to develop software, typically for a specific client project. Companies engaged in subcontracting are EPAM Systems, Exigen Services and Luxoft. Though less well-known than those mentioned above, they easily qualify as truly global companies. These companies operate below the parapet, since their names do not appear as brands; they are hidden suppliers, the brains behind the code in your laptop or smart phone.

Captive software development centres, established in Russia by major international firms, serve the inflow of FDI to Russia. They include Alcatel, Ericsson, Google, Intel, Motorola, Samsung and Sun Microsystems.[8] For the Russian software industry, inward FDI is more characteristic than the outward kind.

Russia's future prospects in the IT sector are bright. There is enough market potential to keep climbing: every year, 200,000 people receive higher education in mathematics, engineering and computer-related sciences, with a significant percentage of them graduating from universities. With too few Russian workplaces to employ these trained people, the industry tends to naturally internationalise into fields that can provide employment, such as that of software for special purposes required by foreign firms.

However, outward internationalisation is difficult to achieve. Russian companies lack both the investment capital that is abundant in the West and professional personnel in marketing and sales, all of which are important requirements for firms wishing to become more involved in the international scene.

High-tech competitive strengths

Russia is ideally sited to become an international outsourcing hub for the high-tech sector, offering a number of reasons for foreign businesses to consider it as an option more favourable than India or China. The main factor in the success of the Russian services industry is the high level of staff training, providing better manpower at relatively lower cost. The ability to deal with non-standard issues is needed to manage high-end complex projects. Russian IT presents itself as being able to do this at a competitive price. It is seen as a bargain in routine software development. It follows that Russia has emerged as having investment potential, thus endowing it with growing sales and a forecast growth rate of 20.4 per cent per year for the period 2007–2011. Russian IT spending is forecast as US$37 billion in 2011.

The Russian software industry is very competitive as a result of its technical skills, sound methodologies, high education level, low labour costs, openness as an industry, low barriers to entry and lack of onerous state regulation. The industry is still young, but a good indicator of its competitiveness is growth in exports – from US$0.4 billion in 2002 to US$3 billion in 2009.[9]

Paradoxically, the crisis of 2008 has revealed itself as an advantage for this sector: their independence enabled Russian high-tech firms (especially IT companies) to preserve the ability to invest even in challenging times. Some companies actually managed to grow during the toughest months of the global financial crisis by exporting software products to new markets. It is most likely that it was the crisis that prompted businesses to proactively scout for new export markets. Partly as a consequence of that, there emerged a group of front-runners in Russia's IT service industry that by now has accumulated sufficient know-how and connections to have received acceptance by IT's global elite.

Software leaders in Russian IT

Luxoft

Luxoft was established in 2000 and now ranks as the number one IT company in Central and Eastern Europe. Gross revenue rapidly increased from US$8 million in 2002 to US$128 million in 2008. The company employs over 5,000 people and offers a wide range of software-related services to industries that range from aerospace to telecommunications.[10] It engages in partnerships with top foreign companies in the industry such as Microsoft, IBM, Informatica, Tibco, Oracle and others. Partnerships with these global majors give Luxoft a strategic advantage since its work links into the knowledge and experience of well-established multinationals.

Luxoft has major clients in a broad range of areas, including the aerospace industry (for example, Aepona, AirData and Boeing), the banking sector (for example, Deutsche Bank) and government (for example, the US Department of Energy). It has development centres in Canada, Romania, Russia, the UK, Ukraine, the US and Vietnam. Furthermore, it has four representative offices in the US and three in Europe (the UK, Germany and Sweden).

The company has also expanded via acquisition. An example, dating back to 2006, is that of the New York based IT Consulting International, a company which has been providing IT outsourcing, on-site staffing and project management services since 1993.

Luxoft's strategy aims at building a network of global delivery centres that meets MNEs' needs with consistency across multiple language and time zones. With delivery locations in place across the globe, Luxoft satisfies a need for multinational organisations seeking to diversify the geography of their sourcing portfolio and improve their bottom line with a mix of nearshore, offshore and onsite delivery suppliers.[11]

Reksoft

Reksoft is an offshore outsourcing company specialising in software development and system integration. It was founded in 1991 and is headquartered in St Petersburg. It has regional sales offices and subsidiaries in Munich, Stockholm and Helsinki, as well as development centres in Moscow and Voronezh.

In 2007 its services revenue grew by 98 per cent, reaching US$22.6 million. Reksoft was the first Russian software-development and system-integration house certified for ISO 9001 compliance by an internationally recognised body.

Its customers include well-known European, North American and Russian companies such as Alcatel, Alfa Bank, Ascom, Avaya, BeeOnline, Benefon, Cubio Communications, Gazprom, Lucent Technologies, Mobile TeleSystems, Ozon, Sberbank, SunTis, Swisscom, Telecominvest and others. The company specialises in the telecommunications, financial services and hospitality and travel industries.

Since 2001, Reksoft has been very active in the Scandinavian market. It opened a representative office in Stockholm to serve the needs of its Scandinavian customers. And the efficient workforce at its headquarters in St Petersburg, which looks out on Scandinavia, lends it competitive advantage in the international field, as does its below-EU pricing for quality software development and maintenance services.

Among Reksoft's technology partners are Documentum, IBM, Macromedia, Microsoft, Microsoft Business Solutions, Siemens Business Services and Sybase. These links mostly relate to development centres, project services and on-site/offshore work.

It has also networked by joining the IT-Företagen association, the largest Swedish IT organisation, being the first Russian company to become a member. The association aims at promoting and furthering IT as well as monitoring conditions for IT enterprises in Sweden's economy and politics.

Kaspersky Lab

Kaspersky Lab, a Moscow-based computer security company, opened to business in 1997. Its founder, Eugene Kaspersky, was a specialist in information security whose interest in the field was aroused after a virus infected his laptop. He undertook an analysis of the virus and was able to develop a cure for it. That event led to the appearance of the now widely known Kaspersky Anti-Virus system. By the second half of the 2000s the database of this system had become one of the most complete in the world.

By this time, Kaspersky Lab had also grown into an international company, employing over 1,500 computer specialists. It was represented the world over, in more than 100 countries, and had regional offices in Europe (the Netherlands, Germany, France, the UK, Poland, Romania, Sweden), Asia (Japan, China, South Korea) and the United States.[12]

The company's most valuable assets are its pool of highly skilled employees and a knowledge base that has been growing by the year, allowing it to offer anti-spyware, anti-spam and anti-intrusion products. Its most famous and most important product – Kaspersky Anti-Virus – has in the meantime established itself as a leader in the industry as well as a front-runner with consumers. The product has won several awards over the years.

One of the reasons Kaspersky Lab has been successful is its Russian origin. Russia's low standard of living (the *Economist* standard of life index ranks the country 105th, sandwiched between Botswana and Uzbekistan) coupled with its high standard of technical education made it one of the world's centres of cyber-crime: a fact that brought forth and generally motivated the upright developer Kaspersky.

Financially, the company has performed well. Europe was its biggest market, with US$196 million in sales. Japan, in contrast, was a small market, with only US$2 million in sales. How they ranked elsewhere is shown in Table 4.2.

While many businesses in the software industry – especially large companies – grow through mergers and acquisitions, Kaspersky followed a path of organic development. As it aimed at global growth it sought new-enterprise-orientated solutions, regional expansion and increase in partnerships. In 2000 the company launched an online shop, which enabled customers to purchase Kaspersky's product over the Internet. This became the fastest and most convenient way of purchasing anti-virus software for most customers, as it offered immediate delivery following instant payment. With the launch of Internet sales the company had a complete line of distribution channels, including distributors, resellers and retail sales networks.

Since the Internet is worldwide, by using it a company instantaneously establishes for itself a worldwide presence. Having done this, Kaspersky then proceeded to set up a network of distributors abroad. The first step in its expansion, and also the most common one, therefore took the form of export.

The next step, destination USA, turned on engaging in partnerships. So in 2001 Kaspersky Lab announced a partnership with Itamigo, a developer of managed Internet security services. This partnership had the advantage of low upfront investment and shared risk. This was important for a young company, which was not yet fully established in the market and operated on tight capital.

Penetration of the US market deserved priority because it was the most advanced market for Internet matters. Having learned its lessons there, Kaspersky then took aim at the equally important European market using largely similar means for entry. Perhaps more significance was attached to making the product available in major retail stores, because online shopping in Europe was not as developed as it was in the US. In addition, there was more accent on selling to small and medium-size businesses, which abound in Europe and were early entrants to the use of the Internet – and early victims of malware attacks.

To add drive to its targeting, Kaspersky opened regional offices in European countries for better oversight and coordination. In 2003 a regional office in Beijing was opened, demonstrating the intent to enter Asian markets. Africa followed, signalling a calculation that, although the continent lagged in industrial and financial development, it did show strong growth in terms of IT.

Table 4.2 2008 sales along regional segments

Region	*Sales (US$ million)*
Europe	196
EEMEA	90
Americas	19
APAC	22
Japan	2

Source: Kaspersky Lab.

Kaspersky Lab did not employ a large staff to handle its international activity: the business division was to grow to 200 people, the regional divisions to 600 and R&D/engineering to 500. But it sufficed to make a contribution to the process of cross-cultural adjustment, so desirable in an internationalised venture.

With partners all over the world, Kaspersky Lab was able to climb to, and then stay at, the top of the industry. Among its strategic partners there were Microsoft, Intel, IBM, Novell, Check Point and Linux Solutions. Microsoft betokened its regard for Kaspersky Lab by promoting it to its so-called Gold Certified Security Solutions Partner list. It joined Kaspersky in an international organisation calling itself the National Coalition Against Spam, of which Kaspersky had actually served as a founder.

To date international software companies still dominate the Russian market, but the locals are gaining a higher market share and improving their image. The locals' problem here is that global giants such as Microsoft or Intel greatly outweigh what Russia can offer as competition. In this situation Kaspersky Lab has managed to show a great potential for further growth on both its domestic market and the international one. It is the great success story of Russian IT.

Sitronics: strategic alliances for growth

Sitronics is one of the biggest high-tech firms in Central and Eastern Europe, as well as in the CIS. It provides products and services in 62 countries of the world to more than 3,500 customers, ranging from middle-sized companies to large ones. The remit of these is wide and includes organisations in the public sector. Sitronics led in information communication and microelectronics in Russia in the 2000s, providing innovative solutions for large and middle-sized firms and businesses.

Sitronics was launched in December 2002 in Zelenograd. It was rooted in the Russian microelectronics firm NIIME & Micron and the Czech manufacturer of software and telecommunications equipment, STROM Telecom.[13] Subsequently it renamed itself Sitronics Telecommunications Solutions. Its first step into internationalisation was the acquisition, in June 2004, of the controlling stake in a Ukrainian company Kvazar-Micro, the largest IT company in Ukraine. It was that acquisition that began to lead Sitronics into the IT services line. On 14 November 2005, consolidation of assets with some other firms led to the formation of Sitronics as it stands in the present day. Following that, the company's headquarters shifted from Zelenograd to Moscow.

Sitronics' next notable step on the road to internationalisation was the purchase, in June 2005, of a majority holding (51 per cent) in a Greek company called Intracom Telecom. The reason behind the deal was to widen access to the markets in Southern Europe, Africa and the Middle East. The acquisition was costly, at around €120 million. Subsequently, in April 2006, Sitronics and Siemens signed a contract for creation of a joint venture, the Centre for Innovations and Research. Its aims were R&D in the fields of security and data-protection systems. In February 2007 Sitronics placed 17.5 per cent of its shares on sale on the London

Stock Exchange. This yielded US$356.4 million, which was then spent on new technologies and other avenues of company growth.

By the end of the 2000s Sitronics was a fully vertically integrated company. The operating activities of the firm were organised into three business streams: Telecom Solutions, which dealt with developing and manufacturing software and hardware for fixed and mobile communications operators as well as for corporate customers developing communication services; Information Technologies, which handled technological and managerial consulting, enterprise management systems, system integration, distributing, software development, training and after-sales services; and Microelectronics Solutions, which specialised in designing, manufacturing, testing and selling computers' chips, smart cards and other microelectronics products.

In each of these streams the company was highly active internationally. Partly deriving from a Czech company, and then merging with a Greek one, Sitronics became a leading provider of comprehensive solutions in the field of systems for support of operations and business activities, next-generation networks, broadband-access networks and solutions for digital television in Russia, the CIS, Central and South-East Europe, Africa and the Middle East.

As time passed, integrated solutions and professional services offered by Sitronics were increasingly in demand in more than 60 countries. Major markets were Russia, the CIS, the Middle East Asia and Africa. Partners that collaborated with Sitronics along its way included Cisco Systems, Oracle, Alcatel, Motorola, Ericsson, Agilent and Hewlett-Packard (HP).

Sitronics has worked on dozens of projects for leading Russian and foreign telecoms companies. Important Russian customers were MTS, MGTS, Komstar-OTS and CenterTelecom, while foreign clients included VivaCell (Armenia), Moldtelecom (Republic of Moldova), Vodafone (Greece, Czech Republic), Callax (Germany), Warid Telecom (Uganda), Shyam Telelink Ltd (India), STE (Syria) and Zain (Bahrain).

Sitronics Information Technologies, which was founded in 1990 and only later became a subsidiary of Sitronics, is an international IT company and one of the leading suppliers of solutions, products and services in the field of information technology in Eastern Europe and the CIS countries. Its activities include management consulting, system integration and introduction of corporate control systems, software development, services and training. Sitronics Information Technologies weighs in at more than 1,100 employees with wide experience in the fields of IT and management. Its partners include leading players in the world's IT market such as Microsoft, Oracle, IBM, Sun Microsystems, Cisco, HP, Nortel, Motorola, Lucent and others.

Via its division Micron, Sitronics has at its disposal a powerful R&D centre collaborating with academic scientific research institutions and design bureaus on an ongoing basis. The R&D sold from there amounted to 17–19 per cent of annual revenue, which is common practice for innovative business worldwide.

By the end of the 2000s, a significant part of R&D shifted from Sitronics' centres to its business streams. Reorganisation of R&D within Sitronics rechannelled but did not change its ongoing collaboration with leaders in the high-tech industry.

Apart from R&D, collaboration also continued in the telecommunications area via joint projects with Ericsson (3G network designs) and Cisco Systems (network solutions for fixed and mobile communications).

Sitronics was interested in venture projects which could provide the company with access to young companies or groups of developers having promising products or designs. It took part in a number of ventures in the field of telecommunications in the US, Israel and parts of Europe. A key partner in several of these ventures was Sistema/Coral Fund.

Since its inception, Sitronics has acted in collaboration with governmental bodies in Russia in the field of infrastructural transformations: for example, it was a major partner in supplying the government's requirements in microelectronics.

Foreign operations by regions

Sitronics has worked with more than 3,500 customers. The firm has offices and subsidiaries in 32 countries, and has exported to more than 62 countries worldwide. Based on its experience in collaborating with leading international technological companies, Sitronics offers solutions, and supplies telecommunications equipment, for communications networks.

Countries actively updating their economical infrastructure were given priority for service by Sitronics. Such countries included fast-developing ones of the CIS, the Middle East, Asia and Africa, but also some developed ones in Europe and the Americas.

In CIS countries, Sitronics contracted into several large projects during the first decade of the twenty-first century. In Ukraine it introduced office automation in Verkhovna Rada, the State Border Guard Service, in regional administrations and in the State Air-Search-and-Rescue Service. It also installed an up-to-date information system to serve the State Statistics Committee. Meanwhile, it continued to work with big business and the banks of Ukraine as well as providing services for such CIS countries as Belarus, Tajikistan, Armenia, Kazakhstan and Uzbekistan.

As for the market of Western Europe, in Austria the company was in solutions for housing and communal services. It also provided multifunctional remote systems for registering and measuring electric energy consumption at the behest of the municipal public utilities operator Stadtwerke.

Servicing Eastern European countries has been a promising line of business for Sitronics. A trend towards the amalgamating of the economics of Eastern and Western Europe has involved updating the infrastructure of the east. Having experience in West European markets, Sitronics has stood prepared to introduce Western best-practices to the markets of Eastern Europe. This proved profitable.

Both in the Czech Republic and in Romania the company has production facilities for assembling electronic equipment for communications systems. Major customers in Eastern European countries are telecom operators, manufacturers of communications equipment and governmental bodies. Sitronics snared contracts here owing to its expertise in wireless solutions for national operators. It supplied equipment and provided service support to practically all Eastern European countries.

Africa and the Middle East, too, were actively investing in updating their economies by transforming infrastructure and developing communications. Sitronics had paid close attention to these challenging markets and positioned itself in them as a partner for both governmental and private ventures. Being reseller and vendor at the same time, Sitronics was in a position to provide customers in these countries with comprehensive solutions. Betokening this is the company's implementation of a number of large-scale projects in wired and wireless IT.

In Syria Sitronics took part in building a national wireless network for public institutions, which included emergency lines. In Uganda, IT infrastructure for telecom operator Warid Telecom was deployed. In Jordan Internet Protocol television (IPTV) solutions were installed for the operator Jordan Telecom Group under the brand name of Orange. In Bahrain a WiMax network was built for one of the leading operators of the country, Zain Bahrain.

Fast-developing telecommunications markets in Asian countries, especially in India and China, opened new opportunities for promoting and introducing IT solutions. Sitronics actively expanded into this area, in 2008 building a radio communications network for Indian operator Shyam Telelink in the state of Rajasthan. In China, Sitronics implemented solutions in the field of telecommunications and microelectronics. Its business stream Microelectronics Solutions handled these and sold up to 25 per cent of its own produce to Chinese manufacturers of electronics. The enterprise had its offices and facilities in the People's Republic of China, Hong Kong and Taiwan. In 2008 the company set up a joint venture with the leading Chinese Corporation ZTE to engage in the manufacture of communication components and electronic equipment.

In the advanced telecoms markets of North America, Sitronics has managed to compete with some success in supplying IPTV services.

Entry strategies

Sitronics' international expansion strategy typically has two phases. First, the company invests heavily for its first projects. Then it fortifies its presence in the market. Its strategic plan for subsequent years includes the following tactical steps: expansion into fast-growing markets; partnership with the Russian government; joint venturing with Rusnano; targeting the banking card market; expansion into the vertical organisation of oil and gas; and special interest in monitoring and safety.

The strategy for its international activity set by the company's management is focus on fast-growing verticals: telecoms, financial services, certain industries and the public sector.

But the strategy also has its 'secret sauce': a number of big projects and contracts won over the past decades relied on strong partnerships with big global and regional players. One does not change a winning recipe, so Sitronics is forging strategic alliances with big operators such as Cisco Systems, ST Microelectronics, Infineon and Giesecke & Devrient. In addition, it has vendor relationships with Siemens, Ericsson, Motorola, Oracle, Intel, Sun Microsystems and Microsoft. One may conclude that Sitronics has taken care to be allied with success.

Of late, the firm's pursuit of success has led it to the fastest growing IT market in the world, India. The group started up there provisionally in May 2008 and targeted initial work in education, with the objective of introducing the complete range of Sitronics products and solutions to the Indian market in due course.[30]

Expansion and development of services in India provided the firm with numerous opportunities for activity even in more difficult times. In late 2009, it announced the launch of a billing platform for the pan-Indian telecom operator Sistema Shyam TeleServices, which trades under the MTS-India brand. The new platform, after being implemented in Mumbai, is to be rolled out to other regions of the country.[31]

Another important deal took the form of a joint venture with the prosperous city of Hangzhou in eastern China. Sitronics holds a 51 per cent stake in the joint venture, with ZTE Corporation owning the remainder. The aim of the new enterprise is to migrate manufacturing and production from Europe to South-East Asia, thereby improving efficiency and reducing costs.[32]

Sitronic's partnership with Nokia Siemens Networks (NSN), a global enabler of communications services, is a further significant international link. Within this partnership, NSN has signed an initial framework purchase agreement with Sitronics, which becomes the official global supplier of analogue power management electronic components for NSN.[33]

Besides the few prominent examples above, Sitronics has engaged in aggressive international regional expansion by means of geographical, vertical and product-expansion strategies. It has used strategic partnerships and international joint ventures in order to infiltrate new attractive markets, thereby enjoying cheaper resources, lower risks and usufruct of the established networks. The strategies Sitronics used can now be said to have succeeded in bringing positive results in both market share and revenues.

Companies in Russia's high-tech sector are relatively small. They have generally focused on software and are all privately owned. Because of growing demand for system suppliers, some Russian companies have started offering such services as well.

When it comes to the strategies of Russian firms in foreign markets, hunting for partnerships and scrambling to be innovative had to make up for lack of significant size. The successful software company Kaspersky Lab has been notable for this. It has a significant reputation despite its relatively insignificant size, as its feat of launching itself as an online shop transformed it into an IT boutique. If you will, it is the Fabergé of IT.

Russian software companies act differently from their foreign cousins. In Russia, it comes more naturally for software companies to form partnerships with governmental institutions, since imported software is not favoured by politically linked institutions. The Russian government saw this as a way to assist an incipient industry in need of help. Offering services to government and staying in close contact with it can thus earn a company bid-money support. This can be very beneficial in times of financial crisis, because governmental services have to be kept running at all times.

Russian companies' good intellectual base helps them gain a useful reputation abroad. Kaspersky Lab is a good example: being small in size, it contrives to gain wealth in the company of much larger firms by bringing intellect to a shared task. Having thus achieved a good standing in foreign markets, the company's image helps it create new partnerships to fill niches that its intellectual base contrives to discover. On the block, Kaspersky is the geeky kid with the wire-rimmed spectacles.

Today, in the home country companies that stay close to Russia, or scrupulously toe the line, as does Sitronics, play it yet another way and are successful. Not only is the government a big buyer, but, as noted, it also affords precious support, such as funding costly R&D and research centres that are crucial to the high-tech sector. It greatly fortifies, thereby, the competitiveness of Russian companies on their own domestic market.

Foreign companies are interested in outsourcing from Russia because of its undeniable intellectual skills, its often low-cost labour and its advantageous taxation. Reciprocally, Russian companies are interested in the West as a new market where they can offer quality at sub-EU pricing. In conclusion, it appears that Russian companies tend to enjoy greater advantages over their Western competitors when operating on the Western market than do Western companies outsourcing from Russia.

5 Opening subsidiaries

The banking industry

International strategies of Russian banks

'Bell, book, and candle shall not drive me back, when gold and silver becks me to come on.' These words of Shakespeare nowadays seem suitable to apply to modern banking, except that today's bankers have long run past just gold and silver. Supported by the latest technology, banks are beavering away inventing new customised services, brainstorming innovative strategies and eagerly following the call of new market opportunities.

To be precise, banks offer five product categories: credit, securities, asset management, financial services and insurance. They target five client types: governmental clients (nation states, supranational institutions), corporate clients, institutional clients (other banks, asset managers and insurers), retail clients and private clients. Progress in the deregulation of global finance has extended, but also tightened, the web of banking activity, resulting in an increased convergence over the past decade between banks that handle only investments and those that only handle commercial business.

As of 2008, the global banking industry succeeded in generating assets of US$90.9 trillion. Behind this figure is annual growth of 16.4 per cent for 2004–2008. In comparison, the European and Asia-Pacific industries grew in value to US$49.2 trillion and US$17.7 trillion, respectively. In the last year of the period under discussion here, they grew by 7.2 per cent.

The Russian banking sector's background

The evolution of the Russian banking sector since the 1998 crisis cannot be understood without reference to its origins. As in all socialist economies, the Soviet Union had a monopoly banking system. The single state bank (Gosbank) operated both as a Central bank and a commercial bank. In 1988 the government established a two-level banking system, consisting of the Central bank and five 'specialised' banks (Agroprombank, Promstroibank, Sberbank, Vnesheconombank and Zhilsotsbank), each assigned to fund specific state programmes for agriculture, industrial construction, people's savings accumulation, foreign trade and housing construction.

In the same year, the government allowed the creation of so-called 'zero banks', which were formed by private investors but often benefited from official financial sources. Simultaneously, many large companies created 'pocket banks' that acted primarily as account agents for themselves, their subsidiaries and their business networks. By the time Russia achieved statehood in 1992 the number of licensed banks had exploded to 1,300.[1]

Hyperinflation in 1992 and 1993 generated vast revenues for banks, as Russian mattresses emptied out in a rush for safety from inflation. Having prospered from this, banks then founded another source of exceptional revenues in 1994. The government began financing its deficit by issuing treasury bills (GKOs). They were denominated in roubles and had maturities of up to 12 months. The Central Bank of Russia, acting as issuing agency and as market maker, sold GKOs only to a select group of banks. In this manner, the banking industry managed to successfully exclude foreigners from the market.

Despite its protective mantle, the Central Bank of Russia claimed in 1998 that the Russian banking sector was solid and reliable, given the high capital/asset ratios and the adequate loan provisions. The crisis, however, revealed the underlying deep structural flaws of the banking sector. As Sberbank's quasi-monopoly in the retail sector crowded out private banks, they borrowed abroad. As of July 1998, 75 per cent of foreign currency liabilities were concentrated in the 20 largest banks, where they represented 20 per cent of total liabilities.[2]

No major bank privatisation has ever occurred in Russia on the scale that was seen in Central European countries. The state has retained control over some of the Soviet-era sectoral banks, notably the major savings bank Sberbank and two foreign-trade banks VTB (VneshTorgBank) and VEB (VneshEkonomBank). The large state-controlled banks have been significant players in the market throughout the post-Soviet period.

The corollary of this is that Russian private banks are mostly new creations, established in the early 1990s. Initially, Russia had a very large number of private banks, most of them miniscule and many of which were believed to have had little if any exposure to the interbank markets. However, the number of banks operating in Russia has decreased significantly over the 2000s, although the banking sector as a whole has grown substantially.

Recent events and going global

The Russian banking landscape was highly fragmented at the end of the 2000s. There was a rapid increase in banking and financial sector services in Russia during the period 2000–2008. More than 1,200 banks operated in the country in 2009, and even the largest privately owned banks held at most 4 per cent of the market. State-owned banks, being considered as more reliable and secure, held about 50 per cent of the market, even though they were perceived to be overly bureaucratic and less dynamic than the privately owned banks.

In 2008, the share of the top 200 banks in terms of asset volume reached 93.9 per cent of total banking sector assets, and the share of the top five banks was

46.2 per cent as of 1 January 2009. The proportion of the market held by the top 10 banks has remained more or less constant for several years, with the big state-owned banks (Sberbank, VTB and Gazprombank) having dominant positions. The proportion of the market controlled by foreign banks was less than 10 per cent and, despite significant increases since 2006, it remains relatively low by comparison with other emerging markets (the average in Central and Eastern Europe is closer to 70 per cent).

The banking industry in the 2000s has been characterised by two important trends, strong state support and consolidation. The first of these explains why the top ten banks were the most active in the internationalisation process. They had the best access to cheap public funds and the state policy pushed them to represent themselves as the new financial centres of the national economy. For example, Sberbank was an overwhelmingly dominant institution in terms of deposits and branch network. Overall, the top five banks accounted for the majority of banking sector assets, retail deposits and total loans. The second trend, consolidation, resulted from legislation of the Russian Federation which demanded that banks with capital below 180 million roubles (US$6 million) raise their capital significantly. Since most of the smaller banks were extremely unlikely to meet the new requirement, many of the banks that provided credit for small and medium-sized businesses could survive only by merging or being taken over.[3]

Competitive advantages

One important feature of the sector was that many banks possessed sophisticated and distinctive advantages that were created, developed and honed over many years, such as partnering with (or even heading) business groups, supplying government with credit, developing e-banking and fast transactions via the Internet, owning networks of ATMs and, hence, getting customers close. Besides, they were able to benefit from home-country location factors, including access both to cash-rich natural resources companies as clients and to cheap funds. The wider range of sources from which Russian banks derived their advantages is often considered to require an extension of the theory of transnational corporations.[4]

Owing to the sheer size of the country there was wide regional variation in Russia's banking system. Roughly half of the banks were registered in the capital, Moscow, and the other half were headquartered in the rest of Russia's 86 regions. Only the larger banks had regional networks to speak of, and the majority of Russian banks did not conduct major operations outside their home regions. Out of the 1,100 banks operating in 2008, fewer than 300 had branch offices in other regions.[5] Despite the impressive number of banks, there was thus wide regional variation in the availability of banking services.

International expansion

The main motivating factor for the internationalisation of Russian banks has been following and serving their clients, especially when that expansion was orientated to the European Union. The second significant reason for operations within EU countries was desire to be present in an international financial scene.[6]

When aiming for overseas expansion, Russian banks first considered opportunities in the EU, the CIS countries and the USA. Approximately half of the banks' plans related to the establishing of subsidiaries in these markets or the making of acquisitions.[7] The Baltic States and Eastern European countries, in contrast, were less important as target regions for future operations.

The expansion of Russian banks overseas happened mostly because of their big clients. Independent expansion was in most cases limited to non-commercial forms such as opening representative offices to carry out marketing functions, to analyse business potential abroad and to gauge the foreign waters if an entry is decided. A representative office is the easiest way to explore and then penetrate a foreign market from a legal point of view. Furthermore, the expenses involved are lower than those associated with establishing affiliated banks and branches.

By the late 2000s, Russian banks had opened around 50 representative offices, of which one-third were in the CIS countries. The remainder were opened in far-abroad countries such as the UK, Germany and China.

If representative offices were booming the same cannot be said of subsidiaries and branch offices. Here, by the late 2000s, the network of Russian banks abroad counted only three branches. This slowness lay in more stringent procedural steps, since permission from both the host country's supervising bank authority and the Bank of Russia were required. Opening these branches was more difficult that creating an affiliated bank.

The poor quality of the financial reporting of the majority of the Russian banks was one of the basic obstacles to expansion through a branch network. In addition, the serious restrictions imposed on operation between the central office and branch made branch creation projects ineffective.

The best regional players were Sberbank, VTB and agro-financing specialist Rosselkhozbank. All three had massive networks that covered the whole country. However, in spite of partial privatisation they were still viewed as policy banks, in which profitability was not an overriding consideration.

Overview of key players

Sberbank

In the 2000s Sberbank was the largest countrywide branch network, with 18 regional head offices and more than 19,100 retail outlets with about 245,600 employees. Outside Russia, Sberbank operates subsidiaries and holds assets in Kazakhstan (Teksaka Bank) and Ukraine (Bank NRB) and is contemplating entry into Belarus (Belpromstroibank); it targets a 5 per cent share of these markets.

Sberbank's international activities involve direct settlement agreements, correspondent accounts with over 220 credit institutions, trade finance operations and membership of a number of international financial organisations. Close business ties and wide recognition by foreign counterparts have enabled Sberbank to expand abroad.

The bank's strategy for international development called for different approaches in different regions and has included both build and buy tactics. Sberbank has acquired existing operations and has established banking and non-banking financial companies outside Russia. Significant potential for growth in the Chinese and Indian financial services markets and the growing interest of Sberbank's corporate customers in these countries have driven the bank to establish a presence in both markets. In view of the barriers and risks linked to market entry, Sberbank focused on establishing limited 'beachheads' (in the form of representative offices or single branches) and then used these to assess further growth and expansion options.

Gazprombank

Gazprombank has been active in the banking market since 1990, when it was founded by the world's largest gas producer and exporter Gazprom (see Chapter 3) to provide banking services for gas industry enterprises. Since then, Gazprombank has become a leading player which is ranked among the top three banks of Russia. The bank delivers banking and investment services to over 45,000 corporate and about 3 million private clients. The bank's corporate clients are companies in all principal sectors of the economy: the oil and petrochemical industry, metallurgy, machinery, the nuclear industry, electric power industry, real estate construction, transport, telecommunications and trade.

By the end of the 2000s Gazprombank's worldwide reach was extensive: eight subsidiary and affiliated banks in Russia, Belarus, Switzerland and Armenia; representative offices in China and Mongolia; and 43 domestic branches throughout Russia. Among noticeable assets abroad were IDF Anlagegesellschaft (Liechtenstein), Arosgas Holding AG (Austria) and stakes in European gas-related companies. Gazprombank also had shareholdings in two foreign banks: General Banking and Trust Co. (Hungary, 26 per cent ownership) and Belgazprombank (Belarus, 34 per cent ownership). In Hungary, the bank operated ten branch offices. Besides these units, the bank completely owned the Dutch-based Gazinvest Finance. In France, the bank has possessed a 30 per cent share in Sofraci since 1999.

The total number of offices delivering banking and depository services under the single brand name of Gazprombank exceeds 500.

Other operators

Several banks were first movers in establishing international operations. One was Promsvyazbank, which was set up by telecommunications companies and provides services mostly for high-tech industries. The bank established a branch office in Cyprus in early 2002. Among the banks having at least one representative office abroad were Centrocredit and Krasbank (both in the UK), and the Moscow Industrial Bank, with an office in Austria.

Although the Russian banking sector is not globally competitive,[9] international expansion has occurred nonetheless. For example, all five leading banks (as well as some other financial institutions) have subsidiaries or affiliates in several countries.

The most publicised recent coup for the Russian banking industry was the deal made by the largest Russian investment company, Troika Dialog, which bought out the 33 per cent owner of South African group Standard Bank for US$200 million.[10] Standard Bank was then integrated into Troika Dialog.

Standard Bank was the largest banking group in South Africa on assets and profits, with offices located in 17 African countries and 20 other developing economies, including Russia, Brazil and China. By 2009, the assets of the group exceeded US$162 billion and the market value was approximately US$9.5 billion. The largest shareholder of the South African bank was Industrial and Commercial Bank of China. By entering this alliance, Troika Dialog also found a new partner with developed competencies and strong resources, large geographical coverage and a wide product range and client base. Considering the strong position of Standard Bank in emerging markets, Troika Dialog can expand substantially both its range of services and coverage of the markets using a well-known brand and the assistance of the foreign partner.

Despite several successful and efficient entries of Russian banks into the international space, most of the attempts were sporadic and careful. Technologies in Russian banking sector were somewhat simplistic, with corporate loans usually extended against collateral rather than against forecast cash flows. Fee-based products played a negligible role, rendering many Russian banks overly dependent on interest and trading income. In addition, most banks were organised by region rather than by business segment, which sometimes led to an insufficient focus on the customer.

Gaps in Russian banks' strategies and capabilities, as described above, provide substantial opportunities for big foreign banks whose funding, brand reputation, product expertise, customer service skills and risk management experience are often superior to those of their Russian counterparts. Russian banks have found it easier to catalyse international expansion by setting up subsidiaries in neighbouring CIS countries. The case studies of Alfa Bank and VTB, presented below, illustrate this growth strategy in further detail.

Alfa Bank: establishing control under operations

Founded in 1990, Alfa Bank Group offers a wide range of products and operates in all sectors of the financial market, offering corporate and retail lending, deposits, payment and account services, foreign exchange operations, cash handling services, custody services, investment banking and other ancillary services to corporate and retail customers.

Its corporate and retail client base has grown considerably during the last several years; by 1 September 2009 Alfa Bank Russia counted over 55,000 corporate and 3.6 million retail customers, while the branch network stretched to 341 offices across Russia and abroad, including a subsidiary bank in the Netherlands and financial subsidiaries in the US and the UK.

By mid-2009 Alfa Bank Group's total assets had decreased to US$23 billion, down 15 per cent from its level at the end of 2008 (US$27.1 billion). This drop resulted from a persistent weakness in the economy accompanied by a reduction in the loan portfolio and a general deterioration in the credit quality of corporate and retail borrowers. The gross loan portfolio decreased by 20.2 per cent to US$15.3 billion within the same time period.

Alfa Bank was founded as a commercial bank, with its first subsidiary office in Moscow. Its banking licence was obtained from the Central Bank of Russia. When launched, Alfa Bank also obtained domestic and foreign exchange licences. First accounts were opened with six foreign banks.

Alfa Bank was the first Russian bank to open a subsidiary bank in Alma Aty (Kazakhstan). In the mid-1990s the bank sat up a representative office in London, and in 2000 Alfa Bank acquired a 76 per cent stake in Ukraine's Kievinvestbank. In the 2000s the international activity of Alfa Bank was impressive. The company opened a subsidiary in New York – Alfa Capital Markets, specialising in brokerage and investment services – and acquired Amsterdam Trade Bank N.V. outright.[11]

Alfa Bank became the first Russian private company to sign an official agreement with the Overseas Private Investment Corporation (OPIC), a US government agency. Together with Merrill Lynch it won a tender issued by RAO UES to advise on the financial and investment aspects of reform of the power and energy sector.[12] With Gazprom it signed a strategic cooperation agreement.

By the end of the 2000s the bank operated over 200 branches in Russia and the CIS, as well as foreign subsidiaries in Kazakhstan, the Netherlands and the US. Alfa Bank's wholly owned subsidiary in the Netherlands, Amsterdam Trade Bank N.V., possesses a European banking license and serves clients mainly in import/export finance.

One of Alfa Bank's priorities was expanding investment services to foreign clients. Alfa Capital Markets in London and Alforma Capital Markets in New York, a NASD/SIPC-registered broker-dealer in New York, serve clients throughout the EU and North America.

Foreign markets entry and operations

Much of the bank's past success has been the result of its comprehensive knowledge and understanding of emerging markets, in particular those of Russia and the CIS countries. The bank employs a mix of Western and Russian management, which means that it both offers in-depth knowledge of the Russian market and applies the highest standards of Western financial practices.

Since the early 2000s the company's management has considered emerging markets as great opportunities, and the international operations of Alfa Bank have reflected this approach. Several countries were of special interest for bank's expansion. In Kazakhstan the company established operations in December 1994 and has since become one of the most reliable and progressive banks in the country. It became a full-service bank with a branch in Astana as well as three representative offices in Karaganda, Ust-Kamenogorsk and Ekibastuz. Alfa Bank Kazakhstan prioritised fast and high-quality financial flows between Russia and Kazakhstan. In Belarus Alfa Bank made its first move in 1999. Until 2008 the company was represented by Mezhtorgbank (Bank for International Trade and Investments). In July 2008 a consortium of Alfa Group companies completed the acquisition of around 90 per cent of the bank. By the end of the 2000s Alfa Bank Belarus offered its services through its head office in Minsk and 17 offices in other regions of the country. The bank became one of the leaders of the Belarussian market for carrying out operations involving most forms of securities: government bonds, short-term National Bank bonds, corporate bonds and shares.

In Ukraine, Alfa Bank has entered as a part of the international Alfa Group. Relatively quickly the bank established a prominent position in all segments of the Ukrainian banking sector. According to National Bank of Ukraine statistics, the bank was the seventh-largest in Ukraine in terms of total assets and among the leaders in terms of corporate customer accounts at the end of 2009. Alfa Bank Ukraine also held the leading position in terms of attracting savings: the bank's retail customer accounts grew by 5 per cent to US$285 million for the first six months of 2009, bucking the market trend. The bank also successfully launched a deposit programme for SME clients as well as offering wealth management for the growing number of VIP clients.

Since 2005, the bank's strategy was aimed at becoming one of the top five players in the local market by 2010 – an ambitious plan given the present gap between Alfa Bank Ukraine and the market leaders. By the end of the 2000s, the bank was in the process of establishing a number of corporate centres to cover major regions of Ukraine and around 70 small support offices for servicing SME clients.

In the UK operations of the company were established in 2000 through Alfa Capital Markets, an international investment banking business based in London. This business has played a key role in attracting international investors to the Russian equity market. Alfa Capital Markets is authorised to deal in a broad range of securities transactions in the UK's financial markets. It is also a member of the London Stock Exchange. The branch has a well-established and highly regarded equities business, offering its international client base access not only to Russia and CIS countries but also to one of the leading financial markets of the world. With its experience on the London Stock Exchange, the branch also acted as corporate broker and had a special focus on supporting LSE-listed companies with operations in Russia, Ukraine and Kazakhstan.

In Cyprus, the investment firm Alfa Capital Holdings was established; this operated successfully in the UK through its branch Alfa Capital Markets from January 2005. In the US, Alforma Capital Markets was established in July 2001 to provide brokerage and investment services to US institutional clients investing in Russia and the CIS. The office was staffed by professionals with extensive experience in the brokerage industry and knowledge of emerging markets.

In the Netherlands, Amsterdam Trade Bank N.V. (since 1994) was launched as a fully owned subsidiary of Alfa Bank. It provided standard and tailor-made products in Russia-related trade and project finance, corporate banking and international money transfers. Since 2003 in the Netherlands and since 2006 in Germany, Amsterdam Trade Bank became active in the retail market with its saving and deposit products offering high interest rates. By the end of the 2000s it was the only bank with private Russian capital operating within the European Union. Amsterdam Trade Bank was supervised by the Dutch Central Bank (De Nederlandsche Bank) and carried out its activities in strict accordance with all Dutch banking regulations.

VTB Group – challenges of international expansion

The VTB Group is a universal financial and banking institution with a strong presence in Russia and expanding international activities in the CIS, Western Europe, Africa and Asia, through both organic growth and a series of strategic acquisitions. At the end of 2009 VTB's equity reached RUB 583.8 billion (around US$20 billion) and its assets RUB 2,696.5 billion (some US$90 billion). According to 2009 results, VTB ranked 65th among the world's largest banks.[13]

The organisational structure of the bank is based on its active participation in the authorised capital of 12 credit and nine financial institutions.[15] VTB Group's operations included two subsidiary banks in Russia and a number of financial companies (including VTB Leasing, VTB Insurance and VTB Capital), subsidiary banks in Ukraine, Armenia, Georgia, Belarus and Angola, six banks in Western Europe (the UK, France, Austria, Germany, Cyprus and Switzerland), and a financial company in Namibia. VTB Bank also has representative offices in Italy, Kazakhstan, Kyrgyz Republic and China. VTB Capital plc (United Kingdom) operated a subsidiary in Singapore. In addition, VTB operated in the Vietnamese market through Vietnam–Russia Joint Venture Bank (VRB). VRB did not actually belong to VTB Group, but the bank had considerable control over its activities through a large stake of VRB shares.

Nevertheless, the core of VTB was its Russian banking business, which was complemented by a geographically diversified branch network for corporate and retail services and financial companies. VTB possessed an extensive network of branches and subsidiary and associated banks located in the most significant and dynamic regions of the country, and several subsidiary companies offering a wide range of ancillary services. As at the end of 2008, VTB Group's Russian branch network comprised 693 points of sale.

VTB's origins lie in October 1990, when the Russian Ministry of Finance and the Central Bank established the Bank for Foreign Trade (VneshTorgBank) to assist Russia's foreign economic transactions and stimulate integration in the world economy.

VneshTorgBank (VTB) provided several business lines, including servicing and funding entities engaged in foreign economic activities, international settlements and interbank operations and precious metal trading. In November 1991, VTB was among the first Russian banks to join SWIFT (Society for Worldwide Interbank Financial Telecommunication) and to handle real-time international payments. Within two years VTB had covered the globe with a correspondent network, including over 200 leading banks in Europe, America, Asia, Africa and Australia. The world's leading banks and export insurance agencies from developed economies recognised VTB's guarantees.

Thanks to its dynamism, VTB joined the ranks of the top five largest banks in the country and become a leading Russian currency market maker. Several important government tasks were granted to VTB, among which were the raising and servicing of external loans related to funding large investment projects and the exclusive right to sell precious metals in the external market on behalf of the Russian government and the Bank of Russia. VTB also serviced the National Currency Reserve of the Russian Federation and the Stabilisation Currency Fund of the Bank of Russia.

In 1997, the government transformed VTB from a closed joint-stock company into an open corporation, although the Bank of Russia retained the largest shareholding, with 96.8 per cent of stock. During the financial crisis of 1998, VTB preserved its solvency, helping the bank to strengthen its reputation.

After a change of management team in 2002, it took less than five years to transform VTB from a highly specialised bank with a small branch network into one of Russia's largest credit institutions. VTB grew significantly faster than other large Russian banks. Along with achieving a rapid increase in the volume of its domestic operations, VTB focused on creating the first international banking group in Russia, which would be able to compete with top Western lending and financial institutions, and provide high-quality banking services worldwide.

Until January 2007 the Russian government had held a 99.9 per cent stake in VTB. However, at the World Economic Forum in Davos in 2007, VTB's CEO announced that the government would retain a stake of 50 per cent + 1 share, while the rest of the company's shares would be privatised. By the end of the 2000s, the government still owned around 77 per cent of the bank via the Federal Property Agency.[16] Nonetheless, VTB's IPO marked the beginning of a new period for the bank. One of the world's largest, the IPO raised almost US$8 billion, with shares publicly traded in Russian and international securities markets. Leading global investment funds showed interest, and more than 120,000 Russian citizens became VTB shareholders. With the funds collected, VTB became one the world's top 100 banks in terms of capital. Furthermore, in October 2007, despite the global financial crisis, VTB successfully placed a US$2 billion Eurobond loan, a first for Russian banks.

In the late 2000s, VTB, as one of the cornerstone banks, played a special role in supporting the Russian economy. It significantly expanded its volume of lending to strategically important companies. This lending was funded by the state in order to support key sectors of the Russian economy. In particular, VTB extended loans to metallurgy, automotive, transport, military, oil and coal mining companies.

International expansion and entry strategies

After Russia, VTB's second priority region has been the CIS, where it has aggressively expanded its footprint by acquiring and opening new banks. The bank's strategy was based on the total coverage of all CIS countries where it deemed such presence to be economically viable, providing banking services to Russian, local and international corporate customers as well as actively developing the retail business.[17]

VTB's third priority region consisted of emerging markets, primarily in Asia and Africa. In these markets, VTB intended to serve the interests of customers from Russia and the CIS and foreign customers doing business with Russia and the CIS, and to participate in joint investment projects. Therefore, the choice of host country related to whether the country is, or will be, of interest to Russian and CIS businesses.

In the CIS region, the presence of VTB was most active in the countries that had the most significant trade turnover with Russia. Furthermore, the economic reforms made in CIS countries also become a particularly important factor for the internationalisation of Russian banks in this region.

Since 2005, VTB has established subsidiaries in Ukraine, Armenia and Georgia. By the end of the 2000s, the management of VTB started to consider Azerbaidjan as the most promising CIS market; its industrial and trade potential were very high, and the region was attractive for investment.[18] Therefore, in 2009, a new subsidiary called VTB Bank Azerbaidjan was set up in Baku.

VTB expanded in the CIS markets mostly through M&As. In 1996 VTB acquired the controlling interest in Slavneftebank (Belarus) and has integrated it into the VTB Group with the name of VTB Bank (Belarus). VTB Bank (Georgia) was established in 1994 following the merger of three state banks and in 2005 became a member of VTB Group. Furthermore, VTB has opened representative offices in Kazakhstan and the Kyrgyz Republic. Financial analysts thus agree that VTB's international expansion was based on trade operations with ex-Communist countries enjoying traditional strong ties with Russia.[19]

In Europe, the bank's activity was also impressive in the 2000s. Europe had been in the bank's strategic plan for quite a while, but one of the main obstacles on this path was the strong competition. Many powerful European banks competed successfully with VTB not only abroad but also in Russia. Meanwhile, the majority of Russian banks did not have access to cheap financial resources and were not able to attract resources from abroad, so their position in the international market was rather weak. VTB's expansion plans in Europe were usually supported by the government, however, since such acquisitions can have a positive impact for foreign direct investment into Russia.

VTB, when still a state-owned bank, had acquired many of its banking assets abroad with government backing: for example, the 85 per cent of Donau Bank in Vienna originally controlled by Central Bank of Russia were transferred to VTB. In developing its banking network abroad, VTB founded Russian Commercial Bank both in Zurich (Switzerland) and in Limassol (Cyprus). VTB later reinforced its international presence by becoming a shareholder of East–West United Bank (Luxembourg) and Ost-West Handelsbank (Frankfurt-am-Main), and increased its participation in Donau Bank (Vienna). However, the Russian Central Bank also held shares in most of these.

Within VTB Group its London-based investment business, VTB Capital, had a unique position in Europe. Owned by the Russian government (with a share above 75 per cent), it was traded in London, and was the only Russian bank to operate a fully licensed British unit. However, VTB Capital was mostly developing operations in Asia, not in the European region.

In June 2009, VTB Capital launched its Middle East office in Dubai, receiving a license from the Dubai Financial Services Authority to operate as an authorised firm in the Dubai International Financial Centre. VTB Capital also entered into a partnership with a subsidiary of Kuwait Finance House to provide financial services in Russia and internationally, and has inked an agreement with Fouad Alghanim and Sons Co, a Kuwait civil engineering group, to develop power generation projects in Russia and the Gulf. The management of VTB Capital considered VTB's entry into the Middle East as giving an access to a region with many deals to be struck, and hence providing the chance to grow at a time when other banks were downsizing.[20]

In 2006 a Russian–Namibian joint venture, VTB Capital (Namibia) (PTY) Ltd, was established by VTB Capital during the course of the opening meeting of the Russian–Namibian Intergovernmental Commission in Windhoek (Namibia).[21] The main purpose of establishing VTB Capital (Namibia) was to attract Russian businesses, technology and investment to the Namibian market and sub-Saharan Africa in order to implement jointly the most interesting and promising projects in the region, as well as the international financing of those projects. By the end of the 2000s, VTB Capital (Namibia), in cooperation with Russian and Namibian partners, was taking part in several projects in the sphere of mining, power generation and industrial construction.

By the late 2000s, VTB expansion plans included Vietnam and Angola, as well as an expanding presence in Singapore. Given VTB's active role in providing credit for Alrosa (one of the largest global diamond mining companies, of Russian origin) in Angola, the entry into Africa seemed a logical move.[22]

VTB was the first Russian bank to obtain licences and to open its branches in both India and China. VTB Capital also negotiated a contract to start servicing bank cards of UnionPay, the Chinese national processing company.

The efficient international results of VTB during the financial crisis can be partly explained by its role as of 'provider of liquidity' for Russia's economy and businesses. VTB was shielded from potential financial woes by the state. High-ranking officials issued multiple statements expressing their commitment to ensuring the normal operations of Russia's large state banks. Its strong branch network, with more than 1,000 outlets, gave VTB Capital a serious competitive advantage in the retail banking market, which was a top business priority in its development strategy. VTB's status as a 'state bank' thus provided it with the opportunity to expand its client base in the retail and corporate segments both in Russia and abroad.

The global financial crisis had significantly impacted VTB Group's operating environment, however: foreign capital markets were effectively shut, liquidity had tightened, borrowing rates had substantially increased, and the stock prices of Russian companies had fallen while credit risks had risen in both corporate and retail segments.

These developments impacted VTB's ongoing business and its future development plans. Its priorities in the current environment have shifted towards improving the efficiency of its operations and maintaining the profitability of its business by restructuring the asset base, improving risk management procedures and introducing more stringent control over expenditures, the productivity of the network and the profitability of the stand-alone businesses.

In response to the crisis, the bank had postponed a move into its planned businesses in Russia, but has maintained its international expansion. VTB chose one of the darkest moments in stock market history to launch a share trade at its new investment banking unit, which was founded to become Russia's new national champion investment bank.

The big Russian banks have been at the forefront of the industry's global expansion outside Russian borders. All five of the biggest banks have branch networks or operations in several countries, mainly neighbouring CIS countries. This is due to the structure of the industry, which is consolidated at the top and fragmented at the bottom. Thus only the big few have the resources to go abroad. A second-tier bank, say a regional entity in the centre of Siberia, will hardly ever have the resources to go abroad. Furthermore, it is likely that the smaller banks would attempt to grow within national borders before testing unfamiliar foreign waters.

The major motive for the banking industry's internationalisation has traditionally been the sector's clients. Here the banking sector followed the same rules of global expansion as have other Russian industries. As corporate customers of Russian banks ventured abroad, they demanded that their banks had a foreign presence to help finance their foreign activities.

Russian financial institutions and large companies thus worked in synergy for their respective global expansion, with Russian banks considering countries suitable for their international expansion if these countries were of interest to large banking customers – especially for mining, metallurgy, oil and gas companies, and other strategic industries which benefit the whole national economy. Another goal for Russian banks operating abroad is to attract inward FDI into the country. They offer financing to foreign companies planning to enter local markets. Here, state-owned banks are capable of benefiting the Russian economy. Both avenues of international expansion – helping Russian industries go abroad and greasing the wheels of inward FDI from foreign clients – help increase the wealth of the nation by generating export income and long-term investment.

The entry methods for Russian banks have usually been acquisitions and greenfield investments. In countries where the banks are doing brisk business, they have acquired existing competitors. For new and unfamiliar markets, the process has usually been sporadic and cautious, typically beginning with the establishment of a representative bureau, which evaluates the market as to business potential and timing for full entry. Most Russian banks establish foreign operations through several subsidiaries, typically spread throughout the world.

The most salient features of Russian banks' internationalisation are as follows. First, there is a geographic affinity to the CIS, and to a lesser extent EU and BRIC countries. This is explained by traditionally close ties; some existing brand awareness; demand by large corporate clients active in the markets (for example, large Russian MNEs); and high demand for financial services in the rapidly developing economies.

Secondly, the choice of establishing subsidiaries (i.e. local branch networks) as an entry mode is arguably a forced one. The nature of financial services combined with the unstable Russian economic environment makes 'low-involvement' options impossible and encourages banks to look for total control over their foreign operations. The example of VTB shows that attempts to establish wholly owned subsidiaries in developed markets can be successful. However, unless domestic business conditions improve and the state reduces its control over Russian banks, this strategy can probably not be replicated.

Thirdly, the cautious expansion approach is again the result of the domestic business environment, namely the perceived country risk. More aggressive expansion behaviour into less developed markets would mean giving up on the need for full control over foreign operations. All key features of Russian bank expansion are thus dependent on domestic economic conditions.

On the one hand, the largest banks are state-owned and sometimes even affiliated with resource giants whose liquidity surplus is comforting; on the other hand, however, Russian banks do not possess an 'export option' when entering foreign markets. Banks need to physically establish their presence. Adding complexity, most countries consider banking to be a sensitive area, and it is protected by strict regulation that limits the leverage of the Russian government's support. Regulation also implies a side-effect: common measures of international activity, such as UNCTAD's Transnationality Index, become useless, as the value of foreign assets, for example, indicate not the financial position of the company but the restrictions in place. As with other service industries, the number of personnel abroad, number of deals with foreign agents and indirect ways of assessing company performance also show a distorted picture, thus making performance evaluation and comparison a tricky task in itself.

As compared with other industries, banks have proven to be rather conservative investors. The most popular route has been expansion to neighbouring and familiar CIS countries via subsidiaries, in most cases followed by expansion to stable Western European and US markets and in some cases China and India. This might be considered a wise move, as Russian banks definitely need their domestic clients.

Another interesting feature of Russian banks' internationalisation was their growing attachment to building subsidiary networks and their attention to local retail customers, in addition to following large Russian companies and servicing their needs. This, along with very limited political accompaniment, suggests that Russian banks' foreign expansion is truly business-driven and not politically motivated. By and large, it is not the government that uses the banks it owns to achieve its goals, but, when necessary, vice versa.

6 FDI from Russia

The metallurgy sector

Strategies of Russian metallurgy firms

In the first years of the twenty-first century metallurgy, with all its soot, smoke and clamour, had some truly golden years. Producing metals from raw mineral ores, via some high-energy alchemy, was a booming activity, and nicely profitable at that.

More recently, metallurgy has been booming again. Construction in emerging markets has fuelled a boom and prices of natural resources are once more skyrocketing. Metallurgy could barely satisfy demand, despite prices at all-time highs. With the onset of the world financial crisis in 2008, however, the industry was forced to throttle down to accommodate the decreased demand from its customers in the West.

As a result, some of the metallurgy companies restructured to operate more vertically. Upstream, they added stakes in mining companies, while downstream they started producing semi-finished goods such as construction materials. Yet, for all of this, the production and refining of metals remained the core of their business.

This line of business is capital-intensive, requiring significant investment to support and expand production and raw materials bases. For example, the most progressive method for smelting steel — in electro arc furnaces — incurs extremely high electricity costs. Equipment used for mining, processing and metal production at all stages is as a rule very costly.

As a result, the industry has high entry barriers. First, as noted above, the capital investment requirements are very substantial. Next, competition is tough. Access to raw mineral ores is also a factor, since many production facilities are located near the mines that provide the raw materials. Lastly, the economies of scale enjoyed by large companies make it difficult for small companies to compete successfully in either ferrous or non-ferrous metals.

One distinct characteristic of the metallurgical business is its high returns — in 2007 the average EBITDA (earnings before interest, taxes, depreciation and amortisation) stood at about 30 per cent. Companies having their own natural resources have significantly higher margins and lower risks. Vertically integrated holdings, which control the whole technological cycle from mining ore to making final products with high added-value (the margin on such products may reach up to 40 per cent), are the most efficient.

Many of Russia's current metallurgy players formed up in the 1990s. This process tended to follow a pattern in which an existing large smelter or mining company, in the course of Russia's period of privatisation, bought an asset in which to hold subsidiary assets (production, natural resources, energy generation), and owned a production suite from ore to finished product.

The leading Russian metallurgic holdings are already closely integrated into the global economy and target foreign consumers. For example, Russia's giant Mechel Group exports half of its production; its associate, MMK, some 46 per cent.

Market segmentation

Russian smelting comprises enterprises which extract and enrich ferrous and non-ferrous metals and non-metallic materials. The basic market segmentation is thus by type of product.

These various smelters produce pig iron, steel, rolled products, steel pipes, metal products, ferroalloys, refractory materials, coke, aluminium, copper, nickel, cobalt, lead, zinc, tin, antimony, mercury, tungsten, molybdenum, niobium, tantalum, rare earth metals and non-ferrous metals (aluminium, titanium, magnesium, heavy non-ferrous metals). Often as by-products, they also produce carbide, carbon, semi-conductor products, recycling scrap and waste and certain types of chemical products. It is a large and complex conglomeration, and is even equipped to do its own R&D.

At the end of the 2000s, Russia was fourth in world steel production (behind China, Japan and the US) and third in steel-pipe production as well as in export of metal products (exports of rolled steel in 2007 amounted to approximately 27.6 million tonnes, while those from China were 52.1 million tonnes and from Japan 35.6 million tonnes). In the production of aluminium, Russia lies second, after China; but it is number one in aluminium export. Russia leads in the production of tin and the export of nickel, and is second in titanium.

There is a strong tendency toward integration in both the ferrous and mining industry and in the non-ferrous sector, in which aluminium is one of the most prominent industries. Cross-border M&As have been taking place for several years. Usually the intention behind these mergers is technological updating and creation of new products. But it is also through integration that companies tend to strengthen their position, drive down production costs and expand into new markets.

With regard to the non-ferrous sector, the Asia-Pacific region is the most lucrative, generating up to 50 per cent of the global aluminium market's aggregate value. Europe accounts for 25 per cent of the global aluminium market, and America more than 25 per cent. The main factor of differentiation in this industry is the availability of bauxites. There are only seven bauxite-rich areas: Western and Central Africa (mostly, Guinea), South America (Brazil, Venezuela and Suriname), the Caribbean (Jamaica), Oceania and Southern Asia (Australia, India), China, the Mediterranean (Greece, Turkey) and the Urals (Russia).

The aluminium industry is highly concentrated. It consists of a limited number of large multinational players, offering similar products and services. As a result it is extremely hard, even impossible, for smaller and weaker companies to enter the market. Exit barriers are high, too, because many of the major tangible assets are highly specific to the industry and thus hard to sell. It is no easy matter to find a buyer for a used aluminium smelter. So, to enter metallurgy costs a lot and to leave it costs a lot. In this situation, players are strongly motivated to remain in the industry even when conditions are difficult, as they were during the recent crisis.

The Russian government protects domestic producers with quotas and tariffs as well as by creating favourable conditions for exporting. It also aids companies in buying foreign assets and makes great efforts to persuade other countries to reduce trade restrictions against Russian steel products.

In 2009, after some years of development, the Russian Ministry promulgated a programme, 'Development Strategy of the Steel and Iron Industry in the Russian Federation'. This consisted of a set of practical measures that were to be taken, by both the industry and the government, to attain certain objectives by the year 2020. Owing to its observation of these measures, the Russian industry had prospered in the 2000s. New tax breaks, one of the measures, encouraged Russian metallurgy to enter new markets.

Russian companies in ferrous metallurgy have greatly increased their international operations over time. Their main mode of entry was acquisition. Domestically, the industry remains internally competitive but has become top-heavy. At the end of the 2000s only four companies (Severstal, Evraz, Novolipetsk steel mill and Magnitogorsk steel mill) together produced 75 per cent of Russia's steel, and nine metallurgical companies accounted for nearly 90 per cent of the country's steel output, leaving the remaining two dozen to produce the rest.

Main players – ferrous metals

The largest metallurgy company in the world is ArcelorMittal, which produces almost three times as much steel as its closest competitor, Nippon Steel, and accounts for almost 8 per cent of the world's production of steel. The rest of the top ten producers account for only some 2–3 per cent.

The largest Russian steel maker is Severstal, which produced some 17.3 million tonnes of crude steel in 2008. Other major Russian steel makers are Evraz, MMK, Mechel and Novolipetsk, all of which belong to the world's top 25 producers. The Mechel group is a vertically integrated corporation which controls the whole technological chain, from mining ore to the manufacture of goods with high added-value. It is the second-largest coal miner and the sixth-largest producer of metallurgical goods in Russia. About half of the group's product is exported.

The company has divisions in mining, metallurgy, ferroalloy and energy. Coal mining (both coking and steam), iron ore and nickel generated up to 30 per cent of all revenue and up to 65 per cent of the company's EBITDA, with an EBITDA margin of above 40 per cent. The group's mining assets are concentrated in Siberia, Kazakhstan and the US. Metallurgy (production of profiled and sheet-rolled steel, hardware, stamping pieces and forged pieces) generated some 70 per cent of the company's revenue and 35 per cent of its EBITDA, with an EBITDA margin of 9 per cent. The group's steel-casting assets are located in Russia, Lithuania and Romania. Ferroalloy capacities are located in Russia and Kazakhstan. With internationalisation ever in mind (Mechel shares are traded on the New York Stock Exchange (NYSE)), the group is making large-scale investments in expanding its raw materials and processing assets domestically, predominantly in Siberia.

Magnitogorsk Metal and Steel Works (MMK) is one of the 20 largest world steel producers, and is Russia's second-largest metal producer, with 17 per cent of the domestic market. MMK's main production asset, JSC Magnitogorsk Metallurgical Plant, generates about 60 per cent of the group's revenue. The plant's technological cycle includes all processing stages: mining and preparation of iron ore, smelting of cast iron and steel, rolling and the making of final products.

Until recently, MMK had practically no sources for raw materials of its own. However, in 2006 the company won an auction for the right to develop the Prioskolsky deposit in Belgorod Oblast, while in 2007 it signed a 10-year contract for the delivery of iron ore from the Sokolovsko-Sarbaiskaya Group deposit, which became its main supplier. MMK also bought 51 per cent of the shares of the Bakal ore deposit management company in Chelyabinsk Oblast, thereby increasing its self-sufficiency in iron ore to 20 per cent. In 2009 MMK acquired 82.6 per cent of Belon, a Russian coal-mining company. The aim of this deal was to cover some 40 per cent of company needs for coking coal concentrate, with the long-term goal of raising this to 80 per cent. In the same year MMK acquired a company named Profit, the capacity of which covered practically 100 per cent of MMK's demand for scrap metal. MMK generates about 90 per cent of its own electricity needs from its own power plants.

Also powering MMK's drive to achieve more perfect integration was at least one significant international deal. In 2007 it bought some 5 per cent of shares in the Australian company Fortescue Metals, with a plan to increase its stake in the future. While Australia holds further potential for MMK, its key export region is the Middle East. To strengthen its position in this market MMK has invested in a steel production project in Turkey called MMK-Atakas. The company's present strategy is to refine its palette of activities to become a producer of high value-added metals.

Main players – non-ferrous metals

A noteworthy player in the non-ferrous sector is Norilsk Nickel, the world's largest producer of nickel and palladium and one of the leading producers of platinum and copper. It also produces various by-products, such as cobalt, chromium, rhodium, silver, gold, iridium, ruthenium, selenium, tellurium and sulphur. The company is involved in prospecting and exploration for and extraction, refining and metallurgical processing of minerals, as well as in the production, marketing and sale of base and precious metals. The main domestic production units of the company are vertically integrated.

Norilsk Nickel's production facilities are located in five countries besides Russia: Australia, Botswana, Finland, the USA and South Africa. Norilsk Nickel's Australian businesses are three-fold: a laterite nickel ore production and leaching facility; three sulphide nickel producers; and a large sulphide nickel ore exploration project. In Botswana, Norilsk Nickel is active in sulphide nickel production. In Finland, the company owns the only nickel refining plant. In the USA, the company holds a major stake in the leading producer of platinum group metals. And in South Africa, Norilsk Nickel holds a 50 per cent interest in the Nkomati nickel mine.

The company has an R&D base abroad in Norilsk Process Technology, a research and development centre in Australia. Another research facility is the domestic Gipronickel Institute in St Petersburg. Norilsk Nickel is multinational not only in terms of having production facilities or natural deposits abroad: it also has a global network of representative and sales offices in Russia, the UK, China, the USA and Switzerland.

Another player on the non-ferrous metals market is the Russian Copper Company, the third-largest Russian copper producer (behind Norilsk Nickel and Ural Mining and the Metallurgical Company group), which produces 164,000 tonnes of cathode copper annually: 18 per cent of the Russian market and 1 per cent of the world market. The company also produces zinc concentrate and precious metals. The group owns the rights to natural resources use at 14 copper and copper–zinc deposits with overall reserves of about 280 million tonnes of ore.

Russian Copper Company's 12 main subsidiaries comprise a fully vertically integrated technological cycle: purchases of scrap metal and ore extraction, production of copper concentrate and blister copper, production of copper cathodes, copper rolled wire and finished products from copper and its alloys.

The company operates in four Russian regions and in Kazakhstan. Its main foreign clients are located in Europe and South-East Asia. In the very near future the company may feel a strong necessity to internationalise more thoroughly in order to better serve final customers and come closer to its suppliers. That, indeed, is what some of its competitors are already doing.

Discussed in case studies below are three firms: Rusal, which is in the aluminium sector, and Severstal and Evraz, in steel. Rusal seems to follow the more typical mode of internationalisation, heading in the direction of least resistance. The other two have opted for aggressive expansion into notably resistant developed economies. Severstal is something of a special case, as it stands almost alone among Russian MNEs by attempting to leverage its brand value.

Going backward: Rusal

The high level of consolidation in the Russian industry is demonstrated by the fact that today there is only one large company in aluminium: United Company Rusal. Before their merger in 2007, there was still rivalry between two firms – Rusal (75 per cent of the market, and the world's top producer) and Sual (about 25 per cent of the market and listed among the world's top ten aluminium companies). Sual's primary specialisation was bauxite mining, while Rusal did downstream smelting of aluminium.

Founded in March 2007, UC Rusal was a result of the merger of Rusal, Sual and the alumina assets of Glencore, a Swiss company. It is headquartered in Moscow. In 2010 Rusal accounted for 10 per cent of the global output of primary aluminium and 10 per cent of the world's alumina production.[1]

The company operates in 19 countries on 5 continents, employing approximately 75,000 people. In addition to its aluminium and alumina businesses, Rusal also comprises such assets as bauxite and nepheline ore mines, foil mills and power-generating assets, and produces alloys and packaging materials. The five business divisions of the company are: aluminium, alumina, packaging, engineering and construction, and energy. Rusal owns 16 aluminium smelters, 12 alumina refineries, 8 bauxite mines and many other assets.

Rusal produced 4.4 million tonnes of aluminium and 11.2 million tonnes of alumina in 2008, making the company the most significant player in the industry. In 2007, at the time of the acquisition of Sual and Glencore, managers of Rusal targeted an increase in the output of aluminium of up to 5 million tonnes. However, the economic crisis intervened and the target was not met.

The company primarily operates in Russia, the US, China, Japan and Singapore. The automotive, construction and packaging industries are key clients, and the relationship with these figures strongly in company strategy. Another strategy of the company is to encompass similar businesses as much as possible, which can help the company to be more stable. Overall management is exercised divisionally.

Though Russia does not have its own large reservoir of aluminium, the country still recommends itself to manufacturing for its low labour cost and the bargain electricity needed for production. It also saves on transportation costs because it has a network of smelters and plants which provides favourable options in the transport of materials to plants and transport of finished product from them.

Company history

Rusal was founded in 2000, when Sibirsky Aluminium and Millhouse Capital agreed to manage jointly the aluminium and alumina assets they controlled.[2] As a result Rusal became the owner of the main aluminium manufacturers both there and in Ukraine, and one of the largest and most powerful aluminium companies in Russia.

In the beginning there were several powerful individual stockholders of the company's shares who ranked as oligarchs, a term both descriptive and censorious. However, all of them, except Oleg Deripaska, sold their shares, making him the principal stockholder of the company.

One of the main aims of Rusal was to turn global. The first step in this regard was the purchase of the Friguia alumina refinery CBK in the Republic of Guinea. Subsequently, the company acquired 20 per cent of the equity of the world's second-largest alumina refinery in terms of production capacity, Queensland Alumina Ltd in Australia. Following that, in 2006, the company turned to opening new markets for its manufacturing. China and Italy were chosen as targets. The company acquired Arcima Mining in 2006. In the same year, it acquired the ALSCON Aluminium Smelter in Nigeria, purchased a cathode plant in China and completed privatisation of the Friguia alumina refinery in the Republic of Guinea. Today Rusal manufactures and pursues other activities, such as refining and smelting in Guinea, Nigeria, Armenia, Ukraine, Italy, Kazakhstan, China, Ireland, Jamaica, Guyana, Australia, Sweden and Russia.

In 2007 Rusal signed a contract with Corporacion Venezolana de Guayana to jointly explore opportunities in and then to develop raw material and aluminium projects in Venezuela. Moreover, the company entered a cooperative venture with the Indonesian state-owned company ANTAM to construct a bauxite and alumina complex in Indonesia. Entry into these two markets was intended to hoist the company to the world's number one spot.

Rusal's international activity peaked with its acquisition of Glencore in 2007. By this acquisition Rusal not only outran its competition in the industry, but also crossed the finish line as the largest aluminium company of the world. In the event, Rusal reached the capacity of 4 million tonnes of aluminium a year and 11 million tonnes of alumina, equivalent, as noted above, to approximately 11 per cent of global aluminium output and 13 per cent of global alumina.

This acquisition was fateful for the company. Before the Glencore deal, Rusal was limited in alumina production (2.7 tonnes per year before) because it could provide only 70 per cent of the bauxite that it needed for its targeted volume of alumina production. With its acquisition of Sual, mentioned above, it bought more bauxite than it had the capacity to process. Acquiring Glencore, however, enabled Rusal to process that excess. In April 2008 Rusal acquired 25 per cent plus 2 shares of Norilsk Nickel, the world's largest nickel and palladium producer, a move that slightly lessened the proportion of shares held by Oleg Deripaska.

Figuring among Rusal's biggest deals was the putting into commission of the Khakas aluminium smelter, one of the most advanced aluminium production facilities in the world. The investment channelled into this project exceeds US$750 million and provides the company with an additional capacity of 300,000 tonnes.

Entry decisions

One of the main characteristics of the aluminium industry is the high level of consolidation as a result of a scarcity of and fierce competition for the raw material, bauxite. As a result, companies with insufficient supply either have to buy it on the free market – and thereby put themselves at the mercy of price fluctuation – or join forces with bauxite mine owners. In this situation the main tool for enhancing market position is M&As, and this is the most common tactic for the sector. Rusal is an example of a company that uses the strategy of buying competitors' refineries or smelters to enter new foreign markets. It uses M&As to increase the volume on its domestic market.

One priority destination for Rusal was African Guinea, where the company was represented, at the end of the 2000s, by three active production facilities. These were an alumina refinery in Fria, which was privatised by Rusal in 2006, Compagnie des Bauxites de Kindia (CBK), which has been managed by Rusal since 2001, and Compagnie Guinéenne de Génie (CGG). The company's establishment in Guinea was yet another critical step in achieving its goal of creating an international and diversified energy and metals corporation. High strategic value was attached to Guinea because of a close relationship with Moscow dating back to the Soviet Union, but also because Guinea held two-thirds of the world's bauxite deposits, or around 18 billion tonnes.[3]

In 2002, UC Rusal obtained control over Guinea's Friguia (ACG), the only alumina refinery in Africa, allowing the company to become more resource-independent. In 2006 Rusal and the government of Guinea reached an agreement on privatisation of the refinery through the sale to Rusal of 100 per cent of the shares of Friguia and a 15 per cent stake in the managing company Alumina Company of Guinea Limited, owned by Guinea's government. The price of this deal was about US$300 million.[4] The estimated capacity of this refinery was 640,000 tonnes of alumina and 1.9 million tonnes of bauxite per annum. According to the agreement with the government of Guinea, Rusal planned to increase the production of these companies almost two-fold.

Rusal continued its shopping spree in Guyana, on the other side of the Atlantic, in 2004 starting exploration of the Bauxite Company of Guyana deposit through licensing instruments. It finalised acquisition in 2006 by buying the state mining company, Aroaima Mining Company (AMC), and wholly transferring its assets to Rusal. According to the agreement with the Guyanan government, Rusal's investment obligations were US$22 million. The purchase of deposits in Guyana was intended to ensure a stable supply of bauxite for loading supplementary capacities at the Nikolaev Alumina Refinery (Rusal), thus allowing alumina production to be increased.

Although UC Rusal mostly used M&As for foreign expansion, these were not hostile deals. One of the Rusal's principles was to seek compromise in forging agreements with partners. It proved to have skill in this. One of its gambits was to concede its willingness to invest and renovate after acquisition. Rusal also exploited the advantages of licensing, as with the Compagnie des Bauxites de Kindia and in a few other cases. Despite its prominent investments abroad, however, Rusal's domestic export still was estimated at about 80 per cent of the company's whole output.

Strategy for foreign markets

A primary goal of UC Rusal remains the creation of an international and diversified energy and metals corporation big enough to be a global leader. To attain this it had to assure sufficient supply of two requisites: bauxite and alumina, the raw ingredients of aluminium. There are only few deposits of these in the world and, as a result of their scarcity, the main players on the aluminium market have already secured these deposits for themselves. For an ambitious company the task, therefore, is to contrive to buy deposits and then to develop them. The tried-and-tested instrument for accomplishing this is M&As. Rusal was not innovating in taking this route.

Another strategic factor that plays into company development and internationalisation is energy, of which the production of aluminium requires massive amounts. Thus, aluminium-smelting plants are located in areas where there are abundant supplies of inexpensive energy, such as hydroelectric power. However, proximity to hydroelectric power does not solve the problem of remoteness from bauxite and alumina. Producers face a dilemma: do I produce near the bauxite mine or near the source of energy?

That is why aluminium producers leave industrially developed countries and shift to countries that not only produce cheap energy but also have cheap raw ore. Rusal is in the forefront of these moves, acquiring foreign assets and modernising some of them.

The aluminium industry is core to Russia and figures significantly in its GDP, impelling the government to support it. Without such support it would be too costly to compete internationally, as the rivalry for deposits and smelters is fierce and worldwide. Rusal, as one of five so-called economy-forming companies in the country, is a persuasive proponent of the idea of government support for overseas expansion and the Russian government has seen fit to help the company not only with domestic projects but also with foreign ones. The deal that Rusal has successfully made in Guinea is an example of such international support, and has proved beneficial not only for Rusal but also for the whole Russian economy. What help (among other things) to maintain Rusal's Guinea operations are intergovernmental agreements between Russia and Guinea.[5]

Even so, the Russian state could not afford Rusal quick help to spare it damage from the international financial crisis. Two problems aggravated the situation for Rusal: falling demand for its goods and too heavy a debt load. To cope, the company was finally obliged to sign an agreement on restructuring its debt to international lenders and Russia's banks.

The government sometimes also helps indirectly. When Rusal began developing an IPO plan it intended to finance it by floating up to 10 per cent of its shares.[6] However, because of high debt, Rusal would not be able to pay dividends for several years. Companies responsive to government guidance, such as Sberbank and VTB, signalled interest in the sale, with a market price of US$2 to US$2.6 billion.

To conclude, Rusal's strategy ensures the company's sustainable development, making the best use of its competitive advantages: cheap energy, low costs and security of resources.

To overcome the effects of the lingering crisis of 2008, Rusal intends to work in partnership with other players, as well as with government and financial institutions. It might have saved itself the need for chastening damage control, however, had it confined itself to the production of primary aluminium and avoided diversification into the high-risk market of end products.

Looking forward: Severstal and Evraz

Severstal

Severstal is one of the world's leading steel and mining companies, with key assets in Russia, the US and Europe. The company focused on high-added value products and unique niche products. In 2008 Severstal produced 19.2 million tonnes of steel, accounting for revenues of US$22.4 billion. The company's 2008 EBITDA was US$5.4 billion, while its earnings per share stood at US$2.20. At the end of the 2000s, the company's shares were traded on the RTS (Russian Trading System), MICEX (the Moscow Interbank Currency Exchange) and the London Stock Exchange.

Severstal Company derives from the Cherepovets Metallurgical Plant, the founding of which was announced in 1940. According to the state plan, it was to supply the north-western region of Russia with steel. But in fact it was built only after the Second World War, in 1955. After the disintegration of the USSR Cherepovets Metallurgical Plant was transformed into the joint-stock company Severstal by the first president of the Russian Federation, and only since 1993 has the company developed rapidly. It is integrated vertically, both backwards and forwards, having plants in mining, extraction, pipe manufacturing and other fields.

A decade into its existence, the company could look back on a successful track record of acquiring and operating high-quality assets in North America and Europe. Today, Severstal also owns mining enterprises in Russia and the USA, supplying its own manufacturing facilities with them. The company also has a gold mining segment which manages important assets in Russia and Kazakhstan. Severstal is the sole Russian company to be included into the Forbes 500 (in 409th place). It checked in as the largest producer by volume among companies in the CIS in 2009. This could be attributed to the fact that it had structured itself to international trim and Western standards of management and performance. It was also impressive for having the longest list of international subsidiaries.

The company has three divisions. The division Severstal Russian Steel is one of the leading steel makers in Russia and consists of six segments: steel (Cherepovets Steel Mill, Sheksna Weld Pipe Mill, Kolpino processing service centre); metalware (Severstal-Metiz); pipe (Izhora Pipe Mill, Sheksna Section Mill); trading (Severstal-Invest); services (Stoic, SSM-Tyazhmash); and scrap procurement (Vtorchermet).

Severstal International is the division responsible for the foreign operations of the company. In the US Severstal has both integrated plants and mini-mills with a significant downstream distribution business and a geographical presence on the East Coast, in the Great Lakes area and within a developing area in the South. In Europe, it works via its Lucchini subsidiary, acquisition of which helped the company to become the prime player in the Italian rail and high-quality wire rod markets. Another enterprise is Ascometal (France), a major in the European market.

The mining division Severstal Resources is Russia's leading producer of iron ore, coal and gold. It was formed out of acquisitions made over the past 12 years and comprises two iron-ore integrated works (Karelian Pellet and Olkon); coal companies located in the north-west of Russia (Vorkutaugol) and in the US (PBS Coals); an iron-ore exploration project in Liberia (Severstal Liberia Iron Ore); and the research institute Giproshakht in St Petersburg, Russia.[7]

International growth

The internationalisation of Severstal began in 2003, when the company acquired Rouge Steel, an integrated steel-making facility based in Michigan, USA, for US$360 million. This successful acquisition led to the further expansion of Severstal (Table 6.1). Overall, the company followed an aggressive international strategy that aimed to acquire steel producers in CIS countries, Europe and North America. In 2006 the company acquired Lucchini Group, a bankrupt steel producer with integrated steel-making facilities based in Italy and France. It provided additional capacity which, unlike Lucchini, Severstal could use. In 2007 Severstal acquired the gold-mining company Celtic Resources, with assets in Kazakhstan. Since 2008 Severstal's acquisitions have rocketed, with seven acquisitions in that year alone. These purchases focused on the USA and Africa.

A noteworthy, albeit modest, piece of internationalisation undertaken by Severstal was the launch of its SeverCorr mini-mill in Mississippi, USA (the plant was later renamed Severstal Columbus). Its most dramatic undertaking, on the other hand, was an attempt at merging with ArcelorMittal, which would have led to the creation of the largest enterprise in the whole steel industry. The project foundered because of conflict with another, more profitable (and probably more politically secure), prospect, a merger with Mittal Steel.

Severstal's recent international expansion through strategic asset-seeking investments was aimed at strengthening the company's position among the world's top steel producers. Acquisitions of under-performing production assets in strategic markets such as the US and the EU provided Severstal with opportunities to increase production capacities and gain market access through local production and distribution outlets. This aggressive internationalisation strategy thus departed from that of many other Russian MNEs, which preferred to

Table 6.1 Severstal acquisitions, 2003–2008

Country	*Name of plant*	*Head office*	*Year*
USA	Severstal North America/Rouge Steel	Dearborn	2003
Italy	Lucchini Group/Piombino	Trieste	2006
France	Lucchini Group/Ascometal	Curbevua	2006
USA	Sparrows Point	Baltimore	2008
USA	WCI Steel	Warren	2008
USA	Wheeling	Willing	2008

Source: Datamonitor; company reports.

gently 'seep' over the border to neighbouring CIS markets. OFDI via acquisition has increased Severstal's competitiveness because of its access to a number of large steel markets, including those of the US and the EU. The strategy selected has considerably enhanced the company's stature in the world steel industry.

Evraz steel group

Evraz Group was founded in 1992 as a small metal-trading company, Evroazmetall. During its first years the company's field of activity steadily expanded and its turnover grew. In the mid-1990s Evroazmetall became involved in settling debts between Russian mining and metallurgy plants. The firm accumulated promissory notes from several steel plants, coal mines and concentrate factories. This led to a decision to acquire equity in mining concerns. In the end of 1999 EvrazHolding was formed in order to diversify into new markets.

This strategy paid off, as by 2009 Evraz had become one of the largest vertically integrated mining and steel- and vanadium-producing companies in the world. The Evraz group is a public company registered in Luxembourg with about 30 per cent of its shares capital in the form of Global Depository Receipts traded on the LSE. In 2007 Evraz smelted impressive amounts of metals: 16.4 million tonnes of crude steel, 12.6 million tonnes of pig iron and 15.2 million tonnes of rolled products; and for the first half of 2008 the consolidated revenues amounted to US$10.7 million and EBITDA a healthy US$3.7 billion.[8]

For its production, the company relied mainly on three Russian steel plants: Nizhny Tagil, in the Urals region, Zapsib, in West Siberia and Novokuznetsk, in Siberia. Evraz has plants in North America, Africa and Europe. In North America the company operates via its subsidiary, Evraz Inc. NA, which comprises several mills (including a Canadian one) along with some pipe business. Evraz's foreign portfolio includes assets in Italy (Evraz Palini e Bertoli), the Czech Republic (Evraz Vitkovice Steel), South Africa (Highveld Steel and Vanadium Corporation) and Ukraine (Dnepropetrovsk Iron and Steel Works).

Because of its mining assets, the company is considered a vertically integrated steel producer. In fact, by 2009 Evraz's own mines covered 93 per cent of its iron-ore and over 100 per cent of its coking coal needs. The world vanadium market knows Evraz well, especially in the US (Strategic Minerals Corporation), the Czech Republic (Nikom) and South Africa (Highveld Steel and Vanadium Corporation).

International growth

Evraz made several acquisitions in 2005–2008 (Table 6.2). Notable among these were the 2005 acquisitions of the rolling mill Palini & Bertoli in Italy and of Vitkovice Steel a.s. – the latter being the largest plate maker in the Czech Republic. This acquisition further diversified the company's product mix into the value-added area, as well as providing access to customers within the EU. It figured as one of the company's first steps toward international expansion.

Table 6.2 Evraz acquisitions, 2005–2008

Country	*Target*	*Head office*	*Year*
USA	Evraz Inc. NA	Portland	2005–2008
Italy	Evraz Palini & Bertoli	San Giorgio di Nogaro	2005
Czech Republic	Evraz Vitkovice Steel	Ostrava	2005
South Africa	Highveld Steel and Vanadium Corporation Ltd	Highveld	2007
Ukraine	DMZP	Dnepropetrovsk	2007–2008

Source: Datamonitor; company reports.

In 2006 Evraz acquired 73 per cent of Strategic Minerals Corporation, USA, one of the world's leading producers of vanadium alloys and chemicals for the steel, chemical and titanium industries, and a 24.9 per cent stake in Highveld Steel and Vanadium Corporation, South Africa, which it increased to 54.1 per cent in May 2007.

Through the Highveld acquisition Evraz gained valuable access to the expanding South African steel and construction sectors, which had strong demand growth, and became an important player in the worldwide vanadium market. And, thanks to the acquisition of Oregon Steel Mills in January 2007, Evraz secured a place of importance on the attractive plate market and in the expanding pipe business in North America, as well as becoming a leading global rail producer.

In February 2008 Evraz purchased an approximate 10 per cent stake in the Chinese company Delong Holdings, which, among other assets, owned Delong Steel. In the following month it announced the acquisition of several assets of IPSCO Canada, a steel and pipe producer. These acquisitions led to the establishment of a wholly owned subsidiary in North America (Evraz Inc. NA), comprising several mills and pipe plants. The idea was to make production and control more efficient, but also to expand marketing and sales capabilities through the new distribution network. Also in 2008 the company acquired a Ukrainian integrated steel mill specialising in the manufacture and sale of pig iron, steel and rolled products in Dnepropetrovsk, as well as, at about same time, several Ukrainian coking plants.

Evraz's reason for internationalisation – that is to say, strategic asset seeking (getting the best possible return on investment) – seems to have been shared by all large steel manufacturers. Evraz sought to expand over the world in order to shore up its main facilities in Russia, and even during the financial crisis its enhanced productive power abroad helped the company greatly. To round things off, Evraz acquired mines in order to overcome a shortage of production resources such as coal and ore.

The metallurgy industry sites itself in areas where its materials are located. Most of the biggest companies have emerging-market origins because the raw materials are mainly located in those countries, and most of these, which formerly concentrated on their domestic markets (for example, Nippon Steel), only lately started looking for growth opportunities abroad.

As the industry is very reliant on access to key resources such as cheap raw materials and energy, a dearth of raw materials, in particular, is what will limit the opportunity of companies to grow organically. You can't just grow more iron ore. The experience of Russian companies operating in the metallurgical industry demonstrates that M&As are the fastest and especially the most efficient way to overcome this handicap. Purchasing companies from developing countries has been the strategy for acquiring key resources, while purchasing companies from developed countries has allowed entry to Western markets, especially for high-end special steels and metals.

The biggest Russian companies in metallurgy have all internationalised to some extent. Consolidation in the Russian industry has made the biggest companies strong in terms of financial clout and raw materials. Russia, as a country of origin, offers domestic companies great advantages when operating in foreign markets and competing with local companies. First of all, access to raw materials is relatively easy because Russia has some of the world's biggest deposits of various metals, minerals and ores. Second, the availability of inexpensive energy is a huge advantage because metallurgical production processes are exceedingly energy-intensive. Third, relatively cheap labour is also available in plenitude. Fourth, because the Russian economy and the growth of the nation's GDP are highly dependent on key industries like metallurgy, oil and gas, the government has been very supportive in ensuring the effective performance of these companies.

The international growth of Russian companies in this sector has profited from the fact that domestic supply has outpaced demand – there has been room for export business. This is not the case elsewhere, namely in South-East Asia (for example, China), where imports are required. The strong growth in demand from manufacturing, construction and other industries, the main users of metallurgical products, explains this deficit. In contrast, Russia is still not refining its materials into final products, thus neglecting domestic diversification but favouring export of lower-value 'commodity' metal.

Rusal, for instance, has mainly concentrated on the acquisition of emerging market companies, especially at locations where the requisite raw materials prevail. The exception is Severstal, which, instead, has acquired companies mainly in developed countries. The purpose of this strategy has been to buy shares of underperforming companies and then transform them to more efficient and profitable ones, and it has also allowed Severstal access to US and EU markets. This, in turn, serves to avoid trade barriers, such as tariffs and duties, imposed by governments anxious to protect their key industries: thus Severstal has established a joint venture with Luxembourg-based ArcelorMittal to fabricate car sheet metal in order to better serve growth in Russian automobile manufacture, because Russia itself does not produce enough sheet metal.

The reason behind the internationalisation of the Evraz group has closely resembled that of other large steel manufacturers like Severstal or ArcelorMittal. It is called strategic asset seeking. Reducing dependency on the home market is also very important not only because of fluctuations in the domestic economy but also to overcome the shortage of production resources. Geographical internationalisation diminishes the risk that staying in one country entails. The acquisition of Italian and Czech assets in 2006 enabled Evraz to increase sales of sheet metal in Europe by almost 150 per cent. At the same time the company also benefited from the construction boom in Russia. It now controls about half of the US rail production through its subsidiary, Oregon Steel Mills (acquired in 2007), and is one of the leaders in the production of seamless pipes. This acquisition has enabled Evraz, at heart a very Russian company, to increase its deliveries to the US and to broaden its product portfolio. Evraz is already a global company and its acquisitions in Europe and the US are likely to be followed by further expansion, probably in the Asian market. It is likely that Japan and South Korea, especially, will be on the company's expansion list.

When we compare strategies of Russian and other emerging MNEs in the metallurgy sector with companies having developed-country origins, we see that generally companies from developing economies have better and cheaper access to resources. This means that developed-country MNEs have less chance to compete in terms of price. Developed-countries' MNEs have thus mainly concentrated on the manufacturing and selling of final products, rather than bulk materials. Russian multinationals in metallurgy still lack the capability of refining their material into more sophisticated final products, and thus concentrate more on selling their materials to companies who then take care of the final purifying. However, this situation is coming into flux as Russia increasingly invests in modern refining, and this trend is likely to continue. It will probably lead to an increase in consolidation of the industry worldwide.

Russian metallurgy has been active not just in horizontal integration but also vertically. Russian companies have decided to operate in a way that differs from that adopted nowadays by companies in developed countries. This means that companies from developed economies concentrate on their core competencies and, beyond that, tend to outsource to supportive operations. The supply of raw materials is such an important factor in metallurgy that more corporate integration than Russia currently practices is needed to fine-tune into the value-added field.

While the Russian market is basically controlled by a few companies, in international markets Russian firms run into competition that is much more intensive and where the number of industry players is much higher. The level of competition in the domestic market is low owing to governmental protection of its players, which spares the homebodies the ferocity of foreign invaders. However, foreign imports are disadvantaged most by Russia's lower production costs.

Evraz has targeted mainly developed countries in its internationalisation process, because its main customers are situated there. Besides Russia, Evraz has gained market leadership status in most of the countries in which it operates, thus gaining strong bargaining power over customers. Evraz is so internationalised that it is not overly dependent on any one market, as well as so geographically diversified in respect of revenue that it is protected from fall in demand in any one country. Because it is specific to metallurgy that companies grow via brownfield investment, Evraz should keep its eye on acquisitions and mergers for future growth. Developing countries especially should be targeted in order to secure good access to resources.

We have seen that Severstal succeeded first and foremost owing to its diversified end-product portfolio. But its presence in countries with developed industries, including automotive, shipbuilding, construction and infrastructure, as well as railways, has by no means hurt it. Unlike Evraz, Severstal has focused on high-added value products and unique niche products, while the focus of Evraz has been in more simple end-products such as pipe and rails. Both companies have probably realised that it would be counterproductive to compete for the same custom, as this would lead to hard price competition and its usual consequence, lower profit margins. Still, the relationship remains competitive, as they both concentrate on steel and in the same markets. North America is one of the main markets for Severstal. To secure its supply of raw materials, the company should now reinforce its vertical integration by acquiring more mines. Presence in various markets provides the company access to a wide customer base, while diversified end markets reduce its business risk.

While Evraz and Severstal have concentrated on the ferrous metals business, for Rusal the core business is non-ferrous metals and especially the production of aluminium. The aluminium business differs from steel as there are fewer deposits of raw materials that aluminium companies can use for their manufacturing processes. Growth opportunities for Rusal are thus more limited than for Evraz and Severstal. Rusal has no alternative to acquiring new deposits and developing existing ones and, compared with Severstal and Evraz, its strategic choices are far more limited. Minimising costs is thus one of the critical success factors in the industry. Aluminium products are mostly substitutes for one another, so pricing is the important factor when a customer chooses his supplier. Besides developing technology, the only way to minimise costs is through inexpensive energy, which explains why Rusal has acquired and developed its own power-generating assets. In contrast, to secure efficiency of production, Severstal has acquired mines and production facilities in developing countries as well as developing extraction and refining technology.

While all companies have their own specific mix of operations to achieve competitiveness, there are also some rules of thumb. These include access to raw materials, a supply of inexpensive energy, a suitable level of vertical integration, proximity to customers and effective supply chain management. These are also the main considerations that affect companies' decision to go international. As the amount of raw material deposits is limited in the world, so garnering the requisite supply of these commodities is essential for business and growth.

Russian MNEs in the metallurgy sector use international expansion as a springboard to acquire strategic resources and make up for their constraints at home. Most Russian metallurgy firms initially tend to dip into internationalisation in culturally related countries such as the CIS. At the same time, Evraz and Severstal have acquired firms in developed countries; this carried a risk, but in succeeding these companies have managed to situate their operations closer to their customers while decreasing the advantage of early entrants in the international markets.

7 Acquiring the customer

The telecom industry

Worldwide telecoms and Russian telecommunications

In its beginnings, the telecommunications sector was run as a monopoly. There are several reasons for this. First, it is a natural monopoly: the installation of a telecom network involves fixed costs, and the installation of two networks costs twice as much, more or less. Second, there is the 'cream-skimming effect'. During the opening of the market to competition, competitors will head into the segments where greater profit beckons (urban telecoms is more profitable than rural telephony). To keep non-urban areas supplied, a subsidy is required. A monopoly is best at cross-subsidising to create an equitable system. Third, there is strategy. Telecommunications carry important security and national strategic connotations. Government monopolies were therefore often entrusted with the initial roll-out of telecom services.

On the other hand, competition has advantages. First, a monopoly means not only control of the prices (usually at a high level) and imposition of a quality level but also limits on innovation and reductions in incentives to provide up-to-date technologies. It limits the range of products and services and the motivation to make valid distinctions between all types of customers. As regards the security factor, nowadays there exist technical solutions to ensure security without having to rely on public ownership. And after the fixed high costs of installation of local loop services, the marginal costs of adding new subscribers is low. A context of high competition will ensure the best price for the customer.

Historical background

At the beginning of the twentieth century, telecommunications consisted of a very few private companies under regulation. In the USA a private telephone company called the Bell Telephone System was set up to focus on innovation in the field of telecommunications. Since its establishment, similar systems have brought into public use inventions such as lasers, fibre-optics and transistors. The oligarchy of regulated companies lasted into the 1980s. Today the oligarchy has been replaced by a competitive playing field, with most companies making a profit.[1]

In the USA, established global telecom players (Verizon, AT&T, Sprint Nextel, Bell South Corp and Qwest Communications) together accounted in the mid-2000s for more than 20 per cent of the industry's overall revenues. The global telecom services industry group generated total revenues of US$1.29 trillion in 2008, growing at a CAGR of 5 per cent for the 2004–2008 period.

Then, in the late 2000s, mobile telephony hit the market. The wireless telecoms segment proved the most lucrative for the global telecommunication services industry group in 2008, generating total revenues of US$673.6 billion, equivalent to 52.2 per cent of the overall value. The performance of the industry group was forecast to slightly decelerate, with an anticipated CAGR of 3.4 per cent for the five-year period 2008–2013, which was expected to drive the industry to a value of US$1.52 trillion by the end of 2013.

Market segmentation

The telecoms industry comprises a wide range of services, including local telephone, long-distance telephone, wireless telephone, paging, Internet access, Voice-over-Internet and many others.

Local telephone service providers are usually involved in maintaining local lines and providing switches with other telephone service providers. In most countries regulations have been developed to protect customers of telephone companies. Similarly, long-distance telephone service providers handle switches between local providers and those in remote areas.

Wireless telephone service is based on different principles from fixed lines as it divides geographical areas into small units called cells. These cells have their own radio channels, transmitters and receivers that enable transmission. There was a particularly spectacular boom in this sector of the industry in the 1990s, when technological innovations within the industry were made and the price of the technology fell. Moreover, the decrease in price was accompanied by continual enhancement of quality.

Recent trends

Recently, some complex trends within the telecommunication industry have been observed. Most of them are related to the Internet, a powerful new factor in the conduct of business in telecommunication.

There is now a tendency in the business to merge and make alliances to provide a full range of services while also providing 'one-stop shopping'. Three large and powerful international alliances of national telecom operators, namely Unisource/WorldPartners, Global One and Concert Communications, went into operation in the middle of the 1990s to service international telecom connections and the new needs of multinationals. In fact, innovation produced so many correlated telecommunication services that customers have come to prize access to all of them with a push one of a single button.

Key success factors

In the 2000s the telecommunication industry used its own products in combination with products of other industries to a point where it became the epitome of rapid technological change. If companies want to enjoy an advantage within their field of business activity, they must fulfil the requirements set by the technological age. First, the biggest players on the telecommunications markets need to achieve on a global scale as far as customer base, cost and networks are concerned. In addition, they need to choose a proper strategy of interaction with other global telecommunication players and develop an excellent customer service system. And last but not least, owing to the very fast innovation process, global players need R&D divisions to keep pace with innovation.

The customer base of a company is largely taken to reflect its market strength, and thus influences the strength of a company in negotiating with its suppliers as well as its pricing and standing as a competitor. If a company has a large customer base it can expect to exert an influence on the way the business operates. Moreover, there is a spread of technological standards which apply to telecommunications products. If a company opts for the wrong technical standard (either already out-of-date, or technically inconvenient), it could lose customers to a more with-it competitor. Changing to implement the right solution can imply a large investment.

Another factor impacting upon the success of a global player in telecommunication is networks. Besides a global network, companies also need to create local networks, especially in the areas where their customers are based. These local networks are interconnected via the global network of a company. This strategy, often followed by big telecommunication players, is called the 'local-to-global-to-local strategy', and could be adopted by means of various kinds of association, such as joint ventures.

In the first stage of this strategy, companies concentrate on the adjustment of their products to the needs of their home customer base, but also develop products that could be sold on foreign markets. During the second stage, companies try to develop products that target foreign markets. According to the local-to-global-to-local strategy, a company creates its own network in its local market where its customers are based. When it has done this, it begins evolving its product mix so as to capture new, marginal customers. This strategy can also help fend off competitors.

The third success factor has to do with economies of scale. When a telecoms company merges with another in a foreign market, they are both able to cut costs. This aspect is of extreme importance because lower costs can either be passed on to customers or re-invested to improve the quality of products and services (or paid out as dividends to make shareholders content).

Within the economies of scale the demand-side variety needs heeding: it demonstrates the increase in the value of a company as it gains more customers. This explains why the valuation of telecoms companies hinges on their subscriber base.

Telecoms going global

Internationalisation affects the telecommunication market structure. The proportion of classical fixed-line telephone services to wireless mobile services changed dramatically in the 2000s as customers emigrated from fixed-line to mobile phones (or skipped fixed lines altogether, as has been the case in emerging markets). This trend is borne out by data on the global fixed-line and mobile operators' revenues. Global revenues in the industry reached US$2 trillion in 2008, with revenues of old-style fixed lines operators exceeding those of newbie mobile operators by around 8 per cent.[2]

There is a stronger trend of growth in the mobile operators' revenues than in that of the fixed-liners: the former grew by 13 per cent a year and the latter by just 2 per cent a year. The highest revenues within the telecoms industry are in North America and Europe, followed by emerging economies in Asia. North America has the highest proportion of fixed-line revenues (38 per cent) while Europe has the largest share of mobile revenues of all the continents.

The internationalisation process engendered severe competition across markets, which, to certain extent, increased customer value. Customers were offered a product mix that could not have been feasible without forging alliances or other forms of partnerships. Moreover, the phenomenon of convergence in technologies brought improvement to the market, including a consolidation of different elements in the value chain, be they telephony, television or computing services.

By the end of the 2000s, the market share of the few big players became gigantic, as giants such as AT&T, Deutsche Telekom and France Telecom formed alliances. The onrush of giganticism, in other words, in fact had nothing to do with new customer acquisition. If anything, it had to do with the formation of a new oligarchy.

Russian telecommunications

The Russian telecommunications and technology sector has recorded extremely buoyant growth in recent years, with mobile telephone, personal computer (PC) and the Internet use all expanding rapidly. This growth was explained by initially low penetration levels combined with strong growth in economic indicators, including real disposable incomes.

Few industries have reflected as clearly the consumer boom and middle-class growth as has the telecom sector. Total telecom sector revenue amounted to US$42.6 billion in 2008, up from just over US$27 billion in 2006. Mobile telecom accounted for 57 per cent of the market, or US$24.2 billion, while the fixed-line market accounted for the remaining 43 per cent, or US$18.4 billion. The share of the fixed-line segment in the total telecoms market has fallen in recent years, owing to a relatively slower growth than in mobile telephony.

Mobile telephony experienced explosive growth in Russia in the 2000s, and the market was the fourth-largest in the world in 2008–2009, after China, India and the US. It has been one of the most attractive sectors for Russian and foreign investors.

Three markets thus shaped the telecom industry in Russia in the 2000s – mobile telecoms, fixed-line telecoms and the Internet. In this chapter we focus on the mobile telecom players, as well on the most prominent international players.

With fixed-line telecoms penetration still relatively low – main lines per 100 inhabitants were estimated to be below 30 in 2008, compared with 36 in China and 44 in Germany – mobile use will remain an essential part of day-to-day life in Russia. As a result, demand for mobile services in Russia may be better protected from adverse developments in the economy than may other sectors, or even other sub-sectors of the telecoms and technology sector, such as computer hardware.

Demand for services in mobile telecoms experienced very strong growth in the 2000s, to the extent that the market quickly became highly saturated and was consequently expected to be growing only slowly by the end of the 2000s. In 1999 only about 1 per cent of Russians owned a mobile telephone; by 2006 penetration had exceeded 100 per cent and, by the end of 2008, according to Economist Intelligence Unit estimates, it stood at over 130 per cent. The boom was driven by several years of robust growth in real incomes and the emergence of a middle class, combined with the difficulty in obtaining fixed-line services and relatively high fixed-line fees. The forecast easing of growth rates in demand for mobile services was in line with the trend in other emerging markets. In the BRIC countries, for example, growth was forecast to fall from 19 per cent in 2009 to 13 per cent in 2010, and to trend down to just 6 per cent by 2013.

The mobile telecom market in Russia was highly competitive in the 2000s. It was dominated by three players: MTS (Mobile TeleSystems), VimpelCom and Megafon, in which TeliaSonera, a Scandinavian company, had a stake. These three companies initially made their mark in the dominant Moscow market and have since expanded by buying up smaller regional operators. Combined, they held 83 per cent of the market in 2009, MTS controlling 34 per cent, VimpelCom 25 per cent and Megafon 23 per cent.[3] VimpelCom was jointly owned by Telenor (Norway) and Alfa Group. However, in-fighting over the past few years between Telenor and Alfa Group over the company's strategy in Ukraine resulted in the seizure of Telenor's stake in VimpelCom by a Russian court in March 2009. The remainder of the market comprises foreign and regional operators such as Norvegian Tele2, and domestic companies SMARTS, SkyLink, Sibirtelecom and Uralsvyazinform, all of which have grown strongly in the 2000s.

All three leading companies were engaged in activities outside Russia. Their international involvement includes operational activities abroad, partial ownership of or by foreign enterprises, and/or seeking financing abroad (for example, stock exchange listings). One of the unique features of the industry was that any international expansion required a direct investment or at least a strategic alliance with incumbent companies, since mobile services cannot be physically exported.

One of the characteristics of the Russian telecom sector at the end of the 2000s was a tendency to make acquisitions. Russian mobile telecoms consolidated during the 2000s. Operators expanded to new regions via acquisitions, which has often been the only way available. Operating licences are required for each separate region. In August 2007, Tele2 sold its subsidiary Severnaya Korona Corporation for US$232 million to VimpelCom. This purchase was concluded because VimpelCom was unable to expand into the Irkutsk region owing to lack of frequencies (and therefore licences) and the only way out was buying a local operator. In another deal, Beeline agreed to let Tele2 use its network for national roaming services for 10 years. This roaming deal has made Tele2 the fourth national mobile operator. Before the deal, Tele2 subscribers were only able to use call-back roaming and could not send text messages to regions without coverage.

A further example is the 2007 purchase by MTS of Bashcell, a mobile operator from the Republic of Bashkir. Contrary to normal practice, this purchase was aimed not at expansion to a new region but at expanding the subscriber base. Another motive for the acquisition was becoming licensed and thereby forestalling the entry of other competitors. The transaction charge amounted to US$38 million, including debt of US$32 million. In 2006 the revenue of Bashcell was US$11 million.[4]

In February 2008 Summa Telecom, a telecom company that has specialised in integration services for the oil and gas industry, won a bidding war against VimpelCom and succeeded in acquiring Esotel-Rustelekom, which owned the licence for Yakutia. Some analysts believe the purchase was made to increase Summa's value before the company put itself up for sale.[5]

The operating environment for mobile firms was difficult in 2009. Although the sector was likely to be much more resilient to the downturn in consumer expenditure than some other sectors, such as automotive, it was nevertheless bruised by the economic crisis of 2008–2009. All three main operators borrowed heavily to fund network expansion across a vast geographical area, and around US$3.14 billion of that debt was due to be refinanced in 2009.[6] Because 82 per cent of its debt was denominated in US dollars, VimpelCom has taken a particularly heavy knock, with MTS suffering also. As a result, the companies needed to re-balance both capital and operating expenditures.

Leader takeover strategy: MTS

Mobile TeleSystems (MTS) is the largest mobile phone operator in Russia and the CIS, with over 91.33 million subscribers (as of 31 December 2008), and 2008 revenues of US$10.2 billion, up 24 per cent over the previous year. Owned principally by Sistema, the largest private-sector consumer services company in Russia and the CIS, MTS is traded publicly. In 2009 approximately 46.7 per cent of the company's shares were floating freely.

MTS never felt constrained by Russian borders, and by 2009 had expanded into Ukraine, Uzbekistan, Turkmenistan, Armenia and Belarus. The main reasons for choosing the CIS as the target market relate to historical and cultural tradition, a common infrastructure network inherited from the Soviet era, and relatively similar business practices. Geographical proximity also plays a role. Yet several of the company's target markets (such as Uzbekistan) are located relatively far from Russia's economic centres. These must be considered exceptions.

With political relations between and within CIS countries tending to develop positively, internationalisation via expansion to CIS countries fits the 'follow your consumer' strategy of Russian companies. Many MTS corporate clients are already active in CIS markets. Human migration within the CIS is also an important expansion driver, since cooperation between mobile operators from Russia and other CIS countries was important in supplying international roaming services.

When MTS established its current brand in 2006 it built upon its reputation as a quality operator and attracted customers in a variety of market segments. The BRANDZ(tm) Top 100 Most Powerful Brands (compiled by the *Financial Times* and Millward Brown) recognised MTS by ranking it in 89th place, with a brand value of US$8.1 billion; it is the sole Russian brand present.

In May 2008 MTS reached number 14 in *Business Week's* InfoTech 100 ranking of the best-performing tech companies. It became the highest-ranked company from Russia, outstripping companies such as AT&T, LG and Microsoft.

History of the company

MTS was established in October 1993 by several shareholders: Moscow City Telephone Network (MGTS), T-Mobile Deutschland GmbH (affiliate of Deutsche Telekom AG), Siemens AG and several others. In late 1996 AFK Sistema acquired a majority stake in MTS and has remained the primary owner ever since.

In 1994 MTS innovated by launching GSM services in the Moscow region. Thereafter, MTS expanded rapidly in Russia, mostly via acquisition of smaller independent players, thus quickly becoming the leading national mobile operator. On 30 June 2000 MTS shares started trading on the NYSE. From the very beginning the company actively focused on the development of its regional operations in Russia, with multiple nation-wide acquisitions. In 2003, MTS acquired a number of leading regional operators, thus achieving virtual national coverage.

MTS's international expansion started in 2002 with the establishment of Mobile TeleSystems LLC in Belarus, a joint venture with Mezhdugorodnaya Svyaz, a subsidiary of Beltelecom, the national fixed-line operator. MTS then aimed for Ukraine, and in 2003 acquired first part and then all of UMC, the leading operator.

For Central Asia, MTS waited another year: in 2004 it took over Uzdunrobita, the leading mobile phone operator in Uzbekistan. Then, in June 2005, it acquired Barash Communications Technologies Inc., the top operator in Turkmenistan. Next came Armenia, when, in September 2007, MTS acquired its leading mobile operator, K-Telecom. In April of that year, MTS also received a licence to build a 3G network in UMTS format in Russia and Uzbekistan, the licence to build a WiMax network in Uzbekistan, and the frequencies for the provision of services in a standard 3G (UMTS) in Armenia.

In December 2008 MTS extended its brand outside the CIS. In India, MTS and Shyam Telelink Limited announced an agreement that allows Shyam Telelink to use the MTS brand. The brand extension to India reflected the brand's increasing success in its markets of operation.

Strategies in CIS markets

In the second half of the 2000s MTS rose to the top of the telecom market of the CIS in terms of outward investments from Russia.

MTS selected Belarus, as noted above, as its first CIS target destination. It ranked as the fifth-largest country of the region, with a population of nearly 10 million and the GDP per capita of about US$1,800 in 2003 (third place among the CIS countries).

Belarus had lagged behind most East European transition countries in developing mobile communications, being the last state in the region to introduce GSM cellular digital standard. From 1993 to 1999 Belarus had used analogue cellular phone services. Despite this outdated technology, mobile phone penetration increased rapidly in the first half of the 2000s, more than doubling from September 2003 to September 2004, to reach a level of about 20 per cent penetration (around two million subscribers). But that did not exhaust the potential of the Belarus cellular market. Two companies dominated there: MTS Belarus and Mobile Digital Communication (MDC). A third company, BelCel, lagged, with only a modest market share.

MTS entered Belarus in June 2002, as noted above, by establishing a joint venture with a local company, long-distance operator Mezhdugorodnaya Svyaz. By 2009, MTS and Mezhdugorodnaya Svyaz held stakes of 49 per cent and 51 per cent respectively. In 2004, MTS Belarus surpassed MDC to become the national mobile leader in terms of subscribers and coverage. After only two years of operations in Belarus, both partners appraised the joint venture as mutually beneficial.

After Belarus came Ukraine, a market of 50 million people that had experienced economic growth since 2000. Ukraine was playing economic catch-up, with higher GDP growth than Russia's. At the same time, GDP per capita remained quite low at slightly over US$1,000, far behind Russia and Belarus. Mobile services were growing dramatically, however. The number of subscribers was skyrocketing (by 140 per cent in 2001, 60 per cent in 2002 and 80 per cent in 2003), reaching about 10 million in September 2004. Two main reasons explained the phenomenal growth: the low penetration rate of fixed lines (24 per cent) and substantial price reductions for mobile services. Ukraine thus became of primary importance for MTS, with its market size of approximately 55.6 million potential subscribers in 2007. When MTS entered Ukraine in 2002 the market was a duopoly of sorts: Ukrainian Mobile Communications (UMC) and KyivStar GSM together controlled about 98 per cent of the market. MTS chose to acquire a controlling interest in UMC (58 per cent of shares), which had been created 10 years earlier as a joint venture between national fixed-line operator Ukrtelecom (51 per cent), TDC AS (Denmark), Deutsche Telekom (Germany) and Royal KPN NV (Holland), with each foreign company holding 16 per cent. Step by step, MTS bought shares from the other owners, so that, by the end of the 2000s, it held 99 per cent of UMC directly and 1 per cent through its subsidiary PPT Telecom Kyiv. The newly established MTS Ukraine (formerly UMC) became one of the largest wireless providers in the country, with a 36 per cent market share in the country.

MTS was one of the largest investors in Ukraine, with US$2.7 billion of total investments in the second half of the 2000s. In 2004–2007 investments were allocated mostly to radio-subsystems (coverage extension and network capacity). Between mid-2007 and the end of the decade, investments have been mostly targeted at IT systems, switching subsystem capacity and back-bone network to prepare for 3G roll-out and the introduction of new services. Recently, however, the investment attractiveness of the Ukrainian mobile market has deteriorated because of economic recession and significant national currency devaluation.

Uzbekistan's low penetration rates in wireless telecoms offered MTS the incentive to develop this market. Here, in August 2004, MTS purchased three-quarters of Uzdunrobita for US$120 million from two private companies. Uzdunrobita was the leading mobile service company, controlling approximately half of the market, and the deal instantly placed MTS as a leading player. An option agreement to acquire the remaining quarter for not less than US$40 million foresaw sole ownership. The acquisition of Uzdunrobita was costly: MTS paid almost US$500 per subscriber.

Since its entry into Uzbekistan in 2004, MTS has maintained its leadership position despite the rapid development of the market and rising competition resulting from the entry of new players. Wireless penetration jumped from 10 per cent to 44 per cent in barely two years (2006 to 2008), thereby catapulting MTS to the number-one provider of mobile telephone services in the country, with approximately 2.8 million subscribers and nearly 48 per cent of the Uzbekistan market. Annual revenue grew by 58 per cent year-on-year to more than US$391 million as MTS continued to expand its subscriber base in the country. As a result of the company's successful marketing campaigns and the introduction of popular tariffs, MTS more than doubled its subscriber base during the year 2008, adding over 2.8 million customers to reach more than 5.6 million.

Since then, the company has continued to invest in its network to gain full capacity and coverage. It has also started to roll out a 3G network in its drive to promote data usage in all of its markets of operation and to better serve the needs of its customers generally. Toward the end of 2008, MTS launched services in Tashkent and Samarkand, with a further three cities, Bukhara, Urgench and Khiva, added in January 2009.

At the beginning of 2005 the USA-based Barash Communication Technologies Inc. (BCTI) was the only mobile communication company in Turkmenistan. BCTI owned the entire range of frequencies required to establish GSM and 3G networks. The only other mobile communication licence belonged to the Turkmen Ministry of Telecommunications. Using a strategy similar to that employed in its previous experience in Uzbekistan, MTS decided to enter the Turkmen market by purchasing the leader – BCTI. The deal value was estimated at about US$55 million. Immediately after the acquisition the Turkmen government, which wanted to prevent the formation of a Russian monopoly on its soil, gave MTS some difficulty regarding its presence in the country.

However, MTS continues to dominate the Turkmen market, having increased its subscriber base by 94 per cent to 356,260 by the end of 2007 from 183,788 at the end of 2006. This represented an increase of market share by around 5 per cent, with an 88 per cent share of the total market in 2007. Penetration in Turkmenistan was still very low – it grew from 3.2 per cent in 2006 to 7.4 per cent in 2007 – but the country's economic growth and low fixed-line penetration seemed to bode well for MTS's mobile line. Things could only get better. And, despite limited competition and an under-penetrated market (only 19 per cent at the end of the 2000s), MTS nonetheless played a vital role in the development of Turkmenistan's telecommunications industry.

In Armenia, MTS acquired an 80 per cent stake in K-Telekom, operator of the VivaCell brand, in September 2007. At the end of that year, VivaCell counted 1.4 million subscribers and had a 73.9 per cent market share. The overall wireless penetration in Armenia at this time was 58 per cent. Barely one month after the acquisition, K-Telekom was allocated frequencies valid for 10 years to offer 3G services in the UMTS standard for the entire territory of Armenia. Since the entry into Armenia in 2007, MTS has successfully built on the accomplishments of its K-Telecom subsidiary and increased its market share of subscribers from 74 per cent to 79 per cent (representing over 2 million subscribers). Through the introduction of new tariff plans and the expansion of the number of customer service centres to 95, MTS has built strong relationships with its customers throughout the segments of its service. It has structured its transactions so that they provide for local management and 20 per cent local ownership.

Since the acquisition of K-Telecom in Armenia, MTS has increased in market share there. In April 2009 MTS launched 3G services to stimulate data usage and to further improve service quality. To reinforce its image in the country the company contributed to a number of charitable causes as part of its social responsibility programme.

All had been going smoothly for MTS before it attempted to penetrate Kazakhstan. At the time, competition on the market there was confined to two clear leaders (GSM-Kazakhstan and KaR-Tel), as well as two smaller companies. Initially, KaR-Tel was a Kazakh–Turkish joint venture. However, the Kazakh side accused its two Turkish partners of breach of contractual obligations and had a court deprive them of their shares. In August 2004 the remaining Kazakh owners organised a tender for KaR-Tel. Eight companies participated in the tender, among them the Russian mobile operators MTS and VimpelCom. The latter won the tender and purchased the whole of KaR-Tel.

So far Kazakhstan is the only CIS market that MTS has tried but failed to enter. Yet, with its relatively low penetration level and importance as a large and rapidly developing market it remains a challenge for the leader of Russian telecom. The deepening of economic integration between Russia and Kazakhstan favours penetration by Russian companies. Many of these are corporate clients of MTS, and this may encourage the company to repeat its attempt to enter the Kazakh market.

By the end of the 2000s, MTS's only joint venture was in Belarus. It penetrated other countries by taking over a native leader.

Perhaps the similarities between Russia and its neighbours help MTS understand the region better than do its Western competitors, therefore providing a competitive advantage. Nevertheless, the main threat to MTS's ambition would most probably come not from national telecom service suppliers but from large Western telecoms with commanding financial resources.

In March 2008, the company began providing GPRS and EDGE technology. This allowed MTS subscribers to enjoy high-speed wireless Internet access, an area that remains in a nascent stage of development. By December 2008, MTS was also starting to offer its own Internet modems and tariff packages.

Russian telecommunication operators have been expanding aggressively in the CIS since the early 2000s, yet no major deals were recorded in 2008 or 2009 (Table 7.1). The move on the part of Russian operators toward diversification into areas other than the CIS, uncertainty over the fate of Svyazinvest (the national state-run fixed-line holding), the high cost of establishing telecommunication assets, and, of course, the restriction on investment caused by the financial crunch have all contributed to the break which Russian operators have taken from their drive to expand in the CIS market. Nevertheless, investment activity is likely to resume in the near future.

The most attractive countries for investment by Russian telecom operators were those of Kazakhstan, Ukraine and Uzbekistan, with their substantial populations and a comparatively low telecom penetration. Russian operators were also interested in Belarus, but the fixed-line and broadband markets there were monopolised by Beltelecom, the state-owned company, and two of the three GSM mobile operators were sold to Western investors.

As the mobile markets have already been tapped by Russian operators in most of the CIS countries, these companies have started expanding into fixed-line and broadband markets. Over the next decade these could turn into the busiest area in

Table 7.1 Russian telecom operators: major acquisitions in CIS countries, 2001–2009

Year	*Operator*	*Country and acquisition target*	*Stake*	*Amount invested*
2001	Megafon	Tajikistan: TT-Mobile	75%	Co-founder
2002	MTS	Belarus: MTS Belarus	49%	Co-founder
2003	MTS	Ukraine: UMC	100%	US$373m
2004	VimpelCom	Kazakhstan: KaR-Tel	100%	US$350m
2004	MTS	Uzbekistan: Uzdunrobita	74%	US$121m
2005	MTS	Turkmenistan: BCTI	100%	US$47m
2005	MTS	Kyrgyzstan: Bitel	51%	US$150m
2005	VimpelCom	Ukraine: URS	100%	US$231m
2005	VimpelCom	Tajikistan: Tacom	60%	US$12m
2005	VimpelCom	Georgia: Mobitel	51%	US$13m
2006	VimpelCom	Uzbekistan: Buztel	100%	US$60m
2006	VimpelCom	Uzbekistan: Unitel	100%	US$200m
2006	VimpelCom	Armenia: ArmenTel	100%	US$475m
2006	Altimo	Kyrgyzstan: Sky Mobile	100%	n/a
2006	Comstar UTS	Armenia: Callnet	75%	n/a
2006	Comstar UTS	Ukraine: DG Tel, technology System	100%	US$5m
2007	MTS	Armenia: K-Telecom	80%	US$425m
2009	Megafon	Abkhazia: Aquafon, South Ossetia: Ostelecom	51%	US$28.5m

Source: Rosstat and UNCTAD 2010.

the CIS. However, this might apply only to those countries with high population densities: in countries with low densities, a harder sell, operators might prefer to wait for the next generation of mobile services, endowed, as it will be, with the extra attraction of high-speed broadband.

Getting knowledge via mergers: VimpelCom

VimpelCom is a leading Russian company in the field of mobile communications, with over a quarter of the national market. It provides voice and data services through a range of mobile, fixed and broadband technologies under the Beeline brand. In Russia, the market penetration in this field has already reached 136 per cent. In addition, VimpelCom has focused its resources on the CIS countries where mobile coverage was still at such a relatively low level as would invite expansion.

Company expansion

VimpelCom[7] was established in September 1992, after a three-month pilot run in which 200 clients participated. In January 1993 the company was licensed by the Russian Ministry of Communication to service Moscow. In 1994 a new network of 10,000 clients was launched and the company started to generate profit in June of that year. The company introduced its trademark, Beeline, at this time. Since then the company has expanded to other areas of Russia. In 1995 VimpelCom took the lead in establishing Association-800, uniting 22 members who were then licensed to provide communication services under the Beeline brand. In November of that year it became the first Russian company in 90 years to float shares on the NYSE. This helped to attract new capital for the company's development.

At the beginning of 1998 VimpelCom signed an investment contract with the Norwegian communication company Telenor. Pursuant to it, Telenor bought 25 per cent + 1 voting shares of VimpelCom for US$162 million. It made Telenor an influential and strategic partner. At the time VimpelCom was just beginning to expand by offering national roaming to other companies.

By the middle of 1999 it had introduced technology to offer Beeline roaming to 50 countries, including in Europe, North America, South-West Asia, the Middle East and Africa. Beeline also introduced per-second charging, allowing customers to save up to 20 per cent.

In 2002 the number of company subscribers grew from 2 million to 5 million, and the number of regional networks in operation increased from 10 to 38. VimpelCom regained leadership in the key Moscow market in terms of number of subscribers. Financial performance improved, with net income reaching approximately US$130 million, compared with the US$47 million reported for 2001. In November, VimpelCom, Telenor and Alfa Group jointly invested US$175.5 million into VimpelCom-Region, the company's vehicle for coverage of Russia in its entirety.

In 2004 VimpelCom took an important strategic step by acquiring KaR-Tel, a wireless operator in Kazakhstan. At the end of 2004 the company served approximately 860,000 subscribers in Kazakhstan. At that time VimpelCom's capital investments in network development, infrastructure and support systems stood at about US$1,242 million. In addition, the company spent about US$440 million in acquisitions.

In 2005 the company started to enter new markets in the CIS: Ukraine and Tajikistan. During 2006, VimpelCom successfully developed its operations in Russia and Kazakhstan, while also achieving substantial subscriber growth through newly launched operations in Ukraine, Uzbekistan and Tajikistan and entering new markets in Georgia and Armenia.

In 2007 the company's board approved a new strategy aiming at expansion into adjacent businesses and geographic areas outside of the CIS. In step with the new strategy, VimpelCom established a telecom joint venture in Vietnam and launched the acquisition of Golden Telecom, a leading provider of integrated telecommunications and Internet services both in Russia and in the other countries of the CIS. All this has transformed VimpelCom from a regional wireless telecoms company into an internationally integrated telecom operator.

The acquisition in 2008 of Golden Telecom gave the company access to a large fixed-line market in Russia and the CIS, which included corporate telecommunications services, wholesale services to telecommunication operators and the rapidly growing broadband Internet market. The combined company realised synergies from the integration of transport networks, tautened operations and provided better sales and marketing coordination. It aided VimpelCom's expansion of reach beyond the CIS, despite the 2008 crisis. Joint ventures in Vietnam and the subsidiary in Cambodia gave the company a footprint in South-East Asia, with its fast-growing population, burgeoning economies and rapidly growing telecom markets.

Entry strategies and operations development abroad

VimpelCom increased its international activity in the 2000s by entering the markets of Armenia, Cambodia, Georgia, Kazakhstan, Tajikistan, Ukraine, Uzbekistan and Vietnam. At the end of the 2000s the purview of the company turned to Asia, where it strove to build mobile networks: in 2008 it established a joint venture GTEL-Mobile in Vietnam in which it had a 40 per cent stake, and acquired a 90 per cent stake in Sotelco in Cambodia.

Recently VimpelCom bought a controlling stake in the Laos mobile network for US$66 million. Twenty-two per cent of the company's shares still belong to the Laotian government. The top management of VimpelCom described the entry into Laos as the first step in that part of the company's strategy that focuses on the South Asian market.

VimpelCom has indeed come a long way since it first started internationalising. That was back in 1998, when it and Scandinavia's Telenor established a joint venture. They started on their way by instituting national roaming in Russia and then progressed to international roaming. Since then they have become global players.[8]

M&A strategy in CIS countries

In Armenia, VimpelCom started its M&A activity in November 2006 by acquiring 90 per cent of ArmenTel from the Greek telecommunication company Hellenic Telecommunications Organisation SA for around €341.9 million. In addition, VimpelCom assumed ArmenTel's debt obligations of €40 million, later on also purchasing the remaining 10 per cent of the company from the Armenian government. Toward the end of the 2000s, ArmenTel started operating under the Beeline brand, although the legal entity's name remained the same. The acquisition conferred significant benefits, as ArmenTel was a leading Internet provider in the region with a market share estimated as 40 per cent.[9] It had licence rights to provide services in GSM – standard 900 and CDMA. ArmenTel's client base consisted of 608,500 fixed-line residential users and 452,000 standard GSM mobile users.

In the same year, VimpelCom moved on to Armenia's neighbour, Georgia. There it acquired 51 per cent of Mobitel, a part of GMC Group, for US$12.6 million. Later it exercised an option to buy the remaining 49 per cent of shares. This allowed it to participate in a deal with Alcatel to establish a new mobile network in Georgia. This network commenced trial activity in the end of 2006. Its initial capacity was 300,000 subscribers, with potential to increase the number to 1 million. When trials ended and commercialisation of the network took place in 2007, VimpelCom was permitted under the licence agreement to expand its coverage to the cities of Tbilisi and Rustavi. Permission to serve the entire region followed in 2008. The Beeline brand was used throughout.[10]

VimpelCom's penetration of Kazakhstan began in August 2004, when the company acquired the local telecommunication company KaR-Tel for US$350 million, plus its debt of US$75 million. In 2010 the Russian company increased its share in KaR-Tel by acquiring a further 24.9 per cent from the Cyprus firm Limnotex Developments Limited. With that, VimpelCom's share in KaR-Tel increased to 74.9 per cent. As in previous cases, VimpelCom obtained access to a significant network of subscribers through this acquisition: already in 2007 KaR-Tel had more than 4 million.[11]

In January 2005 VimpelCom announced its acquisitions for US$12 million of 60 per cent of the shares of Tacom, the leading mobile operator in Tajikistan.[12] In September 2006 Tacom began to provide its services under the Beeline brand. At the end of 2007 the number of Beeline subscribers in Tajikistan reached 100,000.[13]

VimpelCom acquired Sky Mobile, one of the largest mobile operators in Kyrgyzstan, at the end of 2006. The purchase price was estimated at some US$400–500 million. At the same time, Sky Mobile itself acquired all the assets of the biggest Kyrgyzstan mobile operator company Bitel. The ownership of Bitel was legally contested by other Russian companies, including Rezervspetsmet and MTS.[14] In June 2009 Sky Mobile changed its brand to Beeline.

In January 2006 VimpelCom completed its US$60 million acquisition of 100 per cent of the shares in Bakri Uzbekistan Telecom (Busted), the fourth-largest mobile operator in Uzbekistan. In addition, in February 2006, it announced a second acquisition in Uzbekistan: for US$200 million (plus debts of US$7.7 million), the company had bought the second-biggest mobile operator in the market, Unitel. In July 2006 Busted and Unitel were officially integrated, and in September Unitel started providing mobile phone services under the Beeline brand.

One of the owners of VimpelCom, Alfa-Group, acquired 43.5 per cent of the shares in the Ukrainian mobile phone operator Kievstar, which was controlled by Telenor, in 2004. Alfa-Group then sought to hive it off to VimpelCom. Telenor, although partner to VimpelCom, opposed this acquisition. Later, in November 2005, VimpelCom signed a contract for 100 per cent ownership of another Ukrainian mobile network operator, Ukrainian Radio Systems, for a price of US$231 million. As in the case of Kievstar, however, Telenor would not approve. In April 2006 Beeline was officially launched as the name under which VimpelCom was to provide services in Ukraine, and in August 2007 the number of Beeline customers in Ukraine was over 2.8 million.[15]

VimpelCom used M&A strategy not only to penetrate some foreign markets but also to operate in Russia. Through a number of mergers and acquisitions in different regions of Russia it acquired a variety of benefits, notably access to network subscribers and technology development. In 2007, VimpelCom and Tele2 announced the purchase of 100 per cent of Severnaya Korona for US$232 million. That company owned licences for GSM 900/1800 and D-AMPS standards for the territory of the Irkutskaya district. Part of that agreement was a ten-year roaming contract according to which the Swedish operator used the Beeline network to provide roaming services. This acquisition process was finished in 2008 when Severnaya Korona became a part of VimpelCom and ceased being a separate legal entity.[16]

The series of VimpelCom acquisitions let the company not only enter other markets but also strengthen its current market position. At the end of 2010 VimpelCom had 64.3 million subscribers (50.9 million in Russia, among them 11.0 million in Moscow; 6.1 million in Kazakhstan; 2.0 million in Ukraine; 3.6 million in Uzbekistan; 0.8 million in Tajikistan, 0.6 million in Armenia; and 0.4 million in Georgia). The company's market share in Russia also increased compared with 2009, and by 2010 it had reached 24.4 per cent.

Both case companies – MTS and VimpelCom – employed M&A to gain valuable advantages such as knowledge, skills and access to suppliers and customers. VimpelCom acquired a significant subscriber base and the means to apply new technologies to broaden its networks. Furthermore, the fact that a Russian company was penetrating developing markets and then using advanced technology to develop infrastructure there surely played an important role in improving relationships with local governments. Additionally, some of the acquisitions helped the company to overcome competitors by establishing contracts with local companies to make the Beeline network preferable for roaming. This could have significant impact on the power divisions between competitors, giving VimpelCom great benefits.

Nevertheless, not all M&A cases are successful, owing to excessive process complexity and an overload of factors to be assessed. Experience with internationalisation recommends that companies should not only plan the process of the M&A itself but also give consideration to its possible aftermath, especially in regard to public opinion and governmental relations.

Which brings us to the problem of establishing relationships with the governments of foreign markets, as epitomised by the VimpelCom case. The main strategy of this company in entering a new market was establishing partnerships with local mobile operators. This was because the company needed local partners familiar with the specifics of the market, notably its power brokers.

While entering the Uzbekistan market in 2006 VimpelCom first bought Unitel and then Buztel. Both companies merged after a while. Unitel was acquired for US$207.7 million and Buztel for US$62.4 million. Analysts claimed that it was the most expensive price ever paid for such small client base. The reason attributed was that the authorities wanted to make it hard for foreigners to purchase licences. By applying a strong hand right at the start they signalled that they wanted things played so it benefited their country. Having made their point, the licences for GSM-900/1800 that covered all the Uzbekistan area were issued without further loss of precious time.

Both companies, MTS and VimpelCom, have much in common as to their strategies and manner of operation, on domestic as well as foreign markets. First, both companies use strategies that give them effective control over their foreign operations. Accordingly, they go for joint ventures and acquisitions, the latter more often. In most cases they first purchase a portion of the target company, and then increase their share as much as possible over time.

Second, both MTS and VimpelCom began their direct foreign expansion via CIS countries. This decision is based on the perception that these nations have similar cultural, traditional and infrastructural backgrounds, attractive market features, common historical development pattern and soviet heritage, similar business practices and are geographically close. When operating further away, both companies proceed gingerly to gain a better understanding of the environment and ways of doing business there.

While some political tension between CIS countries and Russia persists, there is also a strong trend favouring reconciliation in both politics and business. An air of rapprochement that is both political and commercial attends between these countries. The strategies of MTS and VimpelCom may be seen in this light. Nevertheless, both companies have significant potential in other Asian countries and after gaining necessary experience on CIS markets began expanding to other markets.

Third, in their international and domestic strategies and expansion our two companies have practically the same goals and motives. By acquiring other companies and participating in joint ventures, MTS and VimpelCom strive to obtain access to new subscriber bases, enter new geographic areas, garner new knowledge and expertise, get access to new technologies and fine-tune their adaptability to conditions abroad. They also learn to apply their existing technologies advantageously on a market that is less developed than theirs at home.

Fourth, one of the important goals of international expansion is to obtain local licences. Obtaining a licence not only permits a company to go into business but allies it to strong forces that militate to keep foreign competition out. In this endeavour MTS and VimpelCom on occasion have encountered insuperable problems.

Finally, MTS and VimpelCom usually not only succeed in their entry strategies but also choose the correct post-entry strategies that help them to both penetrate new markets and become stable competitive players there. Their main post-entry strategies include supplying attractive tariffs for subscribers and introducing new technologies and services (for example, 3G Internet).

Nevertheless, some important differences also exist. First, the two companies chose different approaches for their domestic expansion. MTS's approach is based on active penetration in the target regions by acquiring small independent local players in order to become licensed to operate. As a result, it obtains significant network coverage in Russia. Only after achieving a leadership position on the Russian market did the company opt to expand abroad. In contrast, VimpelCom's main focus in its domestic strategy is diversification and expansion of its services and presence by concluding roaming contracts and establishing joint ventures. The company itself is not present abroad though via its roaming activity it provides international services for its customers. So, while MTS operations on the domestic market do not relate to the outside world, VimpelCom's have some international relevance. VimpelCom practises simultaneity in domestic and foreign markets, while MTS does it in two separate stages.

Second, despite the fact that both companies on occasion enter the same countries, the order of market entry is different. MTS tends to penetrate more attractive (in terms of, for example, economic growth, opportunities, market size) countries first, even if this presents difficulty. It also likes the strategy of 'following the customer', seeking to penetrate where its main clients want to go. VimpelCom prefers investing where it is easier to do so, then adding investment tranches when possible.

Third, MTS prefers to employ an aggressive penetration strategy. It has fewer joint ventures than acquisitions, entry into Belarus being the main exception. VimpelCom is more flexible and does not deliberately avoid joint ventures. The MTS strategy is to acquire only leading telecoms companies in order to attain leadership for itself as fast as possible. VimpelCom also tries to acquire market leaders but in some countries settles for less.

Finally, although both companies pay significant attention to developing their brands, tactics differ on occasion. MTS concentrates its attention mainly on brand development and creation of its value, while VimpelCom puts the accent on positioning the company rather than the brand (going public on NYSE demonstrates this). Both strategies have proved successful: MTS, because it leveraged its strong brand name and reputation to snare some important contracts (for example, 3G (UMTS) network development), while VimpelCom's decision to go public on the NYSE opened the way to financing.

Though proceeding their separate ways, both companies gained significant market share and customer approval wherever they tried. Their experiences bear out some basic rules of thumb: assure access to financing, make the right decision in targeting markets and utilise appropriate strategies. Additionally, before starting foreign expansion companies must create strong brands and a strong reputation on the domestic market. Political considerations must also be factored in. A favourable political environment can be very valuable. It can assist in gaining entry and in solving problems that arise afterwards. Choosing to penetrate hostile political territory is tricky, and politics can also affect operation after entry into a market.

Returning to our two companies: MTS mainly chose to gain presence in concentrated markets having an average level of competition. That provided early opportunity to become a market leader. To protect this position it acquired licences (frequencies) to help bar the entry of other foreign competitors. In other words, the company made it policy to strive for monopolistic positioning. That is now mission impossible, however, in CIS and Russian markets, as financially muscular Western players are crowding in. VimpelCom, in contrast, is more flexible. It is accustomed and content to operate in markets where there is some level of competition.

Both companies should think about penetrating the European market, but they would have to brace themselves and go at it proactively. Nowadays the threat of Western telecoms companies' entering emerging markets, and competing in them, is quite high. Therefore, the counter-penetration of Western markets by emerging players could not only lead to further geographical expansion but also protect emerging markets, because Western companies would have to busy themselves protecting their home turf instead of expanding. Additionally, while operating in CIS countries, both VimpelCom and MTS rely heavily on government support to keep themselves shielded from political harm. If something goes wrong in this sphere, companies can be significantly harmed. Entering the European market could hedge against such an eventuality.

It has already been noted that MTS started its business with active penetration into Russian regions and, as a result, attained leadership. VimpelCom was less proactive. The result is evident: MTS is nowadays the leading company on the Russian telecommunication market. Yet it would not be true to say that VimpelCom lost the battle for Russia, because it still remains one of the leaders. Given its strategic options, VimpelCom would be well advised to become more active domestically.

Finally, both companies have significant internal capabilities (funds, resources, knowledge, expertise and so on) that they gained while operating in Russia. This helped them not only penetrate foreign markets but also operate there successfully. They became strong enough to enter underdeveloped markets, forcing domestic competition to let them prosper there. Now the threat of Western telecommunication companies entering countries where MTS and VimpelCom operate is mounting. That being the case, Russian companies should react by proactively entering not only developing countries but developed Western markets as well. This will help them to create additional entry barriers and increase the competition level. As a result, Western companies may face more difficulties in entering CIS and other Asian countries. That being so, an opportunity would be created for Russia.

8 Born to global business

This chapter will treat the rise of three Russian companies that are international by nature. The first, Inter RAO UES, is the distributor for the largest state monopoly in the power generation sector, which transformed itself into a multinational. The second, Rusnano, is a domestically orientated firm which, owing to the highly innovative nature of its business, found that it could develop only through international partnership. The third firm, Yandex, is global from scratch, as it is an Internet company engaged in search systems and the context advertisement business.

Boundless energy – Inter RAO UES

Russian electricity sector

Over the past 50 years electrical energy has become one of the most important developing industries. From the 1950s the world's generating capacity has grown 50-fold, with an annual growth rate twice as large as that of the world economy as a whole. Over the same period the cost of producing electricity has decreased by 75 per cent.

By the end of the 2000s more than half of the world's electricity production facilities – around 3,500 GWt – were located in Northern America and Europe. According to estimates, the share of these regions in the total capacity was going to decrease steadily, while those of South East Asian countries and South America will increase.[1] OECD countries will see their energy demand increase by 1 per cent annually, while that of former Soviet bloc countries will grow by 1.5 per cent, of China by around 3.6 per cent and of the rest of the world by 3.5 per cent. This foresees that by 2020 developed countries will consume about 42 per cent of total produced energy (whereas in 1995 this figure was about 54 per cent).[2]

Russia is the world's fourth-largest producer of electric power. For its electricity production, Russia relies on thermal, hydro-power, coal-fired, gas-fired and nuclear technologies. Faced with obsolete equipment and technology, the government recognised that structural reform was necessary to meet growing demand spurred by economic expansion, and to attract the investment needed to modernise and expand. After an erratic run-up, by the end of the 2000s it appeared as if the industry was at last on the road towards competitive energy generation and transmission.

Overseeing proceedings was the state-owned RAO UES (Russian Public Corporation Unified Energy Systems), a conglomerate established in 1992 and engaged in the generation, dispatching, transmission and retailing of electricity for light and heat. It had detailed plans for the reorganisation of the sector and ultimately for its own wind-up. The process of restructuring between 2001 and 2008 ended with the privatisation of all of RAO UES's 20 regional companies. Thus, while only few years ago RAO UES was one of the most powerful state monopolies, today it is a highly geographically diversified private business.

The energy market under the control of these regional companies was divided, there being no exchange of product between them. The size of RAO UES's contribution to the energy sector of Russia in 2008 was: installed capacity of power plants, 72 per cent; electricity generated by power plants, 70 per cent; heat distribution throughout Russia, 32 per cent.

Regional energy players

In the 2000s only a few regional players operated outside the remit of RAO UES. One was Irkutskenergo, a vertically integrated utility located in the Irkutsk Oblast of Eastern Siberia. In 1992 Irkutskenergo, previously a state enterprise, was transformed into a limited liability company and partly privatised. Its main activities were generation, transmission and distribution of electricity and thermal power. In 2008, electricity and thermal power accounted for 66 per cent and 29 per cent of sales revenues, respectively, with small non-core businesses accounting for the remaining 5 per cent. Sales within the Irkutsk Oblast represented about 95 per cent of its total sales, about 10 per cent of electricity and 30 per cent of heat being sold to local resale organisations. This company is looking into exporting power to China and, in the longer term, to South-East Asia.

The Russian government holds about 40 per cent of the shares in the company. Rusal and Sual, Irkutskenergo's largest customers, control about 40–45 per cent of the company, with the rest being dispersed among employees and small investors.

Irkutskenergo benefits from its near-monopoly position as the sole electricity distributor and supplier in the Irkutsk Oblast. As most of the company's capacity is provided by huge low-cost hydro-power plants, Irkutskenergo is able to offer the lowest prices in Russia.

Another notable player is Mosenergo, the largest regional vertically integrated electricity utility in Russia. Mosenergo serves 4.3 million customers in the City of Moscow and Moscow Oblast, and is the largest of 74 energy companies in Russia. The company is 52.7 per cent owned by the federal government. Mosenergo became a public liability company and was partly privatised in 1993.

Company assets include 21 power plants, 13 electricity grid units and one heating grid subsidiary. Mosenergo produces more than 8 per cent of Russia's electricity and 6 per cent of the country's electricity for heat production, making it the largest provider of the latter in the world. In 2008, the company had about 48,000 employees. About 75 per cent of Mosenergo's revenues derive from sales to the City of Moscow.

Mosenergo is also involved in other activities, such as the construction, maintenance and manufacture of generation equipment. These activities support the core electricity and heat operations, but account for less than 4 per cent of revenues.

Government role in the energy sector

Owing to its low-tariff policy, under-investment remains an acute issue for Mosenergo. In 2002, this resulted in the breakdown of one of the units at Kashirskaya GRES, one of Mosenergo's electricity-only plants. Such problems necessitated change, and they were tackled in the mid-2000s. The idea of reforming had evolved directly from the answers to some very simple but probing questions: who pays, how much, to whom and for what? By the end of the 2000s there existed a number of regional energy companies and large federal power stations, as well as an intersystem of electrical grids. The state owned a controlling stake in most companies, regulating the activities of the energy entities and determining the price of its services and production.

The economic system in the electricity sector did not satisfy the needs of any of its participants. The average consumer was unhappy with the fact that, year after year, there came a hike in price without the corresponding return of a safer and more reliable supply. The search for the party at fault inevitably led the national authority to finger the regional companies, accusing them of constantly asking for too much money and then spending what they got ineffectively. In contrast, the regional companies felt that they lacked input from the national authority in terms of investments and financial benefits. Oddly, both parties were right. It was true that the tariff, set by the regional energy commission, did not cover all the expense incurred by the regionals, many of which lacked the funds to even keep their systems in working order. However, it was also true that the regionals received no effective motivation from upstairs to operate more economically, and no guidance on key performance targets.

The guiding principle of electricity sector reform, in Russia as elsewhere, is to force utilities to operate more efficiently in order to reduce the cost to end users. The way to do so, according to this principle, is to watch the market and respond to its exigencies. But after the Soviet system crashed, a market had to be created which would set prices, and to accomplish this the sector had to be restructured. That took some years and a great deal of harried effort.

For much of the twentieth century, production and distribution in this sector was regulated by the state the world over. In the 1980s command by the state began morphing into command by the market. This resulted in a variety of ways of running things, but it typically involved undoing a vertically integrated monopoly and restructuring it into a natural monopoly.

Energy sector restructuring

Restructuring split the electricity sector into four segments: generation, transmission, distribution and retail. In generation and retail, reformers hoped to introduce competition between independent companies. In transmission and distribution, non-discriminatory access to grids was to be vouchsafed by a strong and independent regulator. The privatisation of the generation and retail segments of the sector tended to be left for later in the day – even though in Russia, as distinct from elsewhere, privatisation of electricity assets preceded restructuring.

High on the list of things that needed to be done to make privatisation work was improvement in the internationalisation of electricity supply. Export of electricity from Russia was in itself no new thing, but it was in need of adjustment to prevailing economic and political strictures.

Russian power was traditionally of great interest to global corporations in terms of its import to Europe, and, as investment became easier at the end of the Soviet era, major Western players soon moved in. Beginning in 2007, the first to make it was the German major E.ON, which took control over one of the largest Russian energy assets, OGK-4; it was followed by Italian utility ENEL as a key shareholder in another huge asset, OGK-5; and, since 2008, the Finnish company Fortum has controlled the former TGC-10.

Russia exports significant amounts of electricity. Its client countries include former Soviet Union members, as well as China, Poland, Turkey and Finland. At the end of the 2000s dual efforts were undertaken to integrate the Russian and Western European electricity grids. The Baltrel programme was designed to create an energy ring of power companies in the Baltic States. Talks were also held between Russian experts and the Union for the Coordination of Transmission of Electricity, of which 20 European countries are members, concerning technical and operational aspects of interconnection.

The Russian electrical energy market differed from the others primarily in having an excess of power-generation. Indeed, it has not just enough extra to fill the predicted internal growth within Russia, but more than enough left over for export. This is in stark contrast to either developed nations that have systems running at capacity, or other BRIC and developing nations where demand far exceeds supply. Couple this with the legacy of the Soviet power-generation system and the need resulted for a large MNC to exploit this asset. Under these promising auspices, enter RAO UES.

Inter RAO UES: background

Inter RAO UES was established as a power distributor daughter company of the RAO UES Group in 1997. In 2001 Inter RAO UES took some initial steps to make large-scale trading possible, establishing its own daughter companies to expand its foreign operations. In 2002 it began exporting large-scale electric power from Russia. In 2003, 40 per cent of the company's shares were sold to another Russian energy company, one specialising in nuclear power, Rosenergoatom. As a result, Inter RAO UES became a unified export and import operator for two of the largest producers of electric power in the country.

The reorganisation of RAO UES, mentioned above, was part of the reform of the power industry which started in 2001. The main goal of this reform was to demonopolise the industry. RAO UES, as noted, ceased to be a government monopoly and instead was split into a number of government and private companies, thus becoming joint-stock company RAO UES. On October 2007, shareholders decided to separate Inter RAO UES from RAO UES. As a result, the newly independent firm became a major generating company that led all the others in the area of export and import of electric power, having been awarded a considerable part of the original company's assets and thereby a notable market share. The total installed capacity of the power plants it owned or managed in 2008 was about 8,000 MW.

By the end of the 2000s Inter RAO UES owned and controlled a group of more than 20 companies based in 14 countries. By acquiring foreign assets, it consolidated its position in the electric power markets of Europe, the South Caucasus, the Far East and Central Asia. The company aims by 2020 to become one of the ten largest transnational electrical-power holding companies globally.

International operations

Russia's first post-communist large international project did not involve Inter RAO UES, however. The year was 2001 and the company was Ignalinskaya AES in Lithuania exporting to Kaliningrad Oblast of Russia and to Belarus. In the same period the first subsidiaries for operations in foreign power markets were established.

Only in 2002 did Inter RAO UES commence exporting, and in 2003 a new period of development of the company began, when, as noted above, 40 per cent of its shares were sold to Rosenergoatom. Aside from changes in the share capital structure this resulted in a considerable increase in Inter RAO UES's potential in cross-border supply.

Inter RAO UES started active purchasing of electric power assets abroad with expansion into CIS countries in 2003. In Georgia, the company received management rights for Khramhesi GES-1 and Khramhesi GES-2; in Armenia, the company acquired trust management rights for shares of Armianskaya AES and purchased the Sevano-Razdanskiy Cascade of Hydroelectric Power Plants (MEK). By the end of that year Inter RAO UES was exporting to 12 CIS countries and to other states. Its purchasing policy necessitated the development of a large-scale investment programme, and from 2003 to 2005 Inter RAO UES and its subsidiaries invested some US$350 million in the purchase of foreign power assets.

In 2004, its subsidiary trading company RAO Nordic Oy became a major business entity in Finland. In 2005, as part of a settlement of electric power arrears of businesses in Kazakhstan, Inter RAO UES was granted ownership of 50 per cent of the shares in a company called Stantsiya Ekibastuzskaya GRES-2. In March of the same year a Russian–Tajik joint venture in Tajikistan called Sangtudinskaya GES-1 was established with Inter RAO UES among its shareholders. Also in 2005, Moldavskaya GRES joined Inter RAO UES. This asset had a strategic value for development of trading operations through Moldova to Europe.

Since the mid-2000s the geography of the company's operations expanded considerably. In 2005 Inter RAO UES acquired 70 per cent of the shares of the Turkey-based company TGR Enerji with the aim of preparing for a scale-up in business activities and implementation of investment projects both in Turkey and in markets of neighbouring states. In 2006 the sale of 100 per cent of Electric Networks of Armenia to Inter RAO UES's subsidiary Interenergo B.V. was completed, and in the following year the company took over a distributor of electricity in Lithuania.

By the late 2000s, Inter RAO UES had an active presence in the markets of a considerable number of countries in Europe and Asia, notably in Russia's near-abroad. It figured prominently in the increase of scale in the cross-border supply of electric power.

The main export destinations in 2008 were Finland, Belarus and Kazakhstan: they accounted for more than 73 per cent of all company exports (51.2 per cent, 11.6 per cent and 10.7 per cent, respectively). Electric power was also supplied to Azerbaidjan, Georgia, Ukraine, Latvia, Lithuania, Mongolia and Norway. In the same year, the main sources of electricity imports were energy systems in Kazakhstan, Georgia and Azerbaidjan, which together accounted for 96.1 per cent of imports (70.9 per cent, 14.2 per cent and 11 per cent of imports, respectively).

In 2009 Inter RAO UES joined a US$1 billion investment pool with the Russian state-owned VTB bank and Kuwait's Alghanim & Sons to invest in electricity projects in Russia, the CIS and Arab countries. It was also bidding in partnership with Rosatom for a contract to build a nuclear power plant in Turkey.

Impact of the financial crisis

The global financial crisis of 2008 changed the investment scene, plunging Russia into its first economic recession in almost 10 years and driving down domestic energy demand. Before the crisis, RAO UES was predicting that Russian electricity consumption, an indicator of economic health, would rise by 4–5 per cent a year until 2012. Instead, demand fell by up to 10 per cent in the late 2000s as the energy-intensive steel and car-manufacturing industries idled.

Although it is unlikely that the government will try to reverse electricity privatisation, there is a risk that the greater involvement of state-controlled companies will place the private sector at a competitive disadvantage because of the former's privileged access to government funds in buying low-priced assets.

Of significant advantage to Inter RAO UES is that its interest and that of the state coincide. The company has an interest in assuring long-term cooperation with new foreign partners and foreign regional markets. It is in the business of purchasing foreign-based assets and using contractual agreements with key foreign players on the global energy and electricity market, and by now holds a solid position within international energy organisations.

This begins to explain that when a company needs to satisfy a client (country), mostly by lowering prices, it may not have to pay much attention to the market side of the problem (profit) if it has a benign and rich government behind it. For the private energy players a lack of profit makes it impossible to keep all its assets performing and thereby sustaining its work force. Inter RAO, thanks to its government relations, can roll the problem away from itself and towards the government.

Smart restructuring

In the light of this, it can be seen that the decision of RAO UES to divide several activities between different corporate units was a truly important one. The decentralisation allowed the organisation to distribute responsibilities between different business units on the sound grounds that it is easier to properly manage smaller portions. The spin-off of Inter RAO UES proved its ability to control successfully an increasingly large part of the old RAO UES giant. By restarting small it learned along its growth path how to be successful when big. This became a case in best practice for Russia.

Inter RAO UES opened the road to the market economy for the Russian energy sector. The emergence of such a large private company lent smaller private companies the spirit to assert themselves and succeed in breaking the state monopoly. Market orientation gained ground, the style of management changed, and the economy gained in verve.

That served also to change the foreign perception of Russians as business partners. Before, such a partnership was felt to be risky or even menacing. Now, with the state relegated to the back burner and partnership with private enterprises made possible, the attitude of foreign players towards such deals improved.

The fact that the private firm Inter RAO UES is nonetheless closely knit to the Russian government apparently did not faze foreign planners. Indeed, the relationship was seen as assuring the Russian company's good fortune. Some of Inter RAO UES's important coups were quite obviously due to its links to government insiders.

Indeed, the alignment of the company's strategic goals with those of the Russian state is core to the birth of this multinational, and is key to its continued success: it is assured as a result of considerable political and financial will to see it succeed. There have been reciprocal benefits for the state in harvesting a share of public approval. As Inter RAO UES has grown, so too has the modernisation of the national grid and attendant better service for a lower price. Thus, the importance of Inter RAO UES's relationship with the Russian state cannot be overstated. There is little doubt, for instance, that individuals have made their political and economic careers as a result of the birth of this company, something which is an inherent competitive advantage for Inter RAO UES, as the fiscal interests of key decision-makers are linked to its growth. While it is unlikely that such closeness would be allowed in the West or in economies with regulated markets, it seems to be the only path available for Russian companies.

In the next two sections we will be presenting two smaller cases of very dissimilar companies with one shared quality: their only chance to grow and internationalise is to be as innovative as possible. The first is Rusnano, a strategic project of the Russian government, and the second is the Internet company Yandex.

Rusnano: who innovates – business or state?

R&D and innovation in Russia

Historically, Russia, as part of the former Soviet Union, has been characterised by a well-developed system of public R&D institutes. During the transitional period, however, this part of the R&D system experienced severe problems, including a critically low level of financial support from both the state and industry, entailing unattractively low salaries for scientists and engineers as well as stagnation of R&D activity in general.

Some Russian companies operate their own research facilities, albeit limited by comparison to those of Western companies, with many of these inherited during privatisation. University R&D is funded primarily from competitive schemes and research contracts with industry and government. Financial and human resources in the higher education R&D sector comprise no more than 5 per cent of the national total.

A majority of Russian R&D (roughly 60 per cent) is financed by the state, yet the bulk of R&D would appear, at first glance, to be conducted by the business sector. This apparent paradox reflects the fact that state-owned companies and branches of research institutes are classified as business entities, and they conduct a large share of publicly financed innovative research.

A key difficulty in the Russian market is the wide gap between what Russian R&D supplies and what the market demands. Private sector R&D investment as a share of sales is low compared with levels in other BRIC countries. Innovation performance indices for Russian companies are also low, not exceeding 10 per cent of the total number of enterprises statistically surveyed by Rosstat over the last 10 years (2001–2010) – three to five times less than the figure in developed economies. Leaders are the aerospace and telecom sectors, with 34 per cent and 36 per cent of innovative enterprises.[3]

The most palpable change in innovation policy occurred in 2006, when the government started to develop indirect measures to stimulate innovation activity. The government has also tried to introduce measures in the area of technical regulations, ecological control and temporary cancellation of import custom duties for types of equipment that are not produced in Russia. These measures were targeted at stimulating demand for innovation from industrial enterprises, mostly through help in updating such enterprises' capital equipment as well as easing access to global know-how.

Further support for innovation infrastructure may come from venture funds and technology parks. In 2007 several government-supported venture funds were created and further development of technology park infrastructure, including the organisation of their management, has been initiated.

Through a series of programmes and policies aimed at achieving competitive companies outside the resource-based industries, the government is thus stimulating the development of the innovation economy. One important programme concerns the nanotech sector development in Russia. By the end of the 2000s the Russian nanotechnology market was at an early stage of development; Russia's share in the global technology sector checked in at about 0.3 per cent, and that in the nanotechnology market at some 0.04 per cent. This was because Russia had turned its attention to nanotechnology developments seven to ten years later than other countries; as a consequence, it lags seriously behind the world's nanotech leaders – the USA, Japan and the EU. The number of international nanotechnology patents in Russia in 2008 was about 30 (being less than 0.2 per cent of inventions worldwide).

Internationalisation of Russian nanotech sector

One reason why Russian companies enter into partnerships with foreign firms (through joint ventures, research contracts and cooperative research projects) is an attempt to get access to the latest technology as well as managerial and marketing experience.

At the same time, Russian research organisations have been very active in mobilising foreign support and research contracts in the 1990s and 2000s. In addition to American and European governmental and non-governmental programmes supporting non-commercial R&D activities in Russia, a growing number of Western companies contracted out research of a commercial nature to Russian research institutes. This reflects the fact that Russia had brainpower available, yet no local uses for it.

Nearly 10 per cent of all R&D expenditure in Russia is funded from abroad. Primary sources of foreign funding were the EU, the USA and Asian countries including China, Japan and South Korea. The resources of Russian enterprises devoted to research have been reported as being limited owing to lack of finance, narrow strategic focus, preference of foreign innovative R&D and absence of state support. According to the analysis of international cooperation agreements made by the Russian Ministry for Education and Research, one important focus was on cooperation with major nanotech players in Japan and the USA and with the emerging players in Argentina, Brazil, China, Egypt, India, Malaysia, Mexico, South Africa and South Korea.[4]

Russian policies regarding the internationalisation of nanotechnology were defined in a variety of official documents. The 'Concept of state policy of the Russian Federation in international science and technology (S&T) cooperation' that was approved in 2000 emphasised the intensification of cooperation with the EU in the framework of European S&T programmes. Another priority was the cooperation with leading countries in nanotech, especially the USA, Germany, Japan, France and the UK, in order to acquire new knowledge for domestic research and foreign experience for the reform of the Russian nanotech sector.

The European Parliament stated the importance of collaboration with Russia in the area of science and technology, confirming plans of joint projects in the area of international nano cooperation, as Russia 'has made it clear that it sees the EU as its long-term priority in nanotech cooperation'.[5]

Rusnano: involved globally

The Russian Corporation of Nanotechnologies (Rusnano) was established in 2007 by Russia's government in support of state policy in the field of nanotechnology. It co-invests in projects that have high potential in terms of commercial or social benefits. The policy is to encourage private companies with promising projects to start up.

As a start, Rusnano seeded contacts relevant to its mission abroad. In the year 2009 alone, delegations from Rusnano visited the US, Germany, Sweden, Finland, Japan, Israel and Canada. There they contacted governmental agencies, business associations and scientific groups relating to nanotechnology in order to develop cooperation.

By the end of the 2000s some important results of this activity were: an intergovernmental agreement between Russia and Israel on industrial research and development; an agreement of cooperation with the Ministry of Employment and Economy of Finland; and an agreement on the development of a joint investment programme with the Finnish state investment fund Tekes (the Finnish Funding Agency for Technology and Innovation).

In addition, several memorandums were signed with, first, organisations in China and Korea based on earlier agreements of cooperation with the ministries of Science and Technology of the People's Republic of China and the Republic of Korea; second, the European Bank for Reconstruction and Development, under which financing from the bank for nanotechnology projects in the territory of the Russian Federation will be considered; third, Alcoa (United States); and, fourth, Singapore-based investors.

In addition to prospects in Singapore, Rusnano set up a Chinese joint venture in early 2010 with Thunder Sky Group. The two companies agreed to develop lithium-ion technology for batteries for electric buses and minibuses. The batteries can also be used in uninterrupted-power-supply units in IT, telecoms and renewable energy. With an investment estimated at US$466 million, this joint venture is expected to generate annual sales of US$450 million by 2015. Rusnano will invest US$72 million in cash and provide credit of US$189 million. The Chinese partner will also invest US$72 million in cash, technologies and intellectual property in the project's equity and provide a loan of US$134 million.[6]

In Europe, Rusnano is working on two fronts. In collaboration with Sistema, Rusnano is planning to acquire a stake in the French electronic components manufacturer Altis Semiconductor, of which 50 per cent was held by the German-based company Infineon Technologies.[7] In addition, Rusnano and the major Russian financial-industrial group Renova have developed plans to build Russia's largest solar module manufacturing facility based on technology provided by Swiss company Oerlikon Solar. This represents a 20.1 billion rouble investment.[8]

Rusnano is also cooperating with US firms in energy efficiency, medicine and other advanced spheres. In autumn 2009 the company participated in a new Russian venture fund put together by VTB Group and Silicon Valley's Draper Fisher Jurvetson (DFJ). The initial investment was US$100 million, of which Rusnano and VTB were pledged to commit US$50 million each.[9] The fund, baptised DFJ-VTB Aurora, will invest in promising nanotechnology innovations from Russia and abroad. It will also attract foreign investment to build Russian nanotechnology production plants. DFJ-VTB Aurora was the first international venture project in which Rusnano participated. Among other projects, two were particularly notable. The first was with the international venture investment fund Burrill Capital Fund IV and involves a fund of up to US$500 million, US$200 million of which will come from Rusnano. This project focuses on research and development in medicines, diagnostics medical equipment and medical and industrial biotechnologies. The second was the setting up of an international fund managed by Harris & Harris Group, Inc., which was aimed at technologies transfer projects from the USA to Russia. This fund will be worth up to US$250 million; Rusnano's share will be US$125 million, or up to 50 per cent of the total investment. The total budget of these projects and funds reportedly exceeds US$1 billion, including Rusnano's investment of US$468 million.[10]

Reaching out to Russians abroad

Rusnano's *modus operandi* stressed contact with fellow Russians living abroad and working in nanotech. Numerous meetings took place in 2009 between company executives and representatives of the Russian diaspora – scientists and businessmen – in the US, Israel, France, Finland, Switzerland and other countries in order to explore collaboration potential.

As of the end of 2009, of the more than 100 foreign requests (including from CIS countries) for co-financing that had been submitted to the corporation, 65 had come from groups in which managers or key participants were Russian. Of the 84 projects submitted to the corporation from applicants in 12 countries (excluding CIS countries), 42 had been prepared on the initiative and with the participation of Russians working abroad.

At the end of the 2000s the company announced a tender for selecting the partner (managing company) to establish a Russian–Israeli investment fund. This fund should become one of the elements of the foreign technology transfer system and will allow increasing numbers of Israeli technology-based investment projects to go into production in the Russian Federation. The fund's target size was US$100 million, up to 50 per cent of which would be committed by Rusnano. The rest was expected to be contributed by the managing company winning the tender. The total fund size might be extended up to US$200 million, if sufficient projects can be identified.

Rusnano's global reach is interesting in itself, but is also different from that of most of the companies discussed in other chapters here. In the field of nanotechnology Russia was far behind other practitioners. The only way to catch up was through the help of nanotech companies abroad. Fellow Russians working in the field abroad provided entry leverage.

A trick of fate, one might call it, but Rusnano, founded as a business having a domestic role, certainly not being a company specifically aimed at foreign markets, found itself forced to become international practically from the very beginning of its existence.

Internationalisation of Yandex: natural or virtual?

The Internet market in Russia

In the 2000s the Internet in Russia fell short of developed-world standards in several areas, but most notably in broadband, academic networks and e-commerce. Fast out of the starting block, by the end of the 2000s Russia had the fastest growing IT in specific areas, such as social services (gaming portals), online stores, national projects in IT, news, analysis and entertainment.

In 2003 only 3 per cent of the Russian population accessed the web daily; by 2008 the figure was 10 per cent and, as of autumn 2009, there were 42 million Internet users in Russia, or 36 per cent of the country's adult population. Compared with the previous year (from autumn 2008), the number of Internet users in Russia increased by 22 per cent (7.6 million people) and the growth of daily users was 35 per cent (6.2 million).[11] The majority of Internet users lived in the two largest cities (Moscow and St Petersburg), where most affluent Russians live and where 90 per cent of government spending is concentrated.

In 2009 there was a decline in the amount of new Internet activity due to a dearth of funding. The impact of the global financial crisis was felt more deeply here than in many other industries. The sharp decline in advertising, primarily from the hardest-hit banks and investment companies, has led to nervousness in management attended by serious cost-cutting expressed in the reduction of staff and even in the freezing of some projects.

Nonetheless, at the end of the 2000s the prediction was that by the end of the century Russia would become the second-largest Internet market in Europe (behind Germany), having more than 40 million Internet users. It was also predicted that more than 40 per cent of Russia's population would be using the Web by 2012, up 70 per cent from the 2007 level.

Moreover, a significant review of advertising budgets was expected to favour the Internet. In a crisis priority goes to the most effective advertising platforms, and the Internet ranks high. Therefore, unlike most of the traditional types of advertising (television, print, outdoor), advertising on the Internet continued to gain share on the others despite the slow-down.

In addition, a positive factor was that Russian Internet advertising is highly contextual, which allows its effectiveness to be tracked with high precision. When there is austerity, this is important. To be sure, Russian advertising is not massive enough to sustain Russian Internet industry by itself, and fee-based services are still needed to sustain Internet viability.

Yandex – background

Yandex is the leading Internet engine and one of best-known brands in Russia, with more than 15 million visitors and users. The name 'Yandex' made its first appearance in 1993, when the engineers at CompTek began development of a programme which would become one of the first search engines in Russia.[12]

Yandex was separated from CompTek so as to provide web-browsing services. It was launched almost immediately after Russia was 'plugged into' the Internet in 1997. In the same year the companies Rambler, Mail.ru, List.ru and Apport also popped up.

Yandex, like any other Internet company, was born global. Yet the only physical international asset that Yandex has abroad is its subsidiary, Yandex Labs, which was founded in 2008 in Silicon Valley in California. It is used for research, rather than to provide services in the USA.

On the Russian market Yandex is a pioneer in contextual advertising. In 2004 its revenues from advertising as a whole skyrocketed in growth, and in 2005 revenue from this source was US$100 million, 80 per cent of which was from contextual advertising. Yandex's major competitor in Russia remains Google, which far outstrips Yandex's experience and client base.

Yandex's innovation on the market was an introduction of the 'pay per click' system, where a client pays per entry to the Yandex website. Under this system the client is paying regardless of whether he finds the goods sought.

During 2009 two domains were opened: in Ukraine (Yandex.ua) and in Kazakhstan (Yandex.kz). Both domains work in Russian, but are geographically orientated towards Ukraine and Kazakhstan in terms of keywording. The Internet markets of Belarus and Poland are Yandex's next important targets. Most of the population of Belarus speaks Russian and uses it in daily life (along with Byelorussian). As far as Poland is concerned, many obstacles are expected. Only a few among the population understand Russian or read the Cyrillic script. Besides, an aversion to all Russia-related things lingers, and Yahoo and Google are very strong on this market. Both companies have their domains in Poland running in Polish.

Western markets are highly attractive for Internet companies as they can be easily entered without any significant outlay in terms of facilities or labour force. That makes it easy for them to crowd in and that, in turn, makes for ferocious competition. This explains why Yandex felt impelled to open a subsidiary in the US that works in Russian and therefore serves almost exclusively Russian expatriates living there.

Competing with Google

One interesting part of the Yandex strategy is the permanent competition with Google in Russia. In many of the countries worldwide Google dominates as the search engine of choice. Even so, by the end of the 2000s some countries remained where local search engines still manage to have a larger market share than Google. In 2009 Yandex led this category, with a 56 per cent share of the search market in Russia (compared with Google's 23 per cent).[13]

Several explanations can be adduced. First, Yandex invested in the Russian market long before Google. Second, the company's technology was perfectly aligned with the language. Third, innovations were offered that Google has to copy to be able to compete. Fourth, strong brand awareness and loyalty from

Russian customers already existed. And, finally, Yandex successfully explored the formation of partnerships and strategic alliances with local companies at an early stage.

Although one of the founders of Google (Sergei Brin) is of Russian origin, this company did not look to enter the Russian market until 2005. Google prioritised its entry into developed markets. At the end of the 2000s Yandex was among the top 10 search engines in the world, but its market share was only about 1.5 per cent, while at the same time Google had 62.4 per cent of the market. This was the reason for enormous difference in these companies' revenues: US$160 million versus US$16 billion, respectively.

Google dominates the global market in searching and context advertising. Around 70 per cent of searches all over the globe in the 2010 were via Google.[14] To achieve this, Google crushed English-language rivals such as Yahoo, AltaVista and others. As a result, other English-speaking countries became Googlers, including India with its population of 1 billion. Google's next targets were the Spanish Terra.es and the German subsidiary of AltaVista. Google was appreciated by the global market for the same reason that Yandex is appreciated in Russia – quality of search.

Yandex prevailed on its home market by doing what came naturally: operating in Russian, with a Russian mentality, for Russian users. While Yandex was already gaining in popularity, Google was just starting to develop its own search morphology for Cyrillic searches, and was able to apply it only in 2006. Only then could it pile on added services suited to Russian needs, such as Russian news, maps and so on. That, apparently, has brought it some gain.

Rusnano and Yandex are two very different companies in unrelated businesses. They do, however, share a similarity. They had to innovate in their struggle for growth in an internationalised milieu.

Rusnano emerged from the well-developed yet fading remnants of the old Soviet system of public R&D institutes. Even though belatedly privatised, Rusnano conducts its business in ways suggesting its old, statistic self. In fact, it seems to hang, chameleon-like, somewhere in between, at times more on the private side, at others more like government. Can this company be seen as a paragon of private initiative for the many international agreements that Rusnano entered into? Or should it be seen as a successful political agent performing on behalf of Russian foreign policy? Was it, at bottom, Rusnano that entered into those big-money contracts, or was it the Russian state? Possibly the answer is that it should be celebrated less as a business success than as a considerable political one.

Yandex, on the other hand, is a software firm that develops and maintains an Internet search engine primarily for the Russian market, where it has a strong brand. It introduced innovations to the industry in the form of the pay-per-click system of pricing for advertising and contriving to operate successfully in Cyrillic. However, competition with Google has stiffened in recent years, and Google is one of the most daunting competitors a company can have. Where Yandex has a strong, established brand in Russia, Google is even now expanding into Eastern

Europe with technology that is fully attuned to the Cyrillic alphabet, something it long lacked. Google and Yandex are now in direct competition, and that on level ground, in Russia, Belarus and Ukraine.

Certainly, it is questionable whether it makes sense to study the process of internationalisation of an Internet company as, from the very beginning, such companies are accessible from all over the globe. This is one of the main advantages of Internet companies that process search queries for anybody on the web, and can monetise clicks regardless of their country of origin.

Yandex and Rusnano are two companies that were helped by the innovative nature of the industry to grow internationally. However, did these companies grow internationally by themselves being innovative? Rusnano set its sights on the world in order to further the field of nanotechnology in Russia, but it has not itself innovated in that field. Rather, it has innovated in the field of Russian foreign policy, which was born internationalised.

Yandex is different. It has, indeed, brought some innovation to the field of online advertising pricing; however, this has not helped it to expand internationally. It might be argued that the barrier of the Cyrillic language hampered development of its internationalisation. But, in fact, it scarcely internationalised beyond its birthright as a search engine. That left it a loser in the race with its highly internationalised rival, Google. It will therefore come as no surprise that, as of now, Google is positioned to swallow up Yandex as it has swallowed up other search companies. It seems that even if you are born international, you must keep working at it to survive.

9 Strategy emphasis

Government stake or brand power?

The role of the state in the development of national companies, including their overseas expansion, is both overestimated (as in the case of resource-based industries) and, in contrast, underrated (as in the case of relatively small companies in less resource-based sectors).

With regard to oil and gas, the state involves itself to a different degree depending on the company (for example, Gazprom as opposed to Lukoil). The same applies to businesses outside the natural-resource-based sectors (as in the cases of Kaspersky and Sitronics).

The importance of the industry to the national economy does, of course, affect the degree of the state's involvement. Automotive, metallurgy and petroleum companies receive more government attention and support than do those in construction, food and software. The explanation for this is that heavy industry is the largest contributor to the state's budget and also the most important token of the state's productive power. Businesses that orient toward the individual consumer have in the eye of the state a lesser significance and are thus deserving of lesser support. This category of business must rely on its own capabilities to promote its brand, develop the loyalty of its customers and innovate in distribution. It must compensate for the lack of strong political and financial government support with good marketing of its own. Here internationalisation plays a part.

This chapter will present two extremes in the way Russian companies use internationalisation to attain their ends. When entering and operating in foreign markets, Russian MNEs that are not favourites of government mostly focus on marketing (and branding) as well as aggressive investment. Favourites of the state receive strong support because in return they make it their job to work in the state's interest. To illustrate this ambivalence in state–industry relations cases of food and beverage businesses will be pitted against nuclear power and military companies.

Glowing government: nuclear energy

The military industry and the nuclear power sector are both strongly supported and monitored by the government. This is facilitated by the government's customary stake in companies in these sectors. In particular, international operation is strictly controlled. This section will discuss two Russian firms – one in the defence sector and the other in the nuclear power industry – that are strongly influenced and controlled by the government. For the purposes of the present study, these firms are also interesting for the way they internationalise for business and political ends.

The nuclear power sector

In the present day economic growth is crucially linked with increased energy consumption, which is a characteristic part of the lifestyle of economically developed countries. As a consequence, nuclear power has boomed. Certainly, the disaster at Chernobyl put a crimp in Russia's construction of nuclear plants abroad. In the aftermath, Russian construction in Romania, Poland, China, Cuba and Libya was frozen or stopped, and equipment earmarked for these projects was sold or laid up. That led to the need to look for alternative markets. The reorientation that followed tended toward China and India.

The reorientation was not predicated on a firm expectation of regaining the full extent of the industry's past stature. Some forecasts, indeed, posited a decrease of up to 5.3 per cent. This was based on changes in attitude in developed countries toward nuclear safety and reliability. Slowdown in production and consumption of nuclear energy will be due to decreasing demand in Europe (approximately 1.1 per cent annually) and a flattening-out in North America. A decrease in the number of nuclear power plants (NPPs) in Europe (except France) will cause construction to seep to developing countries such as China, India, Pakistan, South Korea, Russia, Iran and Brazil. Consumption of nuclear energy in countries such as the US, Canada, Japan and France is expected to grow in coming years and then to plateau.

At the end of the 2000s the estimated volume of the global nuclear market was US$25 billion, with a Russian share of around US$4.5 billion. Nuclear energy accounted for 13.5 per cent of global electrical production. This figure is expected to grow to 16 per cent by 2020 and then over 20 per cent by 2040.[1] The global nuclear industry (GNI hereafter) was expected to grow to US$80 billion–100 billion by 2020, though it is too early to predict with assurance the effect of the disaster at Fukushima (Japan) on these forecasts. By the year 2009, 30 countries worldwide were operating 436 nuclear power plants which provided almost 14 per cent of the world's electricity production. The USA has the greatest share of nuclear power plants (104), followed by France (59), Japan (53) and Russia (31).[2]

One of the trends in the global market in the 2000s was the growing interest in nuclear energy in East and Central Asia. It was inspired by the increase in the price of fossil fuels. A token of this interest is the existence of 103 nuclear units operating in 8 Asian countries with a total capability of 75 GW. Of 34 units that were opened world-wide at the end of the 2000s, 25 were built in Asia, and there are an additional 15 reactors under construction. The most active developers of nuclear power are India and China.[3]

One noteworthy characteristic of the GNI is the tendency toward cooperation between different companies from various countries. This is mainly occasioned by the high cost of maintaining and servicing nuclear power plants and the effectiveness of researching and developing as a group.

Major players in the nuclear power industry are international companies from the USA, France and Russia. In the Russian domestic market, unlike the global market, there were no direct competitors of Rosenergoatom (see below). This results from a combination of factors. One is that the nuclear industry is constrained by the high cost of its technology. Another is the inordinately wide need for research and development. In addition, the industry must operate under the thrall of politics.

Two major players in the GNI are Areva and Westinghouse (recently acquired by Toshiba). These and other main players tend toward close association with Rosenergoatom, rather than competing with it, but it must be said that, in the end, all companies are competitors to some degree.

Areva is a Franco-German company with total sales in 2008 of €13.2 billion and approximately 75,000 employees. Areva works the whole nuclear value chain, from mining to exporting and selling; 62 per cent of company revenue derives from nucleonics and related activities. The operating income of the company was €417 million in 2008. The company was established in 2001 by mergers of companies with a long nuclear history. Starting with Areva's 'parents', company activity began in the 1960s. By the end of the 2000s, Areva had built more than 90 out of 440 reactors that were then in operation.[4] Areva is a competitor of Rosenergoatom owing to its presence in the same business of building and operating nuclear power plants, as well as in support activities for a variety of safety systems. In addition, it is present on the same markets as the Russian company.

Westinghouse concentrated its activity in the US, Belgium, France, Germany, Spain and Sweden. The company considers its main task as providing a wide range of products and services to make the operation of nuclear power plants safe and effective. It manufactures components and installs technologies for nuclear power plants. As did Rosenergoatom, Westinghouse organises training and education programmes in special facilities to train and improve workforce skills.

One other participant in the GNI is Tractebel, established in 1986 as a result of the merger of Electrobel and Tractionel. After a series of mergers, in 2009 Tractebel became a full-fledged independent company within the GDF Suez Energy Services business unit of GDF Suez. By the end of the 2000s, Tractebel had 3,700 employees worldwide. It was present in 20 countries and handled different energy projects in 80 countries. In 2008 company's revenue was €411 million, 57 per cent of which was generated outside Belgium. Its main activities are in nuclear power (27 per cent), infrastructure (24 per cent), gas (8 per cent), power (39 per cent) and heavy industry (2 per cent).[5]

To describe the situation on the Russian nuclear market the following statistics are salient. There are 10 nuclear power companies in Russia with 31 operating reactors, and they account for almost 17 per cent of all electricity produced in the country. From 1994 to 2003 the growth reached approximately 150 per cent in the sector. In 1998 104 billion kWh was produced, while the potential amount was 156 billion kWh; the amount of energy produced has increased from 1998 to 2005 by 46 billion kWh, attaining 150 billion. In 2010 the output was over 170 billion kWh and was projected to grow to 239 billion kWh in 2016.[6]

Rosenergoatom

The idea of establishing the company that became Rosenergoatom emerged in early 1990, during a period overcast by the post-Chernobyl distrust of nuclear energy and a scarcity of funds. Rosenergoatom was thus founded in 1992 by decree of the president of Russia.

Since the mid-1990s Rosenergoatom had been organising funds for nuclear energy development. It began using these to modernise existing generating plants. In 2002 Rosenergoatom restructured into a United Generating Company, which involved adding 20 state enterprises to the company. That endowed Rosenergoatom with nine operating nuclear power plants and six under construction.

In 2007, for the first time in post-transition Russia's short history, the construction of two new nuclear power plants began. Previously, only units and plants built, or started, in Soviet times existed. One of the new plants was Novovoronezhskaya NPP-2. It consisted of 2 units with capacities of 1,000 MW and incorporated advanced safety measures. It also marked the beginning of 'NPP – 2006', a plan to build a suite of nuclear units, each with a capacity of 1,000–1,200 MW. In August the construction of the second plant, Leningradskaya NPP, began. And in this same year work restarted on the fourth unit of Kalininskaya NPP, having been halted owing to post-Chernobyl fears.

From 2008 a nervous period ensued. Under the press of the world financial crisis the company found itself subordinated to the Nuclear Energy Federal Agency. Still in 2008, another reorganisation took place in which Rosenergoatom morphed into a corporation named Energoatom with 100 per cent of shares owned by yet another corporation, Atomenergoprom. In November 2009 Energoatom transformed into its present identity, returning to the name Rosenergoatom. But it was not to remain the largest in this nest of Russian dolls, for it later became part of the government corporation Rosatom. The two main functions of Rosenergoatom on behalf of Rosatom were supervising and supporting the operations of nuclear power plants.

In addition, the company was responsible for, besides its NPPs, searching for additional resources and administering them on behalf of the state. In short, it was expected to control the efficiency and effectiveness of its remit so that only such state funds as were justifiably needed were called for.

By the end of the 2000s, Rosenergoatom controlled 10 nuclear power plants with 31 units, having a total capacity of 23,242 MW. Among them 15 were pressurised water reactors, 15 graphite-moderated reactors and one fast-breed reactor.[7] This was a commercial empire large enough that the Russian state, ever alert to how its interests abroad were handled, oversaw its giant's internationalisation. Accordingly, Rosenergoatom's foreign sales were assigned to Atomstroyexport, a special unit of Rosatom.

The sort of activity that required watching kept expanding. With global change in the air, Rosenergoatom expanded into the fields of international scientific-technical cooperation; international nuclear safety programmes; foreign economic activities; and organisation of international activities (protocol, customs and export control).

For all this, economic performance indicators of Rosenergoatom in 2007 were impressively moderate: US$2 million from the export of goods and services; over US$90 million from contracts abroad; received technical aid worth US$10 million under 'soft assistance' projects; purchase of licenses and technologies worth US$1.2 million.[8]

In the second half of the 2000s Rosenergoatom was awarded engineering and consultancy contracts for Tianwan NPP (China) during the first overhaul of the plant's first unit. Later Rosenergoatom obtained the job of building and operating new units in Bulgaria (Belena NPP) and India (Kudankulam NPP).

In the 2000s the company became heavily involved in cooperative activities.[9] Under the aegis of various international organisations (World Association of Nuclear Operators, International Atomic Energy Agency, World Nuclear Association, national nuclear societies) it participated in NPP inspections. It also entered bilateral operations with partners (EDF, Areva NP, Energoatom NAEC) in the development of twinning projects (for example, between Balakovskaya and Zaporozhskaya NPPs, and Kalininskaya and South Ukrainian NPPs).

In addition, Rosenergoatom participated in a number of international safety programmes based on inter-governmental agreements aimed at solving problems related to nuclear and radiation safety. Main partners in this sphere were very large international nuclear energy companies such as Areva and Tractebel.

Increasingly it contracted with big international companies on the import of equipment, components, technologies and services in its own name or that of its branches. In this sphere there were several main partners. They were Siemens and, more recently, Toshiba. After purchasing 40 per cent of Inter RAO UES, Rosenergoatom expanded its energy export operations to other countries.

At the end of the 2000s there were multiple international agreements in force. Some of them were framework or governmental agreements, while others were with foreign nuclear operators such as EDF (France), Energoatom (Ukraine), JNPC (China), Iberdrola (Spain) and Exelon (the US), while still others aimed at cooperation towards trouble-shooting specific problems.[10]

The 2008 international financial crisis did not halt the international activity of the company. In any case only a few projects were under way in the late 2000s, the most prominent being the following: in Italy Rosenergoatom cooperated with Sogin on treatment of radioactive waste and spent nuclear fuel at decommissioning; in Finland, the company cooperated with Fortum and TVO on the enhancement of the efficiency of WWER reactors and exchanged experience in the field of new reactor construction; and in Canada the company took part in a joint project with MDS Nordion to produce isotopes for export.

Rosenergoatom's activity appears to depend heavily on three factors. First is European countries' positive attitude toward the use of new technologies in the nuclear sector and the development of new types of reactor; the company is aware of the fact that if it lags behind the pace of progress made abroad it will lose its position in the global market. Second, there is a current shift of NPP construction from developed to developing countries, which Rosenergoatom is aware of and interested in. It aims to increase its presence in China and India, in addition to a target already hit, Iran. In countries of the former Soviet bloc Rosenergoatom is already active, participating in the construction of NPPs in Slovakia (Mohovez NPP), Ukraine (Hmelnizkaya NPP), Kazakhstan (Center for enrichment of uranium) and Hungary (Paksh NPP).

Third, state's willingness to lend a hand with investment is influential. Huge amounts will be needed for the kind of work that is anticipated. The name of that work, especially after Fukushima, is nuclear security. Considering the fact that Russian technologies are fairly old, new ones will need to be developed. The only place to look for the kind of money for this, apart from the state, is cooperation and partnerships with international companies. That can be achieved in several ways, such as via contracts for importing new equipment (as now done between Siemens and Rosenergoatom). But association with foreign firms can also bring new skills to improve technological status.

Blazing government: the defence industry

The military industry, under the strict control of the state, acquires its earnings from the government's weapons programmes. These programmes can be affected by troubles such as cost overruns, delivery delays and unsatisfactory performance, causing possible friction with other states. Companies engaging in military exports to less developed countries fall hostage to regional arms races, international debt and poverty, while also frequently acquiring a poor reputation owing to their tendency to bribery and corruption.

Defence firms and industries have a long history of troubled change. As time passes, so do the spear and the Luger. The major arms companies of the nineteenth century, such as Armstrong, Gatling, Maxim, Krupp and Vickers (machine guns, armour, battleships) have been replaced by new ones, Boeing, Lockheed Martin, EADS and BAE Systems (aerospace, missiles, electronics).

In 2009, the USA was responsible for 43 per cent of world expenditures, distantly followed by the China (7.3 per cent of world share), the UK (3.7 per cent), France (3.6 per cent) and Russia (3.6 per cent).[11] Fourteen companies of the top 20 list of arms manufacturers were located in the US, two were from the UK, one was from Italy and one from Russia. Five companies were involved in projects at the cutting edge of technology:

- BAE Systems, a British company which became the world's leading developer of arms in 2008 and the first non-US company to head the list;
- Lockheed Martin, an American company which was the largest producer of arms in 2008;
- Boeing, an American company which was the largest company in 2007, but fell from first to third place in 2008;
- Navistar, a US-based company, which was a new entrant in the top 20 list in 2008;
- Almaz-Antey, at 18th place in 2008 the first Russian company to make the top 20 list.

In 2009 the global military market represented total revenues of US$743.9 billion, having a CAGR of 4.9 per cent for the period 2005–2009. In comparison, the European market grew by 5.7 per cent and Asia-Pacific by 10.4 per cent, clearly demonstrating the Asian potential. However, the Americas still account for 55.4 per cent of global value, while Europe generates a further 25.7 per cent and Asia-Pacific 18.9 per cent.

Russian arms industry

Russian history has long depended on defence. The Soviet Union acquired its status of superpower by developing its atomic bomb in 1949 and its hydrogen bomb two years later. It currently maintains a full-spectrum armed force of more than five million soldiers.

As one of the highest national priority industries in Russia, this industry satisfies domestic military need, budgeted at US$128 billion for the 2009–2011 period. Orders were expected to rise by a further US$1.3 billion for 2010 and by US$1.9 billion for 2011. Moreover, this industry served not only the domestic market, but also foreign buyers such as China, India, Algeria and Vietnam, which imported US$8.8 billion worth of Russian arms in 2009.

The Russian military industry is the second largest conventional-arms exporter after the United States, with US$8 billion worth of exports in 2008 and with 23 per cent of global arms exports.[12] In 2009, Russia's military industry consisted of over 1,250 firms and employed approximately 2.5 million to 3 million staff.

Product diversification in this industry was highlighted by the report of the Centre for Analysis of Strategies and Technologies in 2009, which gave the share of different weapon types as the following: aerospace: 61 per cent; ground: 21 per cent; naval: 9 per cent; air defence: 8 per cent; and other: 1 per cent.

The top three Russian companies in 2007 were Almaz-Antey (missiles), Sukhoi (aircraft) and Irkut (aircraft). In 2008 the arms sales of Almaz-Antey reached US$4.34 billion, an increase of US$1.22 billion from 2007; arms sales made up 94 per cent of total revenue. The revenue of Sukhoi (a major Russian aircraft manufacturer famous for its fighters) was US$1.86 billion in 2008, an increase of 160 per cent from the previous year. Irkut's revenue rose 22 per cent to US$1.25 billion. Furthermore, companies such as Aerospace Equipment Corp. and Tactical Missiles Corporation were also important players in this industry. Russian military firms follow two operative modes: the profit-driven deal, where the business motive is primarily profit, and the politics-driven deal, in support of foreign policy.

In the 2000s Russian weapons manufacturers operated on the construction and equipment of military bases, cooperation programmes with foreign companies and investment projects in the emerging markets.

Most Russian arms companies, such as Sukhoi, Irkut, MiG and others, focused mainly on export, around 90 per cent of their products going overseas. Russian arms companies had more than 20 international joint ventures, the main ones being in Vietnam, India and Ethiopia. One well-known joint venture was with the Indian company Brahmos Aerospace, which was formed by the Defence Research and Development Organisation of India and the Military Industrial Consortium of Russia in 1998. The firm's capital was financed at US$250 million, with 50.5 per cent from the Indian side and 49.5 per cent from the Russian.[13]

Russia has several military bases in CIS countries (including Armenia, Belarus and Ukraine). The military equipment was directly provided by the Russian military companies, and the facilities and local military industries in the periphery of these bases were also supported by these companies. Moreover, most Russian military firms invested to establish local manufacturing of necessary components. In addition, Russian military companies have invested in more than 10 overseas maintenance and technology centres in developing countries. These centres are responsible for maintenance, technology updates and supply of components.

Rosoboronexport

Rosoboronexport is a state enterprise acting as the Russian state's intermediary for the export and import of military and related products, technologies and services.

Until the end of the 1990s two companies existed in the military sector in Russia: Rosvooruzhenie and Promexport. Rosoboronexport was established in November 2000 by a Russian Presidential Decree which combined the two enterprises. By the end of the 2000s the new company accounted for more than 90 per cent of Russia's arms sales. Rosoboronexport includes more than 1,500 research institutes, design bureaus and manufacturing plants and has established cooperation projects with more than 60 countries during its 50-year history. Headquartered in Moscow, the company has representative offices in 44 foreign countries and in 26 major industrial regions of Russia.[14]

Since its establishment, Rosoboronexport has been supported by the Russian state, which guarantees all its export operations; its influence is thus disproportionate to its size. From the beginning the company has been the sole supplier of the whole range of armaments and military equipment produced by Russian enterprises, positioning it firmly among the world's leading arms exporters. Its role as the state's sole arms trade agency has enabled it to promote long-term partnerships with foreign customers and to sustain Russia's leading position in the global arms market.

Rosoboronexport's annual sales now stand at US$34 billion. The company not only focuses on export, but also sells via subsidiaries in host countries. In 2009 the company management wrote contracts regarding supply of arms to the amount of US$15 billion, a significant increase over previous years.

Nearly 80 per cent of Rosoboronexport's exports used to be to India and China. In 2008 this changed to a more diversified clientele which included Latin American and African and Asian countries which made it necessary to enlarge the product portfolio. It also filled new requirements of old customers. It was for this that an international joint venture, Rosoboronservice, was set up in India to concentrate on supplying large orders of aircraft and components.

In 2006 Rosoboronexport developed a close trade relationship with Venezuela, thereby becoming Venezuela's main arms supplier in a deal worth about US$3 billion. The collaboration of Rosoboronexport with Iran and Venezuela impacted on US–Russian relations, as the Bush administration imposed sanctions on Rosoboronexport. The business relationship between Moscow and Teheran violated a US law known as the Iran Non-proliferation Act of 2000, which aimed at preventing the spread of weapons of mass destruction.

International growth

Being strategically crucial to states, military business operates in an imperfect market where information is not openly traded and where contracts are often based more on politics and geopolitics than on technical or financial considerations. Russia's military industry may be seen as doubly imperfect in a free market, owing to the imperfect fit not only of its industry but also of the country.

Generally, internationalisation remains limited in the military sector when compared with most other industries. This is due to the high development costs associated with new equipment and advanced technology. International strategy is threefold: first, it targets a foothold in various regional markets (for political reasons); second, it acquires state of the art technology (to stay at the forefront of the industry); and, third, it muscles out competition and takes any new opportunity for itself (for profit).

Rosoboronexport employs all three of these approaches, but for reasons which a Western company might not entirely recognise. The company targets markets which will enhance Russia's international clout; it scouts for new technology because the government sees it as in the national interest to do, and foots the bill; and with the state at its back it internationalises because it is economical to do so.

Rosoboronexport, as well as many other Russian firms, makes it its policy to serve the interests of the state. It is able to focus on selling its wares, while leaving the state to pay for the effort needed to improve efficiency and prepare for the future. This approach, however, is akin to attempting to fitten athletes by feeding them, rather than exercising them. Therefore, most Russian firms lag in Western standards of efficiency and must seek their fortune on less developed markets and in state subsidy.

Food and drink: in and out

The food industry in Russia was strongly competitive in the 2000s, with many specialised niches in the segment. The rise in the price of essential food products (bread, vegetable oil and so on) decreased in 2009 as against 2008, which cannot be said of sugar, cheese and horticultural products, which were expected to grow by 13 per cent, as they did in 2008.[15] Russian food and beverage companies showed more resilience than many other sectors during the crisis of 2008–2009 and their results remained satisfactory. The most crisis-resistant sectors, unsurprisingly, were those producing essential food products (crop production/grain processing, cattle breeding, sugar production) while subsidised by the government.[16]

Foreigners in the Russian food market

The main entry modes which foreign companies use to penetrate the Russian food market are acquisitions, joint ventures, wholly owned subsidiaries and export. All this inward FDI focused on processed foods and not commodity food production. There were many examples of acquisition of Russian companies by big MNEs. The most prominent deals were made by Coca-Cola, which bought a juice producer, Multon, and by its long-time rival, PepsiCo, which acquired another Russian juice company, Lebediansky. Among failed but interesting cases was Danone's attempted acquisition of a controlling stake in Wimm-Bill-Dann, a leading Russia dairy-products firm, in 2006. The reason behind these investment projects was the particular attractiveness of the Russian food sector, which has been growing twice as fast as the country's industry as a whole over the past ten years.

By the end of the 2000s exporting food to Russia had become a lucrative business. Yet Russian food producers, unlike car makers or banks, showed no fear of their foreign rivals. According to the Russian Institute for the Economy in Transition, 54 per cent of Russian companies in the sector believe that their products are competitive with imported goods in terms of price/quality ratio, 17 per cent consider imported foods uncompetitive, and only 8 per cent say their output stands little chance against foreign-made goods.[17] The Russians, it appears, don't much care to eat what they don't know.

Many companies unafraid of failure, among them many from neighbouring Finland, established their own greenfield subsidiaries in Russia during the second half of the 2000s. In March 2008 Fazer announced the building of a bakery in the east of Leningrad Oblast. The company was ready to invest €100 million in the bakery to produce a range of breads for the domestic and surrounding international markets (the company had already invested €130m in Russian operations in previous years). Since 2005 Fazer has seen unprecedented growth in the Russian market, with the business growing at a rate of 40 per cent a year. Fazer Russia operated under the Hlebny Dom (Home of Bread) brand name. According to the statistics, Hlebny Dom is one of the leading players in the market of St Petersburg, with an annual output of 130,000 tonnes of bread and other bakery products, of which one-fifth goes to Moscow. In 2009 the company made another acquisition by purchasing a majority stake in the St Petersburg-based BKK Neva bakery, which further strengthened Fazer's assortment of frozen bakery products. Two more Finnish companies – Atria and Valio, in the meat and milk sectors respectively, also had investment projects in Russia in the 2000s.

In general, international companies increased their pressure on the sector during the 2000s. They captured nearly the entire beer market, with over 90 per cent of it being served by the foreign companies. Of the six leaders in the confectionery sector – United Confectioners, SladCo, Nestle, Kraft Foods, Mars and Dirol Cadbury, which accounted for almost 70 per cent of sales – only United Confectioneries was Russian-controlled. Belatedly, Russian food companies have seen fit to rapidly upgrade production and develop brand recognition, as Russian consumers become increasingly quality-conscious.

Global producers of food and beverages such as Coca-Cola, PepsiCo, Mars, Kraft (all USA), Nestle (Switzerland), Danone (France), Campina (the Netherlands), Ehrmann (Germany) and Sun Interbrew (Belgium) have established production facilities in Russia. While development in the market continues to be dominated by foreign investors, however, several Russian firms have by now contributed significantly.

Consolidation through M&As by both domestic and foreign business groups accelerated in the Russian food sector toward the end of the 2000s. The brewery industry experienced the first consolidations, which occurred in the early 2000s; later this trend carried over to the confectionery, dairy and soft drinks segments.

The majority of domestic players in the market are small and medium-sized companies. Large domestic companies, though dominating the juice, meat processing and vodka distillation segments of the market, as well as the fresh foods (bakery, dairy and grocery) segment, have still not consolidated. The Western idea that you have to keep growing has still not fully impacted in Russia. Major obstacles to consolidation in the industry include the country's vast geography, uneven population density and underdeveloped distribution channels.

Yet, in Russia's dairy market, domestic food companies have preserved and strengthened their standing, and there has been some integration. By the end of the 2000s two leaders of the Russian dairy market, Wimm-Bill-Dann (WBD) and Unimilk, had acquired more than 60 companies and controlled about 20 per cent of the market. Danone responded by building a facility near Moscow which helped it to remain the third-biggest producer in Russia.

After the failure of its attempt to acquire WBD (see above), Danone secured its Russian expansion via a deal with Unimilk in 2010. Including operations in Russia, Ukraine, Kazakhstan and Belarus, the merger covers all dairy products and would make Danone-Unimilk the leader for dairy products in the CIS area. In Russia, it will account for around 21 per cent of the total market and hold strong positions in high-value, high-growth segments. The new entity will have annual sales of around €1.5 billion, and can also exploit the momentum in the region's dairy product market. Danone controls 57.5 per cent of the new entity.

Despite integration and consolidation, 100 per cent protection against inroads by foreign companies cannot be guaranteed. The example of soft drinks demonstrates that international corporations are able to bring to bear sufficient funds to overcome the most stubborn of domestic competitors.

Russian food abroad

The major foreign market for Russian food companies remains that of the CIS countries. The main entry mode which Russian food companies use to penetrate these markets is export. When considering Russian firms' international results it should be remembered that Russian companies face restrictions that hamper export. Food safety in Russia has been neglected to the extent that it has lately become an issue of such critical importance that attempts to solve it have brought about complexity and confusion. Food exports are largely on hold until matters clear up.

The leading Russian company in the industry is WBD, with more than 35 production facilities in Russia, Ukraine and Central Asia. In 2005 WBD became the first Russian dairy producer to receive approval from the European Commission to export its products into the European Union.

Another company prominent in the food and beverages sector is Baltika. The Baltika brand is one of the three most valuable in Russia and it is the top beer in Europe in terms of sales. It exports to more than 60 countries around the world, including in Western Europe, North America and the Near East.[18]

In the confectionery sector, The United Confectionery Manufacturers is the leading Eastern European confectionery holding. It consists of 15 firms with over 20 per cent of the market and with key factories in Moscow. The company has been actively developing bonds throughout the 2000s with nations of the former Soviet Union, the US, Israel, Canada, Germany, Greece, France, countries in Eastern Europe, Mongolia and New Zealand.

In the sector of alcoholic drinks, Russian Standard vodka was ranked fourth among the fastest-growing alcohol brands in the world in 2007 according to the industry journal *Impact.* Russian Standard continues to experience extraordinary growth, increasing its volume (in sales) in Russia and 48 export markets by 40 per cent and launching a new brand, Russian Standard Gold. Russian Standard continues to strengthen its position as Russia's number-one premium vodka and the country's only truly global vodka brand. In 2009, the brand increased its global volume by 5 per cent to more than 2.2 million 9-litre cases in more than 70 export markets. According to *Impact*, Russian Standard is ranked forty-second among the top 100 spirits brands in the world.[19]

In summary, Russian food and beverage companies continue to trail foreign companies. Not many Russian companies are present on foreign markets, and generally they penetrate foreign markets through exporting; very few Russian food and beverage companies risk foreign investment. The main trends are consolidation and integration. Foreign companies invest more in Russia than Russian companies invest abroad.

Milking it: Wimm-Bill-Dann

In 2008 the average rate of consumption of dairy products stood at approximately 250kg per person annually (with a total value of more than US$22 billion). The industry growth rate was modest, and the consumption of milk and dairy products grew at a moderate pace. In 2009 consumption rose to 270kg per person, far below the medically recommended amount of 392kg. The slowing industry growth rate led to an increase in competition, which neither deterred foreign MNEs nor discouraged Russian producers from going abroad.

Dairy companies in Russia

Competition between Russian and international companies in the dairy sector is keen enough to be evident. There were approximately 2,000 dairy products manufacturers in Russia at the end of the 2000s, of which only 5 were really large. The two largest Russian companies (WBD and Unimilk) were truly international, as they operated in the CIS markets while also trying their luck at entering the markets of Eastern Europe and Asia.

WBD was established in 1992 and became not only a major player on the Russian market but also one of the leading ones on the CIS market, and on the market of Baltic countries before the onset of the twenty-first century. WBD had created a unified production network in the regions of Russia and the CIS countries, becoming a national manufacturer to Russia. At the time, the WBD group owned almost 40 manufacturing facilities.

Unimilk, although established a decade later than WBD, in 2002, also became one of the major players in Russia and the CIS market. Unimilk engaged in the production of dairy products and baby foods. By 2009 the company had over 30 production centres in Russia and Ukraine. The company focused on the production of traditional and innovative dairy products catering to changing customer tastes, as the post-communist palate developed. At the end of the 2000s Unimilk possessed all the attributes of a mature company – a structured portfolio of national brands, optimal production facilities and a developed system of distribution and sales.

Other market players were Danone, Valio, Campina and Ehrmann, all international firms. Danone is the world leader in the manufacture of dairy products. Around one-third of the group's sales is to developing countries. Despite the importance of Europe as its core consumer market, the company rapidly expanded to different regions, including the CIS and Russia. In 2008 Danone's annual sales exceeded €15 billion.

The Finnish company Valio is the largest exporter of dairy products to Russia. The company has more than 200 large clients in Moscow, St Petersburg, Novosibirsk, Krasnoyarsk, Rostov-on-Don, Krasnodar, Samara, Vladivostok and other cities and regions of Russia. Campina became the very first supplier of yoghurt products in Russia, entering the market in 1992 with its brand 'Fruttis'. After five years of successful operation it decided to further strengthen its position on the market by acquiring a plant in Stupino (Moscow region) in September 1998. In 2000 Campina launched its first local manufacturing line for the production of yoghurt. Ehrmann entered Russia in 1995 via export, but soon decided to open a fully owned production line in Russia, owing to the great popularity of its product. The company decided to set up a greenfield FDI, and in 1998 began building a plant in Ramenskoye (Moscow region). In 2000 the plant went into production, and within six years the company became one of the leaders in the dairy markets of Russia and the CIS.

Company overview

WBD had become a major player on the Russian dairy and non-alcoholic drinks markets by the end of the 2000s, and as noted, one of the leading players in the CIS and Baltic countries as well. It had created a unified production network in the regions of Russia and the CIS countries, from which dairy products accounted for more than 70 per cent of the company's revenues.[20] The group owned

37 manufacturing facilities by 2009 and employed more than 18,000 at the company's production facilities and trading affiliates.[21]

WBD had several highly recognised brands on the Russian dairy market – Domik v Derevne (Little House in the Village), Chudo (Wonder), Vesely Molochnik (Jolly Milkman), Imunele and Lamber, as well as several well-known brands in other food segments. WBD's core markets encompass a population of around 280 million people. These markets, including Russia, Ukraine, Belarus and the countries of Central Asia, are extremely diverse, with dietary habits shaped by many different national traditions, environments and differences in spending power. But they also had things in common. Each country had seen sustained economic growth in the 2000s, and local consumer markets were driven by rising household incomes and the emergence of a mainly urban middle class that was health-conscious and sought high-quality, healthy and nutritious food and beverage products.

WBD's main competitors in Russia are the Russian company Unimilk and foreign producers Danone, Ehrmann and Campina (described above). In the mid-2000s Danone's, Campina's and Ehrmann's market shares had risen, on average, to around 10 per cent each, while WBD had a market share of about 30 per cent.

An important part of company strategy was sustainability: producing dairy products directly in the region where they were to be consumed. The main entry tactic (and expansion strategy) was brownfield investment. WBD started to expand to the CIS with FDI in 2000, when it acquired existing production facilities in Kiev (Gormolokozavod) and in Lithuania (Birzu Dairy Group). In the main, WBD acquires smaller local firms in Russia and CIS countries. A compelling reason for WBD to acquire manufacturing facilities in the CIS was that it was much easier and less expensive to buy them there than in Russia. However, the flip side of the coin is that most CIS production facilities require modernisation. WBD was obliged to invest 13.3 million to upgrade two facilities in Ukraine in 2006.[22]

Joint ventures and partnerships with local producers were not attractive to the company as they could only very rarely provide it with any really useful technology or innovation. WDB focused on the excellent quality of its products in every country, which necessitated significant investment both in quality control when buying a new production facility abroad and in intensive advertising to promote a product at launch.

As elsewhere in the world, customer loyalty to established brands is important in Russia. Abroad, Russian products may be perceived as being of low quality, which makes the process of establishing a brand both expensive and lengthy. So WBD chose another route: acquiring established local brands and operating under their names.

In 2006 Danone made an ultimately unsuccessful attempt to merge with WDB. But in the process it nonetheless bought a significant equity stake and then further increased it. Today Danone owns some 18 per cent of WBD shares. That may be to WBD's advantage, as it is thereby associated with a global firm. As Danone holds an interest in WBD it follows that it ought to show an interest in stimulating, and sharing in, WBD's success.

In terms of exporting, WBD's products face tough customs regulations, norms and restrictions. Here Danone cannot help. What could help is Russia's joining the WTO. Another sticking point is that Russian milk may be regarded as of lower quality because of Russia's blemished ecological image. But, in fact, WBD's milk is good enough to pass EU muster and the bias against it could be overcome by selling it under the Danone brand.

To comply with EU regulations, WBD cannot rely on state support; however, the state is obliged to help the industry as a whole in this matter, in order to contend with protectionism in the EU agricultural sector. Therefore, the government's fixing of the price of milk (the main raw material for dairy products) at a low level (as it does at present) serves to improve WBD's competitiveness in terms of production costs on foreign markets. On the negative side, this can lead to a rise in international firms' interest in buying local manufacturers in Russia.

The government has helped companies such as WBD indirectly, however. Even though half of Russia's milk is produced by small farms and private households, most government support for the dairy industry had focused on larger players with more than 2,000 head of cattle. When the numbers of cattle started declining – as a result of, for instance, reorganisations in the agriculture sector, the privatisation of *sovkhozes* and the rise of the interest of individuals in doing agro-business – the government realised that with the introduction of a little modern technology small producers could make a useful contribution, and government money began to flow to, shall we say, the *kulak*.

This happened at the end of the 2000s: the Russian government made a deal with Swedish company Delaval, which already had a major presence on the Russian market supplying technology and operational service to farmers. Swedish farm equipment is now assembled at the Kirovsky plant in St Petersburg for a project called Rosagroleasing, which leases small-scale production equipment to small farmers, in which Delaval and the Russian government have invested more than €16 million.[23]

Spirit of Russia: Russian Standard

Market background

The Russian spirits market generated total revenues of US$15.6 billion in 2008, but there has been a slow decline of almost 1 per cent annually for the 2004–2008 period. Market volumes declined annually by 5 per cent during 2004–2008 to reach a total of 1.4 billion litres in 2008.[24] The market volume was expected to decline to 1.2 billion litres by the end of 2013.

Vodka sales proved the most lucrative for the Russian spirits market in 2008, generating total revenues of US$9.1 billion, equivalent to 58.8 per cent of the market's overall value.[25] In comparison, sales of brandy generated revenues of US$3.6 billion in 2008, representing 23.3 per cent of the market's aggregate revenues. Despite the fall in market volume noted above, the performance of the market was forecast to accelerate in terms of revenue, with an anticipated CAGR of 1.1 per cent for the five-year period 2008–2013, which was expected to drive the market to a value of US$16.4 billion by the end of 2013.

The Russian spirits market is not highly concentrated. Large companies such as Cristall and Liviz together held only 30 per cent of the market. Vodka dominated, and the leading companies have not diversified greatly beyond this key product. Product differentiation within each spirit category was relatively difficult and, in order to weaken the buying power of retailers, manufacturers invested in brand building, as retailers were obliged to stock the brands that their customers demand. Supplier power was weak because the raw materials for the end product were commonly available. Entry into the market greatly depended on the growth prospects and also on the size of existing players. There were very few substitutes for the products and only major changes in trend can make customers switch over to another product line, such as health drinks.

As regards distribution, supermarkets and hypermarkets were the principal distributors on the Russian spirits market. In 2009 they accounted for 38.8 per cent of the total volume. Specialist retailers distributed a further 36.4 per cent of the spirits market's volume.[26]

Russian Standard history

Russian Standard vodka was launched in 1998 by Roust Inc. By 2002, Russian Standard (or 'Russkiy Standart' in Russian) was selling at US$13 a bottle at Russian airport duty free shops, more than long-established premium vodka brands such as Absolut Blue (US$12) or Stolichnaya (US$8). In outselling these brands Russian Standard topped the market with a 27 per cent share.[27]

To get there, Russian Standard set itself two goals.[28] The first was to become a global umbrella brand. To ensure that the brand would appeal to domestic and international consumers alike, the company engaged professional international consultants and advertising agencies. The second goal was to become the first premium-quality brand bearing a 'Made in Russia' label.

The market-entry strategy for Russian Standard vodka was developed with the help of international consultants from McKinsey & Co. The vodka itself was produced by Liviz, one of Russia's oldest distilleries, located in St Petersburg. In August 1998 Roust Inc. launched its new vodka, positioned firmly in the deluxe category. A trade marketing group was specifically set up to develop marketing programmes to promote the new product.

The launch of Russian Standard vodka was successful, and the new product quickly gained a significant market share in the domestic market. Supermarket stocks would often exhaust faster than production could resupply. In response, production was doubled. A key reason for Russian Standard's rapid success was that it was the first domestic brand to associate itself with a rich mosaic of imagery (product, packaging, pricing, merchandising, communications), contrasting with the concept of quality that draws on tradition and establishment.

Taking Russian Standard abroad

Two years after the brand's debut, its domestic success suggested the idea of taking Russian Standard abroad. In short order Russian Standard was then launched in several European countries, including the UK, Italy, Greece, Estonia and Bulgaria. By the end of the 2000s the brand was being exported to 40 markets around the globe.

When seeking to enter a new market Russian Standard looked for a reliable partner, usually a local distribution company possessing market power. For its entry into the French market Russian Standard went into a partnership with the prestigious French distribution company Lixir, itself a joint venture between William Grant & Sons and Remy Cointreau, which handles spirits, champagnes and wines on the French market. The underlying idea of the new partnership was to reinforce Russian Standard's premium image of elegance at leisure. Owing to this and other partnerships, Russian Standard quickly became a strong competitor in major markets across Western Europe.

More recently, Russian Standard announced a partnership with Maxxium South East Asia to distribute the entire Russian Standard portfolio of brands in South-East Asian markets including Singapore, Malaysia, Indonesia, Vietnam, Cambodia, Laos, Myanmar, Thailand and the Philippines. This distribution agreement included both domestic and travel retail. Maxxium South East Asia is a division of Maxxium Worldwide, a leading global distribution company with operations in over 35 countries. Its portfolio includes some of the world's best-known premium brands. Maxxium has a strong presence in all South-East Asian markets and is one of the top three suppliers in the global duty-free and travel retail industries. In Spain, Russian Standard has a partnership with Zadibe Vinos y Licores, one of the country's leading independent distributors of spirits.

As duty-free is a very important distribution channel in the alcohol business, an agreement with Remy Cointreau Global Travel Retail was signed. As part of the agreement, Remy Cointreau works on behalf of Russian Standard and acts as its distributor to its many duty-free outlets worldwide.[29]

Russian Standard did not shy from covering the smallest market. In witness thereof it even entered a partnership with a niche specialist called Lotus Arts de Vivre to create a Russian Standard Vodka Bar at the Four Seasons Hotel in Bangkok. Through such partnerships abroad Russian Standard sought to acclimatise itself to local acceptance and thereby achieve brand loyalty.

The use of direct export by Russian Standard has the aim of attaining, and then retaining, full control over product management, marketing and distribution. Since exporting does not require that the goods be produced in the target country, no investment in foreign production facilities is required. Most of the costs associated with exporting take the form of marketing expenses.

The push of increasing competition and feedback from retailers have militated for the adoption of a strategy that now has a strong following in the business of spirits. Its main objective is the promotion of international brands. This strengthens the supplier and weakens the dealer, as a powerful brand results in customer demand which the dealer must then satisfy. Hence, marketing and promotion are now essential to the global success of a company in this sector.

Strategy focus: what makes their brands?

The international results of WBD and Russian Standard can be better highlighted by the traditional 4P framework (which comprises product, price, place and promotion), as follows.

Both companies attempt to position their products as being of high quality. They do this because they believe that it creates strong brands. Russian Standard enjoys the advantage of being associated with Russia, the country of vodka's origin. This enables it to claim the noblest of origins, just like its cousin caviar. WBD, unfortunately, cannot make such a claim. That may explain why, when entering a new market, the company chooses to acquire a well-established local brand and takes it from there: when doing large-scale business, it pays to be seen as a homebody.

Russian Standard can operate on the strength of a product portfolio containing only a very few items. In the spirits industry it is usually enough to simply export to foreign markets. Companies in the dairy industry, in contrast, need a voluminous portfolio including many stock products, such as cheese, milk and yoghurt, as well as specialities of the region in which it is attempting to sell. As a result, these companies are encouraged to reduce costs and complexity by siting manufacture in the customers' country. Because of the expense this entails, WBD must choose its target markets very carefully. For WBD, unlike Russian Standard, it is not practical to go global.

Russian Standard's pricing also positions it as a premium-quality vodka, being higher-priced than common-or-garden vodkas. The natural urge to buy the best is there to be exploited. But to attain this cachet, it must indulge in premium-quality sales promotion and marketing, with all its attendant high expenditure. It is costly to establish a luxury brand. In addition, it often takes partners of a similar calibre to make the strategy work locally – and then globally.

For WBD, the lie of the land differs. Being a large company catering to medium-segment custom, it cannot afford to charge high prices. In this sector margins are low, leaving companies to compete on price as best as they can. That is why WBD uses FDI to enter new markets. Having production plants where it sells saves costs, which means lower prices and better addresses the local customer.

Russian Standard aspires to be renowned internationally. For this purpose, marketing is designed to make Russian Standard an umbrella brand, which is to say that the brand will appeal the same way in Russia as abroad – as the authentic spirit of Russia. By working through the largest or most prestigious global distributors, Russian Standard has come to enjoy good brand awareness worldwide. Though penny-pinching belies the brand's image, it does quietly save a lot of money by being able to sell via export.

WBD cannot do this. Unlike Russian Standard, it supplies not just one product but a soberingly wide range of products that it places in large, medium-sized and small retail stores. WBD is mainly present in the CIS countries; going outside this area entails greater risk and expense. That is why WBD, when it does decide to go abroad, uses FDI as mode of entry. That way it acquires production facilities and is able to sell under a locally established brand name.

The government can help or hinder an MNE in expanding into new markets. It can provide funding or pass legislation to help. It can also withhold support and thereby make things difficult. A company left to its own devices will have to rely on its own resources to make its way. It can be hard to secure bank loans or raise equity to finance the way to expansion. Usually, it is also expensive.

This latter situation is typical for Russian food and beverages companies such as Wimm-Bill-Dann and Russian Standard. Such companies must spend heavily on marketing and promotion to have a hope of succeeding, as Russian taxpayer money does not flow to their support, or at least not directly.

Russian firms in the food sector need even more marketing and promotion when going abroad. The opposite applies to the heavy industries (nuclear power or the military businesses). Here the government, typically, helps because it is at least a part owner, often because it sees a strategic interest. Yoghurt and vodka rarely elicit such public sector interest. Hence, private food companies with domestically established brands must go to great expense and trouble to attempt to establish themselves in a foreign market. In contrast, state-owned nuclear and military businesses such as Rosoboronexport, which are little known to the general public, are well known worldwide to their small circle of potential customers. And because they deal in such statist and enormously expensive ware, customers are usually foreign governments, or organisations closely linked to them. The privateers thus expand for lucrative profit, the statists in the cause of Russian foreign policy. To make profit abroad WBD even sacrifices its own name and does business under foreign brands. The statists, on the other hand, sally forth with the flag fluttering afore.

In May 2008 a former chairman of the board of Gazprom (2000–2001, 2002–2003), Dmitry Medvedev, became president of the Russian Federation, and a former chairman of the board of Rosneft (2004–2008), Igor Sechin, became deputy prime minister with supervisory control over natural resources. Thus over the short span of the post-communist period, 1991–2011, the role of government in state-owned business has tightened, whilst private business has become more private. The result has been that Russian private business lags abroad, but Russian government business flourishes there.

At home, in contrast, experts believe that over the past decade state ownership of natural resources has led to a slowdown in output, export and GDP in Russia, while the opposite is true of private ownership.[30] A similar tendency can be detected in business sectors where state ownership is not as pronounced as it is in natural resources. In light of this, the question is why taxpayer money is being spent to increase the state's interest in Russia's large companies.[31]

What justifies this question is that, while official statistics show a decline in state ownership, there is also strong evidence of a considerable increase of control by the Russian government over the largest enterprises of the country. The Russian government justifies this by claiming to create large, vertically integrated structures that are fit to survive international competition, as well to foster diversification of industry away from its present dependence on natural resources.

But should the doldrums of the state-owned large oil and gas companies be read as signifying improvement through diversification? Hardly. What it does seem to show is that state control is justified in just two types of business: one in which very strict control is required, as is the case in the nuclear energy sector and Rosenergoatom; and the second in which foreign policy is paramount, as applies to the military business of Rosoboronexport.

The military industry requires strict monitoring because the security of the nation depends on it. It needs government guidance in the control of export and import of arms. Export should favour allies and be denied to enemies. Indeed, the government should help military business to land contracts with friendly nations, as this would be helpful to both the Russian military business as well as to the security of the alliance. The right dosage of military business can be made to persuade recipients to serve Russian interests.

Nuclear power is another area of business endeavour that needs very strict control to ensure safety. Hiroshima, Nagasaki, three partial meltdowns and one total testify to this. And as this sort of power is seen as being required until other forms of energy are developed to take its place, government's involvement in the business remains necessary and welcome. Elsewhere, however, it comes progressively into doubt.

10 Boundaries of Russian MNEs

In this chapter the problems and failures of Russia's OFDI will be discussed. The causes have to do with the size of the investing firm and the scale of management's expectations. Two sections below will showcase two extreme examples. The first, the attempt of a Russian group headed by Sberbank to acquire the car manufacturer Opel, involves a deal so large that has implications for the future of the entire industry. The other is the story of an industry dwarf, the Japanese cuisine restaurant Two Sticks, that wants to grow.

The most prominent Russian investors are natural resource companies; M&A is the preferred form of their foreign expansion. Hence, in the first part of the chapter, the results of some not-so-successful large-scale acquisitions are considered.

Despite being aggressive in their growth ambitions, small firms often do not have even major preconditions for internationalisation, and in this connection they may have to rely on the selection of the right niche or on the efficient marketing of their product. In this context the SMEs' internationalisation attempts will be examined via the story of KGK – a small firm in the technology intensive business.

More and more mega-deals

The 2000s have witnessed significant development in investment practices by Russian MNEs. The recent increase in foreign investment by Russian firms suggests strong variation in investment motivations between industries. Whereas the initial stage of internationalisation included export-related activities, numerous Russian companies have since evolved to more sophisticated operations abroad. Foreign acquisitions, especially, have become notable, either to acquire assets abroad or to strengthen market positions and access natural resources.

For Russian energy companies, one evident motivation was to internalise control over the complete value chain. By acquiring refineries and sales outlets abroad, Russian MNEs are better able to satisfy foreign demand, processing oil in their own refineries and selling the products via their own filling stations. In the oil sector, the infrastructure assets were of vital importance and Russian MNEs have gained control over several strategic infrastructure assets in Central and Eastern Europe, including seaports and oil pipelines delivering crude oil and products to the Western markets.

Late arrival to foreign markets had one advantage here: many Russian oil and gas champions could avoid some painful lessons that other MNEs from developing and developed countries suffered.

One lesson is the case of Brazilian giant Petrobras, whose previous attempts to internationalise ended in sorry failure. In the 1970–1990s Petrobras chose to invest in poor-quality land deals in South America that were a bad match with its capabilities and portfolio. Similarly unsuccessful was the Algerian company Sonatrach's political entry into the Middle East, where it tried to exploit its desert experience. It pulled out after it realised that it did not have the required technical expertise after all. Finally, Norwegian company Statoil's first attempt to go global, involving partnering with BP to learn operational skills, failed when the political will for Statoil to become a national champion evaporated and it became clear that there were no security of supply considerations in Norway.

As a rule, Russian companies in the metallurgy sector were the most active in expanding their market shares and strengthening their global positions by acquiring assets abroad. The recent large-scale acquisitions by Russia's leading non-ferrous metal companies serve as examples of resource-seeking investments. Henceforth, such acquisitions provide companies with significant additions to their resource bases and assets, and add to the companies' global scope of activities.

Over the 1992–2009 period, according to UNCTAD, the net foreign acquisitions (discounting divestments) of Russian firms exceeded US$58 billion. The first half of 2010 is forecast to tally a staggering US$9 billion. The number of transactions by type (M&As, greenfield projects and strategic alliances) confirms the close relationship between the different forms of FDI. In these data sets, the number of greenfield projects exceeds the number of M&A deals. However, given the fact that acquisitions tend to be larger than greenfield projects, foreign acquisitions are evidently the engines of outward FDI from Russia. Moreover, strategic alliances are becoming popular among Russian companies; their number has fluctuated since 2000, but it has been steadily growing since 2004. It has to be noted that equity-based strategic alliances are counted among FDI statistics, while the non-equity based ones are counted separately. Overall, all three modes of internationalisation were on the rise until 2008. In 2009, owing to the crisis, the number of both greenfield projects and M&As declined (see Table 10.1).

Table 10.1 M&A deals, greenfield projects and strategic alliances initiated by Russian companies, 2000–2010

Type	*2000*	*2001*	*2002*	*2003*	*2004*	*2005*	*2006*	*2007*	*2008*	*2009*
M&As	7	21	20	19	27	45	54	70	108	65
Greenfield projects	–	–	51	120	109	139	155	134	194	150
Strategic alliances	29	21	51	28	15	37	52	89	–	–

Source: Filippov 2010 and UNCTAD 2010.

In terms of shares in cross-border M&A purchases and global FDI, the performance of Russia continued to be strong even in the crisis years of 2008 and 2009. By 2009, the country's share in global FDI flows exceeded 4 per cent, and its share in cross-border purchases exceeded 3 per cent. At first glance, these may seem to be marginal figures, but given the long-standing domination of developed-country multinationals, these shares are quite respectable. Compared to other BRIC countries, in terms of cross-border M&A purchases, Russia is behind China but ahead of both Brazil and India.

By the end of the 2000s acquisitions were significantly driven by industry consolidation and redistribution of oil and gas assets between leading groups. This process was unique in that the government took a direct ownership of companies. This development was reflected in the partial renationalisation of oil assets and the rapid growth of state influence. Both Gazprom and Rosneft were majority state-owned. In vying for key positions in the global oil and gas industry, making acquisitions abroad was an effective way forward.

The internationalisation of non-natural-resource-based companies is a more recent phenomenon in the Russian economy. Led by the high-tech and telecom sectors, the Russian non-extractive companies are rapidly catching up in acquiring foreign assets. Examples of market-seeking acquisitions by Russian firms can be found in the telecoms sector. Through active expansion, Russian telecoms companies have strengthened their positions in the near-abroad CIS region. In that particular market, Russian companies lead the race for market share, pioneering Russian expansion to this lucrative market area.

How do the big Russian companies express their international ambitions? Mega-deals (transactions valued above US$1 billion) are one natural way. Almost all huge deals were very recent: the oldest one (Norilsk Nickel's acquisition of Gold Fields in South Africa) was dated 2004. Since then, these deals have exploded in number: two in 2005, a peak of six in 2007 (the last pre-crisis year), then a moderate slowdown in 2008 and 2009 with five and four deals respectively. Their aggregate value over the period 2004–2010 attained the sum of US$44 billion.

These transactions clearly reflect the strategic ambitions of Russian firms. When they acquire mining assets, they do not do it with the aim of ensuring resources for Russia but with the aim of controlling the vertical value chain globally (i.e. mining, smelting and retail of semi-finished or finished products). When they acquire companies in their own industry, their main aim is horizontal control (market power). This horizontal control is important not only in the resource-based industries which constitute the bulk of these transactions, but also in telecoms, in which Russian firms are equally active. There are also important technology-seeking motivations behind these transactions (especially present in the acquisitions in the automotive industry).

Not all deals work out

As highlighted by the literature on cross-border M&As, a portion of deals fail, mostly because of excessive expectations at the outset or unforeseen or underestimated difficulties. Underestimating difficulties seems particularly relevant in terms of the risks of doing business in the host country environment, as well as the unpredictable areas of social and political considerations. However, the definition of failure is not straightforward. In some cases, it means a complete reversal of the deal; in other cases, it simply means worse-than-expected results.

In Russia, as in other countries, the onset of the financial crisis in 2008 increased the level of failure. Some of the examples were widely discussed in the media, or whispered about by experts in the know. In 2008 several deals were stalled or failed entirely. Russia's fourth-largest MNE, Evraz Group, agreed to buy 51 per cent of Delong Holdings in China. However, the Chinese government has blocked the deal and it is still pending. In Europe, NRK (National reserve corporation) decided to purchase a 76 per cent stake in Oeger Tours Gmbh (Germany) for €120 million. However, NRK did not transfer the cash value of the deal in due time, allegedly because Oeger Tours had failed to provide the financial reports required by the deal, and the deal was cancelled. And in the US, in August of that year, NLMK Steel (Russia's 7th largest MNE) agreed to buy the JMC Steel Group for US$3.5 billion, excluding debts and cash assets. NLMK revoked this agreement in November 2008 owing to changing market conditions.[1] DBO, the parent company of JMC, sued NLMK for breach of contract. In the same month GAZ Group agreed to buy from Penske Automotive Group a 50 per cent stake in VM Motori for US$100 million. According to the contract, GAZ had to pay by October 2008, which it failed to do owing to lack of cash in the midst of the financial crisis.

In December of the following year Sberbank agreed to buy 100 per cent of the shares of Belpromstroibank (Belarus). However, owing to lack of cash, it paid only US$280 million, thus purchasing 93 per cent of the bank.

Several totally failed transactions deserve more detailed attention, and are presented below.

Oil and gas: Surgutneftegas and MOL Group

In March 2009 Surgutneftegas bought 21.2 per cent of Hungary's MOL from the Austrian company OMV for US$1.9 billion. The deal immediately gave rise to a strong reaction from both MOL and OMV.[2] MOL considered the deal to be hostile and accused OMV of collusion with the Russian company and of initially buying MOL shares in Surgutneftegas' interests. MOL also contested Surgutneftegas' rights as a shareholder and insisted it disclose its shareholdings. In April 2009, MOL's board of directors refused to include Surgutneftegas in a shareholder list and the Russian company attended MOL's annual shareholders' meeting in May as an observer. Surgutneftegas has filed a court suit against MOL for the refusal to include it in the shareholder list. However, the court decision supported MOL's position.

The Hungarian firm and the Hungarian government raised various issues which in their view were reasons for concern about Surgutneftegas and its intentions.[3] They contended that Surgutneftegas' ownership structure was not transparent and that the company was indirectly influenced – perhaps even owned – by the Russian government. As indirect proof, they cited the fact that until 2009 Surgutneftegas followed a conservative business and investment policy, focusing exclusively on the Russian home market. A sudden change in strategy, with an acquisition abroad in which Surgutneftegas overpaid for the shares compared to their stock market price, did not make strict financial sense; it could, however, be explained by external influence, such as persuasion by the state to follow broader national strategy objectives. MOL made full use of all the means at its disposal to prevent the takeover, applying its internal rule that limits voting rights to 10 per cent for any shareholder, irrespective of the number of shares they own.[4]

As for the Hungarian parliament, it adopted a law that seriously limited the scope for hostile takeover bids for strategic companies, even if the latter are privately owned (such as MOL). Hungarian resistance to Surgutneftegas can be explained by the fact that the deal hurt various sensitivities: it targeted the sensitive energy sector in a net energy importing country; it affected the largest and most successful firm of the country, which also happens to be largest outward investing MNE; a flagship for the Government and public opinion.[5]

Gold mining: Polyus Gold and KazakhGold

Polyus Gold

Polyus Gold was the leading gold-mining company in Russia and Kazakhstan and one of the biggest in production and reserve volume in the 2000s. By the end of the decade the group controlled 6 of the 10 largest Russian gold fields. Assets of Polyus Gold were located in the Krasnoyarsk, Irkutsk, Magadan and Amur regions and the Republic of Sakha (Yakutia), as well as in Kazakhstan and Romania.

Polyus Gold was officially established in 2006, via the spin-off of the gold-mining assets of Norilsk Nickel group, but its history stretches earlier. In the course of the 1990s ZAO Polyus, the state-controlled company that owned the Olimpiadinskoe gold field, grew to become, by the beginning of 2000, one of the biggest private gold-mining companies in Russia. When Norilsk Nickel began to actively increase its portfolio of gold assets, within a few years it had purchased several companies and some attractive mines, including those of ZAO Polyus. In 2005 it was decided to place all the gold assets of Norilsk Nickel into an independent public company. In March 2006 Polyus Gold was floated on the market with publicly traded shares.

Target company – KazakhGold

KazakhGold Group was Kazakhstan's leading gold-mining company, employing approximately 3,200 people. Its main office was located at Stepnogorsk (north of Astana).

KazakhGold had three gold mines which were located in the Stepnogorsk region and the largest national combined reserves and resources. Several major competitive advantages of KazakhGold attracted many investors. First was a location in a well-established mining area with good infrastructure. Second, it benefited from large reserves, low-cost modern mining and processing techniques, and competitive labour and electricity costs. The third advantage consisted in the local currency stability and modest royalty payments.

In 2005 the group upgraded their operations and implemented several innovative processes. Even so, by the late 2000s the deteriorated condition of fixed assets which had not been modernised in the last 20 years caused financial difficulties. Constant changes of the company operations led to the loss of a significant part of the company's infrastructure.

In 2009, measures to stabilise production capacities and increase the output of finished goods were implemented. These also attracted a lot of investors.

Game-changing deal

In 2009 the family owners of KazakhGold encountered financial difficulties and, to remedy these, agreed to sell a 50.1 per cent stake to Polyus Gold for US$11 billion. The deal was to create a new company called Polyus Gold International. The area of the interest included resource-rich areas of Kazakhstan and Central Asia, licences for mining, an existing listing on the LSE and registration in the jurisdiction of the British crown. It would allow the company to expand significantly and to become international.

However, instead of reaching a completion of the deal, the two parties filed lawsuits against each other, alleging breaches of contract. During the three-month due diligence period, difficulties arose. First Polyus filed a lawsuit claiming that KazakhGold had committed false financial reporting to the tune of US$450 million. In retaliation, the Kazakh government suspended all licences essential for the operations of the consolidated company and filed a counter-lawsuit against Polyus.

In December 2010 a new agreement was signed between AltynGroup Kazakhstan, controlled by the (former) owners of KazakhGold, and the Polyus Group. In a complete reversal of roles, AltynGroup Kazakhstan now proposed to buy Polyus. However, this deal makes business sense only if the Kazakh government returns the licences required.

Automotive: Sberbank and Opel

In 2009 intense negotiations took place between GM and a consortium composed of Canadian car components maker Magna and Russian state-owned bank Sberbank for the purchase of a 55 per cent stake in Opel AG Germany, subsidiary of GM, for about €500 million. In December 2009 all parties were close to a final deal.

Party 1: Sberbank

As of 2009 Sberbank was the largest credit institution in Russia and the CIS, accounting for 27 per cent of the aggregate Russian banking assets and 26 per cent of banking capital. As of 1 July 2010, Sberbank was ranked forty-third in the world in terms of Tier 1 capital.[6]

Sberbank had the largest Russian branch network and more than 18,880 retail outlets, with about 241,000 employees. Furthermore, Sberbank operated subsidiary banks in Kazakhstan, Ukraine and Belarus and had representative offices in some European countries, a branch in India and an office in China.

Sberbank was involved in foreign activities through direct contracts, correspondent accounts with leading credit institutions of the world, trade finance operations and membership in a number of international financial organisations.

Party 2: Magna

Magna International is the most diversified automotive supplier in the world, with more than 96,000 employees in 256 manufacturing operations and 82 product development, engineering and sales centres in 26 countries.[7]

The main company activities included design, development and manufacturing of automotive systems, assemblies, modules and components, as well as engineering and assembly of complete vehicles, primarily for sale to original equipment manufacturers of cars and light trucks in North America, Europe, Asia, South America and Africa. Magna supplied content to almost every automotive manufacturer in the world for many major brands.

Consistent with the Magna international strategy of expanding in new regions, at the end of 2010 Magna acquired seat-manufacturing companies in Brazil and Argentina. Combined 2010 sales for the two seat companies amounted to US$260 million. Also during this year Magna acquired Erhard & Sohne GmbH, a manufacturer of fuel tanks.

Party 3: General Motors

General Motors runs neck-and-neck with Toyota for title of world's largest automaker, with a history that goes back more than 100 years, to 1908. With its global headquarters in Detroit, GM employs 202,000 people in every major region of the world and does business in more than 120 countries.

GM and its strategic partners produce cars and trucks in 30 countries, and sell and service these vehicles through the following brands: Buick, Cadillac, Chevrolet, FAW, GMC, Daewoo, Holden, Jiefang, Opel, Vauxhall and Wuling. GM's largest national market is China, followed by the US, Brazil, Germany, the UK, Canada and Italy. GM's OnStar subsidiary is the industry leader in vehicle safety, security and information services.[8]

GM has interests in Russia; in 2008 a car-manufacturing facility was launched in north-west Russia. Moreover, it invested more than US$350 million for a Chevrolet assembly plant in Kaliningrad.

Party 4: Opel

Founded in 1862, Opel is one of the most technologically advanced automobile manufacturers in Europe. In collaboration with Vauxhall, its sister brand in the

UK, Opel sells vehicles in over 35 markets in Europe. Opel operates 13 vehicle, power train and component plants in eight countries and employs around 47,000 people.[9]

In 2009 Opel sold over 1.2 million passenger cars and light commercial vehicles in Europe, representing a market share of 6.4 per cent. In its domestic market in Germany, Opel holds second position (after Volkswagen), with a market share of 8.6 per cent.

One of the most innovative plans of the company was the launch at the beginning of 2010 of the Opel Ampera, the first extended-range electric vehicle.

The premises and beginning of the deal

General Motors filed for creditor protection (bankruptcy) on 1 June 2009.[10] According to Bloomberg, at the time the company's assets amounted to US$82.3 billion and its debt to US$172.8 billion. As a result of its Chapter 11 proceeding, GM decided to sell its German subsidiary Opel. Among the candidates who lined up to purchase Opel were: Russian bank Sberbank in alliance with Magna; Belgium investment fund RHJ International; Italian carmaker Fiat; and Chinese automotive company BAIC.

The German government did not hide its scepticism about a Chinese acquirer. BAIC clearly asserted that the main goal of purchasing Opel was to transfer Western technology for car-making in China. German government opinion was that there was an obvious danger in the transfer of technology and jobs to China. For Germany, a Chinese deal was not viewed favourably.[11]

Fiat's proposal was not suitable to GM and Opel, since it involved deferred payment or sell-off of tangible assets such as buildings. Such suggestions were absolutely unfeasible for GM.

Sberbank-Magna and RHJ International were thus the two main contenders to purchase Opel. Sberbank-Magna wanted to buy 55 per cent of shares (35 per cent for Sberbank and 20 per cent for Magna).[12] Russian officials appeared happy about Sberbank's intention to buy Opel. They had resigned themselves to the fact that Russia was not in a position to build its own national car-manufacturing empire, and therefore national producers should feel free to acquire shares of world auto leaders.

Sberbank president German Gref claimed that the main goal of buying Opel was to create a transnational company that included a Russian investor.[13] Sberbank then planned to resell its Opel shares to GAZ, the second Russian automotive company, which would have enabled GAZ to strengthen its position and improve its production quality, and even to internationalise its activity. Since the automotive industry was not a priority for Sberbank, it was evident that pressure was being exerted by the Russian government.

Negotiations and changes in attitudes

In September the German government offered its plan for the sale of Opel, with 35 per cent each for Sberbank and GM. The third party, Magna – one of the world's biggest suppliers of auto components – would obtain 20 per cent and the remaining 10 per cent would be distributed among Opel employees.[14]

On the final day of bidding, the managements of Sberbank and Magna changed their minds and decided to divide 55 per cent equally (27.5 per cent to each).[15] The negotiations were complex and drawn out, with some experts saying that GM purposefully prolonged matters in order to enable the American government to bail out the company and save its German operation.

The result and consequences

In the event, GM decided to keep Opel and not sell it after all, playing its cards so as to hold off bidders for as long as possible. First, it waited for government support and finally it was restructured through the procedure of voluntary bankruptcy. Too big to fail, GM received billions of dollars in government help, at the cost of oversight from the government-appointed auto giant. Another factor that played against Opel's divestment was that the former GM top managers who had wanted quick asset sales departed the company. The new top managers were under less financial pressure, given the bail-out money, and reconsidered the sense of divesting themselves of Opel, which was still considered a strategic asset. Third, the global car market began gradually to recover. Under these circumstances GM did not want to sell its technologies to its potential competitors, stating that Opel held intellectual property which GM was planning to use in new products. This factor, above all, was probably the main cause of the deal's failure.

GM now had to restructure an unprofitable Opel on its own, since it could not expect US government aid. This would have to be done in the context of slow-growth European markets. GM would also confront complex negotiations with European trade unions.

GM's refusal was also huge trouble for the German government, which had backed the sale of Opel to the Sberbank-Magna consortium, and had committed to give €4.5 million to Sberbank-Magna for the consortium to save as many jobs as possible. Moreover, it would have been one of the most advantageous of many Russian–German investment projects, for both parties: for Russia, it would have meant a swift entry into the world automotive sector, while for Opel it would have been a mean of rebirth.

Of course, GM's refusal also dashed Magna's plans to become the biggest independent European car producer, and GAZ's hopes to obtain modern intellectual property. As a consequence Russian car-making in the near future will be constrained to assembly plants for foreign automotive giants (GM, Ford, Toyota, Volkswagen, etc.).

On the positive side, GM has claimed that it has plans to enforce collaboration with GAZ. GM plans to increase car production in Shushari (St Petersburg) and Kaliningrad.

After the 2010 deal broke apart, Sberbank requested €60 million compensation from GM, having spent a great deal of money on consulting and auditing. In the end, however, it had to settle for approximately €12 million.[16] German Gref, president of Sberbank, does not regret participating in the negotiations: Sberbank became well-known the world over as a consequence. Indulging in some wishful thinking, perhaps, Sberbank now claims that the negotiations saved it some €250 million in foreign advertising.

SME going abroad: ambition or rational decision?

Large enterprises and SMEs have very different investment motivations owing to their very different operational and financial resources. Whereas large Russian enterprises are engaged in cross-border M&As to improve their global market positions, Russian SMEs predominantly seek niche markets abroad. Market- and technology-seeking investments dominate the international expansion of Russian SMEs. Owing to their relatively low experience levels and tight financial resources, Russian SMEs have thus far targeted assets mainly in the CIS and Eastern Europe.

The SMEs investing from Russia often include leaders in narrow market segments, such as specific electronic appliances or speciality foods. Estimating the total scope of these companies' international activities is extremely complicated due to low public coverage of the operations. Despite the low level of publicity and the private nature of these businesses, numerous Russian SMEs have already entered the CIS and the EU markets.

For SMEs internationalisation is a problem of problems. One of these is that companies have scant resource to undertake it. Another is, if undertaken too early, going global risks losing much more than during later, more mature stages. But when is 'too early'? It is at this point that many SMEs call it a day. Unlike the large corporations, these companies essentially have only one shot at the golden ring because of their limited reach and underdeveloped experience.

Yet there is no lack of incentive for SMEs to internationalise. Exporting can lead to increased productivity through the attainment of economies of scale. Foreign projects can provide a firm with fresh know-how and technologies, which can be combined to develop new competitive strength. They can provide access to cheap inputs, such as raw materials or labour. As large firms increasingly outsource parts of their value chain, opportunities for SMEs arise to internationalise through cooperation with these large firms.

Even so, the majority of enterprises choose to internationalise gradually. This they do in consideration of the following factors: resource availability, the level of acquaintance with 'abroad', the problem of communication, lack of clarity concerning risk and the ability of management to handle itself on foreign turf.

Last but not least, going abroad means having not just one government to deal with. Coping with the rules of the game abroad usually depends on help bought from locals. This may entail costly legal and lobbying services.

To prevail, the entrepreneur usually taps the international experience of his network, his buyers and suppliers. If this input is good, internationalisation can be worth the travail, and, especially in the years directly following entry into a foreign market, both exporting and importing, SMEs may experience very high growth rates.

In the US and UK, small high-tech start-ups are considered 'international' when international sales represent at least 20 per cent of total revenue, and only after five successive years of foreign presence. It can help if the entrepreneur, out of personal ambition, wants to expand abroad to enhance his persona, but four factors tend to favour the chances of success through internationalisation:[17] the global nature of the firm's product or industry; the applicability of the firm's core technology to a foreign setting; the attractiveness of the product to foreign customers; and the extent of competitive squeeze in the domestic market.

SMEs in Russia face a number of obstacles that prevent them from developing and growing as quickly at home as they might in other lands. Most common are poor physical infrastructure (gas, water, electricity, heat); poor enforcement of contractual and ownership rights; administrative and legislative ambiguity (bureaucracy); lack of affordable long-term finance; strong entrenched 'informal' networks between legislative, executive, judicial and business bodies; the protectionist attitude of big business; and more.[18]

Which is to say, enterprise is not as free in the Russia of today as it is in most European countries and the United States. Recent research has probed both motivations for and impediments to starting up new businesses in Russia over the period 1994–2008. It also analysed and compared entrepreneurial needs for training, consulting and other types of assistance. The research's main conclusion was that, though Russia's climate for SMEs and entrepreneurship has improved, it is still a work in progress. The survey found a trend to a younger age range among entrepreneurs and to increasing female entrepreneurship, but was unable to report growth in the size of Russian firms. It found no significant differences between 1994 and 2008 in terms of entrepreneurial motivations and deterrents.[19]

The varying experiences of Russian SMEs' internationalisation is exemplified here by two case studies. The first – KGK – decided to enter the Brazilian market with a transport-monitoring service and thereby succeeded in helping the company grow. The second – the restaurant chain Two Sticks – intended to undertake extensive internationalisation, but then found itself better advised to practice caution and remain in its home country.

Why the difference in results? Was it due to the difference in business lines, the one company being in high tech, the other in the restaurant trade? Or was it in the style of management – the one being very meticulous in selecting its target market and defining the form of entry, while the second ventured out eagerly and with intestinal fortitude, confident in the universal attractiveness of its product?

KGK Global – careful analysis

Defining the right market

KGK Global was established in 2006, after its entrepreneurial founders had initiated the development of its global fleet tracking software in 2004.[20] The system provides solutions for vehicle monitoring, based on the use of GPS and GLONASS. KGK's system allows customers to schedule fleet workload in a precise manner, monitor every step of the delivery process and obtain feedback from the field that provides the fleet operator with important information such as time of loading, time and number of stops, elapsed time in travel, level of fuel and fuel consumption.

KGK began operating at a time when the GPS tracking market in Russia had been in development for nearly five years. Competition was already intense, requiring that KGK offer differentiated solutions to its potential clientele. The company was then, and is now, headquartered in Moscow. It has representative offices in all major Russian cities which provide services to, for instance, trucking and taxi services, ambulances, agricultural services and production-related organisations. KGK's portfolio includes customers such as Sberbank, Severstal, the Moscow oil refinery, Nemiroff spirits and others.

Foreign market selection

The first step in KGK's internationalisation consisted of pinpointing potential markets. Among potentials, company management was especially interested in finding fast-growing markets with a constant growth in the number of vehicles, where cargo is transported by road, and where driving culture requires monitoring.

Developed economies, where transportation systems were already optimised, were trimmed out of the initial research. Of the remainder, the largest markets were three emerging ones: India, China and Brazil. Further analysis showed that China to be too tricky a market to enter. It is frustrating to locate into China because of the problems of intellectual property rights and the Chinese habit of attaining progress by unabashed reverse-engineering of foreign innovation and patented processes. In addition, a great deal of transport there is by rail, which, as elsewhere, has its own monitoring system.

KGK's management then short-listed Brazil and India. Market research on India identified it as a market with plenty of opportunity, but the local management mentality did not accord promisingly with KGK's system. The company therefore settled on Brazil, with its fast-growing economy, freight transportation concentrated on roadways and compatible management practices.

Brazil's road system totalled 1.98 million km in 2002. Paved roads increased from 35,496km in 1967 to 184,140km in 2002. Brazil's railway system has been declining since 1945, as emphasis shifted to highway construction. The total railway network was 30,875km in 2002, actually lower than the 31,848km in 1970. Most of the railway system belongs to the Federal Railroad Corp., with a majority government interest; there are also seven lines which the government privatised in 1997. Large Brazilian logistics and mining companies have been investing in railway transportation as a means of attaining a higher level of competitiveness. At the same time, the efficiency of the cargo sector in Brazil was 4.5 times lower than in the USA. Such were the factors that KGK had to mull.

In comparison, however, it found that the market in vehicles been growing steadily and was expected to keep growing in the future. In 2010 Brazil counted nearly 61 million vehicles on its roads, 55 per cent out of them being cars and light commercial vehicles. It was the world's fourth-largest new car market, having overtaken Germany in the first six months of 2010, with 4.5 million new vehicles expected by 2014.

Along with the growth of production and sales of all types of vehicles, a further reason that KGK targeted Brazil was the crime level, particularly theft of vehicles and cargo. According to national statistics, every 1.5 minutes a car is stolen countrywide: every three minutes in the state of São Paulo, and every six minutes in the state of Rio de Janeiro. Brazil also has one of the highest levels of highway accidents, 10–70 times higher than in developed countries. Only 22 per cent of roads are classified as being in a perfect or good order; the rest are assessed as bad or even drastically so.

This figured into the strong demand for vehicle tracking systems in Brazil. The government encouraged drivers and vehicle owners to use them to help cope with crime. Around 350,000 vehicles are stolen each year, and many of these thefts were violent. The Brazilian government wanted all new vehicles to be fitted with anti-theft telematic systems from February 2010, but this faced ongoing legal challenge. One such challenge, in April 2009, forced the government to ease legislation.

Entry decision

To choose a market entry strategy, KGK found itself obliged to consider who its competitors were and who its potential partners. At first, a list of companies already selling and producing tracking devices was obtained and a few companies were visited. As a result of these visits, the company gained an understanding of who its competitors were, how they behaved and how to pitch monitoring systems to customers. It led KGK to assess its product as offering sufficient advantage on the Brazilian market to be able to outgun other local players, which were found to offer a more limited palette of services, as well as software power that lagged behind the state of the art. In addition, prices charged were comparatively high. Yet the established brands were expecting a rapid increase of demand in the future.

On the basis of its exploratory findings, KGK decided to establish its representative office, with its own sales team, in the city of São Paulo. This site was chosen for its significance as the leading industrial and financial centre of the country. Nearly 35 per cent of the Brazilian vehicle fleet is concentrated in the state of São Paulo.

When registering the company and searching for fitting partners to help start the business, KGK encountered a number of problems, such as product adaptation, difficulty in obtaining needed information, cultural distance and lack of intermediaries willing and qualified to help. Nonetheless, it made enough progress in these areas to be able to foresee growth, after start-up, of at least 4 per cent per year, with the market share growing at least up to 4 per cent per year.

As a technology firm, KGK enjoys firm-specific advantages compared to other emerging-market firms in going global. With the Russian government pushing technology innovation, it is apt to incentivise its ministries and state companies to support innovative made-in-Russia companies. It was possible, therefore, for the government to help KGK domestically and thereby create leeway for it to invest in foreign ventures. Moreover, Russian high-tech firms are lured and pampered by BRIC countries because such companies help local industry to develop.

Two Sticks – hesitation in choosing

To go abroad – where and how?

In late 2002 two Russian entrepreneurs decided to open a restaurant that featured Japanese cuisine, but did so without looking like a Japanese restaurant. The restaurant's designer succeeded in imbuing the restaurant with a pleasingly rugged air. It offered an uncluttered appearance and a certain blandness of expression, while allowing people to circulate and communicate. One particular mark of this style was the restaurant's 'Twin WC'. This arrangement united two toilet bowls in a shared room as an expression of the designer's intent to build the ideal of continuous communication into the space. At the time, Two Sticks was the sole 'Japanese' restaurant where the only thing that related to Japan was the menu.

The first restaurant was opened in mid-2003 and drew a spillover crowd from opening night. This encouraged the company to open new restaurants all over the city of St Petersburg. By 2008, the chain numbered 12 restaurants, which were distributed roughly equally between the city centre and the periphery.

Two Sticks was not the owners' first project. They had experimented with a variety of formats such as fashionable cafés, classical restaurants, nightclubs and fast-food restaurants. Finally, the partners decided to solely focus on Two Sticks. In 2008, the chain served an estimated 150,000 customers a month, with a total turnover of US$30 million.

The market for Japanese food restaurants

In Russia there are three categories of Japanese restaurant: expensive (fine dining) represented by such establishments as Ki Do, Wasabi and Gin-no Taki; mid-price (casual dining), such as Planeta Sushi and Yakitoria; and low-cost, such as Eurasia and Yaposha. Two Sticks belonged to the mid-price category.

The quality of sushi and rolls in all the Japanese-cuisine chains is almost identical; therefore, a key to success in the market is ingenuity: *la petite difference*. It was its stubborn simplicity – a studied air of laid-back post-communism – that made Two Sticks different from other restaurants. And it seemed to click. Market research carried out by the company's management showed that over 60 per cent of the chain's sales were repeat. Occasional visitors did appear as well, but these were fewer.

A restaurant's atmosphere is known to be created by the approach of its personnel. That is why the company management paid particular attention to recruitment. Employees are encouraged to build strong relationships with each other, thus feeling more comfortable sharing ideas, which in turn spawns innovation and brings success. Since employees are considered a major component of a chain's success, the recruitment process uses many filters, such as interviews and tests, to evaluate the suitability of every applicant.

Food and service standards across the spectrum of Japanese-cuisine restaurants are now levelling out, and are expected to reach an equilibrium by 2012–14. This would favour chains like Two Sticks by luring custom to its level from both the levels above and below. Russians are not as sophisticated as Americans or Europeans and often opt for price over quality of service (but they do like to be served).

Two Sticks' advertising campaigns

Advertising has always been very important for Two Sticks in the development of both its clientele and its image. Outdoor billboard advertising draws attention to the presence of a Two Sticks restaurant in the vicinity. The company's creative group even created 18 different messages to convey this, mostly in the guise of instructions to the passer-by, as for example: 'It's seven minutes of traffic jam to Two Sticks from here', or 'You can coast in neutral to Two Sticks from here', and so, helpfully, on. In addition to outdoor advertising, small posters are placed in lifts inside neighbouring apartment buildings. These posters are designed to draw people's attention by being placed close to the list of apartment numbers in the lift.

Another aspect of the campaign has consisted of the development of a uniform for waiters and waitresses. In this, the marketing department decided to avoid dullness and monotony, but impose a unified corporate style. Uniforms had to be identical but allow for touch-up by the individual. In practice it was made compulsory for every attendant to wear a slogan of their preference on the back. Line personnel took part in developing the new uniform. At creative workshops, restaurant employees discussed and decided what the new uniform should look like.

First expansion steps of Two Sticks

Yaposha was the first chain of Japanese restaurants from St Petersburg to enter the Moscow market in 2006. Two Sticks followed in the spring of 2008, with two restaurants.

The company considered entering the Moscow market as a toe-dunk for further regional expansion. The executives believed that the Moscow model was particularly important for the lessons it would hold for expansion to distant operations. If the move to Moscow proved successful, Two Sticks would copy it in other cities.

When the company decided to enter Moscow, the scene was already very competitive. Numerous restaurants and cafés were offering rolls and sushi, even establishments that were not at first sight 'Japanese'. Rent in Moscow was 50 per cent higher than in St Petersburg, and the average bill twice as high.

In their plan to open some ten restaurants in Moscow within a couple of years, the company was aware of such stringencies. In addition to the high rent, they had to go to the expense of differentiating themselves from other restaurants by accenting the atmosphere of its St Petersburg origin – it styled itself, accurately, as more demure and better quality than Moscow establishments. Taking into account these strictures, the company decided against franchising, because it left too much leeway to depart from Two Sticks' distinctive model.

To support the brand's image, two new restaurants in Moscow received about US$1 million each. Each one had floor space of some 5,400 sq. ft, with about 250 seats.

Further expansion: plans and reality

By 2008, the company had proved to itself that the Two Sticks' business concept was exportable to other big cities, provided that they were culturally diversified. There were about ten cities like that in Russia: so Yekaterinburg and Novosibirsk came next. By the end of the year, 40 more restaurants were to be opened.

The company also investigated countries neighbouring Russia. The first restaurant abroad was to be in Kiev, Ukraine. Two Sticks executives started negotiations to rent three premises in the Ukrainian capital. The restaurants were to be financed by reinvesting the company's own money and taking external loans.

Simultaneously, the company started planning expansion to Sweden. Having visited Stockholm, executives initiated entry through a series of meetings with Swedish businesspeople regarding possible cooperation. Estate agents, recruitment agencies and law firms were identified to support Two Sticks' intentions.

However, having thoroughly studied perspectives in the Ukrainian and Swedish markets, the company decided against both. Unlike Europe, Ukraine could not provide a valuable international experience. In Sweden, the major drawbacks were very high investment costs and small interest in Japanese cuisine.

Although the plans for international expansion had changed, Two Sticks had not abandoned the idea, but was merely reconsidering its foreign priorities. New targets were chosen, such as Western Europe and China. As an entry point to the European market, the company tentatively chose London. The Asian casual-dining niche there was seen as reasonably accessible: Japanese cuisine and other variations on Asian food were popular in London, yet Two Sticks, on taking a closer look, could find no more than a dozen big Japanese-cuisine restaurants there. In addition, the ratio between the fine dining, casual dining and low-cost segments in London was similar to that in Russia, and Two Sticks had a hope of attaining a solid place in the mid-price segment.

For entry into London the company intended to adapt the existing concept, starting by translating the original Russian name, Dve Palochki, into 'Two Sticks'. The concept of the restaurant would change as well. Values such as 'freedom and independence', which were promoted by the Dve Palochki brand, would not be as compelling to people in a Western democracy. The St Petersburg version of fun also needed adaptation for Europe.

The UK market became considered as risky, however, when Yakitoria failed there. Nevertheless, other Russian players were not discouraged. Thus, Westa-Center International, a Moscow restaurant holding, opened its first Gin-no Taki restaurant in London in the summer of 2005. But Two Sticks decided, nonetheless, to hold off.

Another market of interest was China. Japanese cuisine is unlike other Asian food, and China is far from market saturation in that niche. Two Sticks' target there was Hong Kong. The Chinese market was promising because Russia and China had similar histories of national development; thus the implementation of Two Sticks' values, primarily 'freedom', had a chance of attracting Chinese custom.

Yet, as of the year 2011, nothing has come of these high-flying plans to internationalise, although the company still insists that it intends to continue internationalising. Is this the result of a realistic assessment of Two Sticks' chances given the foreign market's present state? Or could it be that the process of entry and of adaptation of company marketing and HR policies to other markets' requirements has become too complicated to be worthwhile? The company itself has failed to find such answers, which is remarkable for an organisation previously so adept. It may show that the company may need to re-evaluate the changing environment, the competition and its own capabilities in relation to its intentions to go abroad.

Let's conclude what makes the boundaries for Russian firms' internationalisation and how they can cope or even benefit from the failures. In the study of failed acquisitions, it makes sense to focus rather on the pre-acquisition phase of the M&A, because in all cases the parties did not go further than this stage of the process.

In the case of Surgutneftegas and MOL the failure of the negotiations was largely attributable to the governments of Hungary and Russia, but the companies' managements were not without blame. The deal foundered when OMV, of which MOL is a part, accused MOL of collusion with the Russian company and even with the Russian government. This should have been ironed out in the pre-acquisition phase, to avoid an unnecessary argument between states.

As for the attempt of Sberbank to buy Opel, this could have benefited Sberbank and the Russian automotive industry in general, because of Opel's possession of advanced technologies that Russia still lacks. But although the deal failed, Sberbank made its name the world over and, according to experts, lost no money over it.

A major problem with the majority of big Russian investment firms is their lack of transparency. This issue beclouded the attempted deal between Polyus Gold and KazakhGold on the one hand and Surgutneftegas and Hungarian OMV on the other. Expensive and protracted negotiations failed because ownership by the Russian government had been concealed but had surfaced during the course of the negotiations.

And this is a generic problem. Russian acquisitions and takeovers often target strategically strong, powerful and influential foreign companies. Because of this the governments of the targeted companies scotch the deal, on the grounds of the country's interests or even its security.

In cases of Russian SMEs internationalising, the entrepreneurial perspective can be paramount and government support only incidental. In the KGK case internationalisation was not at the behest of the government. It worked out because the company saw an opportunity to make a profit abroad and did its homework to harvest it. This case demonstrates that the investment climate in the targeted country is an important factor for Russian SMEs. They usually lack the large investment resources that may be required to lobby or litigate their way into a sticky foreign market.

Another problem is that, to be successful abroad, Russian SMEs (especially in high-tech sectors) have to find a niche where they may exert the technological advantage they have gained from the Russian science base and developers. KGK operates in a niche where technological savvy invites foreign demand.

As for the restaurant business, the main driver in this sector is quality, which attracts clients and gives a specific advantage over competitors. Two Sticks considered a franchising roll-out strategy as inappropriate owing to the risk of damage to its idiosyncratic model. At the same time, many restaurants sell franchising rights because, they believe, a limited number of specifications, not absolute purity of identity, suffice to give their chain an unforgettable presence.

Going abroad for profit is often coupled with the hope of gaining valuable experience not obtainable at home. Where there is strong competition such extra knowledge can prove to be crucial. In fact, it has driven globalisation. Europe and the US are over-saturated with service companies, and to succeed entails being unique. Two Sticks in its spread is unique to St Petersburg, but its case also demonstrates that it can be difficult to implant the St Petersburg manner abroad: this laid-back style may not grab people everywhere. For any company – big or small – a key success factor in going abroad is recognising when a window of opportunity exists. Two Sticks grabbed the chance in Russia, but understood that worldwide conditions differ. Two sticks in Russia is better than chopped sticks abroad...

Conclusion

Whither multinationals?

International results of Russian MNEs

Comparing Russia's performance in international competition with other emerging multinationals is something of a rarity. Broad conclusions tend to be seen as premature because internationalising is not yet an established discipline in Russia, and this generalising on the international results of Russian MNEs remains limited.

In different industries the decisions regarding entry to multinational competition and what to do after entering are varied. Whereas some commonalities can be seen among Russian competitors, the individual achievers tend to make up their own rules.

In oil and gas, which is highly diversified, the star performers are Gazprom and Rosneft (both state-owned). It is their practices that are bending the Russian style in this discipline towards inefficiency. Only Lukoil operates in the manner of a profit-seeking company. However, the old methods employed by these Russian majors do have understandable reasons.

Given the global scarcity of oil and gas reserves, there simply does not exist a justification for greenfield investment, which is why all the companies operating in this industry go brownfield when expanding abroad. The aim is to transfer Russian know-how to foreign opportunities in order to expand distribution networks and acquire foreign know-how, technologies and hard cash. Using acquisitions, joint ventures and cooperation agreements, Russian companies exploit the pre-existing frameworks of international business etiquette.

In the case of Lukoil, its core activities (exploration and production) are less internationalised than its less important ones (refining, distribution, marketing), which shows that internationalisation is not, in the oil and gas industry, an absolute requirement for high profit margins.

In the high-tech sector, the typical Russian player is a privately owned small company operating in IT and software. Domestically these firms can benefit from servicing government organisations and practising close cooperation with them. As these firms venture abroad, success is defined by their ability to exploit partnerships in order to become innovative. Larger companies make acquisitions in order to achieve or strengthen a market position abroad.

Sitronics, which has operated in close cooperation with the Russian government, is doing well; not only is the government an important buyer of its goods but it also supports Sitronics and companies like it by funding R&D which is expensive but crucial for any high-tech industry. However, the case of Kaspersky shows that a strong link to government need not be essential; establishing partnerships with foreign software giants can be an equally good way of catching up with the state of the art.

In banking, outward investment destinations are researched and then rated for their potential value for the existing banking clients. But business also includes inward investment, where Russian banks operating abroad aid foreigners to establish themselves in Russia.

Usually the process of penetrating new markets has been sporadic and cautious. It begins with a representative office that evaluates the potential of a foreign market and gauges the appropriate time for entry into it. Most such reconnaissance has been carried out by foreign subsidiaries of Russian banks. Only a few big Russian banks (such as Alfa bank, VTB and Sberbank) have the resources to go abroad; small banks need to grow domestically before they can follow.

In metallurgy, both the rise and expansion of MNEs occurs in the regions where raw materials are found; many of the biggest players are of Russian origin because Russia is a big place containing lots of raw material and Russians therefore have accumulated experience in metallurgy. With that in hand it is natural for them to use their know-how to expand abroad. They are experts in taking over firms in developing economies and they are not shy about acquiring companies in developed markets. The booming commodity markets have meant plenty of cash for investment, so Russian companies in this sector are multinationals by nature.

Evraz and Severstal have made relatively risky acquisitions in developed countries (countries of the EU and the USA, in particular) which allowed them a closer approach to customers as well as a way to overcome trade barriers, tariffs and duties. Rusal, which cultivates brawn over brain, has mainly concentrated on acquisitions of emerging market companies, especially in locations where raw materials sufficient for massive business are located. But even the cleverer Russian metallurgy firms lack the best technical capabilities of the West for refining the metals; they still prefer to sell semi-finished or commodity metals to Western companies that do the final processing. However, they are increasingly investing in modern refining as they get used to the realisation that money can also be made in a more sophisticated way.

Severstal has succeeded first and foremost because of its diversified product portfolio. To secure the efficiency of production, it has acquired mines and production facilities in developed countries. Growth opportunities for Rusal are more limited than for Severstal. It is, essentially, a simpler company. Rusal goes about its business acquiring new deposits and developing the existing ones sufficient to cover the needs of a product line more restricted than is Severstal's. For Russian metallurgy, in general, one important way to lower costs is by securing the supply of inexpensive energy, which explains acquisitions and further development by Rusal of, in particular, power-generating assets.

In telecommunications, M&As are also actively used, but their purpose differs from that in metallurgy, focusing rather on gaining state-of-the-art knowledge from foreign players (which is particularly important in this segment), and thereby expanding its market (obtaining both new suppliers and new customers). While two companies, MTS and VimpelCom, began expanding abroad by entering CIS countries, they have also begun exploring opportunities in large Asian markets such as India. Seeking maximum control over their foreign operations, these companies first purchase a modest stake, and then, to the extent that experience warrants, increase their stake up to 100 per cent.

Strategic differences did exist, however. MTS liked to be more aggressive, having fewer joint ventures and more M&As, while VimpelCom was more flexible and, depending on market conditions, was open to joint ventures. The MTS strategy orientated on takeovers of leading telecom companies in order to attain as swiftly as possible a leadership position in a foreign market, while VimpelCom did make exceptions and also acquired companies of only average market heft. Both companies have paid significant attention to development of their brands, MTS and Beeline, MTS concentrating primarily on MTS as a brand, while VimpelCom emphasised the importance of company (for example, by going public on the NYSE) while letting its brand, Beeline, prove itself.

Several Russian companies are seen as being 'international by nature'. Examples here were Inter RAO UES (the electricity distributor to other countries on behalf of the state), Rusnano (a domestically focused but highly innovative company which requires international partnerships in order to develop) and Yandex (the Internet company which is global by dint of its core activity, search engine services).

In the electricity sector, where the role of the state is much greater than in the high-tech sector, the success of Inter RAO UES could not have been possible without the alignment of its strategic goal with that of the Russian state. While not a monopoly in the strictest sense, the company has enjoyed massive government backing, including inheritance of Soviet era assets. This heritage endowed it with a competitive position such that other players able to construct and operate nuclear plants or power grids cannot compete on price.

In the nanotechnology sector, Rusnano makes for an interesting case. Its internationalisation involves a large nest of agreements and memoranda with foreigners. In sum, these activities have indubitably brought success to Rusnano, but success more of a political than of a commercial sort. Otherwise, Russian nanotech practises internationalisation because thereby it can access state-of-the-art technology that it has heretofore not been able to attain on its own.

In the software industry, while Yandex has a extremely strong brand in Russia, Google has one of the strongest brands in the world, and both are in direct competition in Russia, Belarus and Ukraine. As does every Internet company, Yandex from the very beginning has operated across national boundaries. It has innovated in the field of online advertising, but this should not be seen as a tool for expansion. Yandex was expanded already at birth, was born global; this is no product of managerial deftness.

For Russian MNEs the state was, alternatively, pushy (as in the case of most resource-based industries) or lax (for example, toward companies of relatively small size in less-resource-based sectors). Companies chosen here show two extremes of the strategies followed by Russian MNEs: the one relying on marketing and branding when the government has no interest in a domestic firms' expansion abroad, and the other in which a firm is encouraged by the state to internationalise in the interests of foreign policy.

In the food and beverages sectors the government does not usually support commercial expansion abroad. Such firms are left to expand using their own resources and initiative. Such are the examples of Wimm-Bill-Dann, in dairy products, and the vodka producer Russian Standard, both of whom must rely on their own marketing efforts to compensate for the lack of government support. Both companies have strong and well-known brands in Russia and can expand internationally through brand goodwill.

The interest of the state in the internationalisation of national firms attends two types of companies: those where the business itself requires very vigilant control, as in case of Rosenergoatom, in the nuclear power sector, and those in any other sector where foreign policy impinges, as in case of Rosoboronexport, in defence.

In the nuclear power sector, where massive capital investment is required, the business, at least in Russia, cannot develop without government subsidy. Supporting Rosenergoatom is obligatory lest Russia be denied its own nuclear power industry. In a manner similar to that employed by the nanotech industry, internationalisation in this sector is engineered via involvement with foreign companies and organisations in joint projects.

The military industry, where government involvement serves the cause of national security, is heavily reliant on foreign sales to offset the cost to the national budget, while the government leverages deals for the military industry abroad to help with the industry's budget. Coincidentally, these deals assist in the formation of alliances and other requisites of foreign policy. In other words, to a company like Rosoboronexport a strong government link is the path to custom.

In both cases, improving the technical and financial performance of the firms under the control of the state is an obvious precondition to achieving what the government has ordained, namely improvement of efficiency in state firms. Such new efficiency, it is hoped, will help diversify state firms away from their present rut in natural resources, and thus enrich the economy as a whole.

Though Russia has become eager to internationalise, it still needs to refine its technique. This is attested by discussion of boundaries of Russian OFDI. One major problem is Russian non-transparency. In one notorious litigation arising from this, a Hungarian company charged, successfully, that a deal with a Russian company should be adjudged invalid because the Russian party had claimed to be private while in reality it was but a camouflaged tool of the Russian government.

Instead of using trickery, Russian internationalisation should proceed along the avenue of good entrepreneurial practice. The vehicle-tracking manufacturer KGK sets an example here. Its entry was predicated on a thorough analysis of international target markets, and of own relevance within those markets. Meticulous homework in this case led to a highly successful entry and development. The story of Two Sticks in the restaurant business shows the utility of a 'wait and see' strategy, where it is seen as better to avoid expanding abroad, instead waiting for better times and developing a more innovative approach.

Prospects of Russian multinationals

Future prospects for international expansion of Russian firms remain highly promising, despite the pall created by the world financial crisis for the global economy as a whole.

While good economic growth at home and high-quality human potential are likely to continue to drive investment from Russia abroad, increasing international assets and foreign customer base provides Russian companies with capabilities to compete with more confidence and with opportunities to become more 'typical' MNEs.

The outward expansion of Russian companies is important from two standpoints: one is the development of national enterprises, and the other is the adjustment of the Russian economy to the global economy. Russian firms are becoming more competitive – both domestically and internationally – by tapping the experience gained from investing abroad, establishing partnerships with global companies and developing products for foreign markets.

In the long term, Russia requires a structural reform and improvement in competitiveness to transform the country from a situation in which it is held hostage by its limited natural resources. It needs to liberate itself and turn to activities dependent, instead, on the renewable human resources of technology and innovation. The internationalisation of Russian firms is the best way to make companies accord with this stringency.

The further development of Russian MNEs needs work. The role of the state in outward internationalisation is ambiguous and other institutions in substitution of it are lacking. Hence, the coordination of private, bank and government investment is needed.

As a corollary, information on how to do business abroad must be provided. Surprisingly, whereas much guidance is provided to Western investors on how to do business in Russia, almost none is available for Russian firms thinking of going abroad. The international experience already accumulated by Russian companies is too scant to be generalised, which raises the importance of the transfer of knowledge regarding what works and what does not when going global. We hope that this book may have helped to contribute in its own manner.

Notes

1 The internationalisation of the Russian economy

1 Nove 1992, 5; Fischer 1994, 221.
2 Nove 1992, 6.
3 Fischer 1994, 224.
4 Gregory and Stuart 1981, 52–7.
5 Nove 1992, 236.
6 Ibid., 277.
7 Ibid., 301.
8 Ibid., 359.
9 Frydman *et al.* 1993, 37–8.
10 Sterlin 1993, 215–37.
11 Desai 1995, 1–34.
12 Åslund 1995, 253.
13 Chubais and Vishnevskaya 1993, 89–99.
14 Blasi *et al.* 1997, 26.
15 Ibid., 26.
16 Earle *et al.* 1996, 205–52.
17 Danilov *et al.* 2010.
18 UNCTAD & UNECE 1998.
19 Ibid.
20 Ibid.
21 Ibid.
22 Robinson 2007 245–59.
23 Saleem 2009, 243–56.
24 Lucey and Voronkova 2008, 1303–24.
25 Danilov *et al.* 2010.
26 Golubchikov 2007, 191–215.
27 Colton and Holmes 2006; Goldman 1991; 1994; 2003.
28 Hanson 2004, 421–8.
29 Kalotay and Sulstarova 2010, 131–42.
30 Kalotay and Sulstarova 2010.
31 Aervitz 2009.
32 Panfilov 2009.
33 Belousov 2010, 14–27.
34 Belousov 2010.
35 Aloui *et al.* 2011, 130–41.
36 World Bank 2009.
37 Blasi 1997.
38 Kuznetsov and Kuznetsova 1996, 1173–85.

39 Boycko *et al.* 1996, 309–19.
40 Shleifer and Vasiliev 1996, 62–77.
41 Kuznetsov and Kuznetsova 1996.
42 Burawoy and Hendley 1992, 371–402.
43 Huber and Wörgötter 1998, 81–91.
44 Clarke and Kabalina 1995, 142–58.
45 Clarke *et al.* 1994, 179–214.
46 Huber and Wörgötter 1998.
47 Gaddy and Ickes 1998, 53–67.
48 Ageev *et al.* 1995, 365–76.
49 Puffer and McCarthy 2001, 24–38.
50 Yakovlev 2006, 1033–56.
51 Ibid.
52 Ibid.
53 Kalotay 2008, 85–107.
54 Economist Intelligence Unit 2006.
55 Ickes and Gaddy 2010.
56 Goldman Sachs 2003.
57 Goldman Sachs 2005.
58 Goldman Sachs 2010a.
59 Goldman Sachs 2010b.
60 Ibid.
61 Ibid.
62 Ibid.
63 Ibid.
64 Ibid.
65 Ibid.
66 Ibid.
67 http://www.gks.ru/wps/wcm/connect/rosstat/rosstatsite.eng/ (2010).
68 www.unctad.org (2009).
69 Panibratov and Kalotay 2009.
70 Davies 2010.
71 Satyanand and Raghavendran 2010.
72 Ibid.
73 United Nations Conference on Trade and Development 2007.
74 Lima and de Barros 2009.
75 United Nations Conference on Trade and Development 2007.
76 Ibid.
77 Panibratov and Kalotay 2009.
78 United Nations Conference on Trade and Development 2008.
79 United Nations Conference on Trade and Development 2009.
80 Davies 2010.
81 Ibid.
82 Panibratov and Kalotay 2009.
83 United Nations Conference on Trade and Development 2010.
84 Ibid.
85 Sauvant *et al.* 2010.

2 Multinational genesis

1 Wells 1983.
2 Bartlett and Ghoshal 1989.
3 Elenkov 1995, 66–78.
4 Luo and Tung 2007, 481–98.

5 Tsang and Yip 2007, 1156–68.
6 Jensen 2004, 535–50.
7 Blomström *et al.* 2001.
8 Ramamurti 2009.
9 Filippov 2008.
10 Bulatov 1998; 2001; Crane *et al.* 2005; Filatotchev *et al.* 2007a; Heinrich 2003; 2006; Kalotay 2004; 2005; 2008b; Vahtra and Liuhto 2006.
11 Liuhto and Vahtra 2007, 28–36.
12 Ramamurti 2009.
13 Hamilton 1986; McMillan 1987.
14 Vahtra 2006.
15 Elenkov 1995.
16 Filatotchev *et al.* 2007b, 556–73; King *et al.* 1995, 6–22.
17 Kuznetsov 2010.
18 Economist Intelligence Unit 2006.
19 Kalotay 2005, 9–22.
20 Panibratov and Kalotay 2009.
21 Rugman and Verbeke 2008, 305–13; Sethi 2009, 356–65.
22 Panibratov 2009, 210–28.
23 Luo and Tung 2007.
24 Witt and Lewin 2007, 579–94; Boddewyn and Brewer 1994, 119–43; Kalotay 2001, 259–76.
25 http://www.eiu.com/public/ (2010).
26 Kuznetsov 2009.
27 Dunning 1993.
28 Kuznetsov 2009.
29 Ibid.
30 Kuznetsov 2010.
31 http://rt.com/business/news/kamaz-trucks-china-production/.
32 Expert Online 2009a.
33 Expert Online 2009b.
34 RAO Bumprom (Russian Association of Pulp and Paper industry).
35 http://www.datamonitor.com/store/Product/airlines_bric_brazil_russia_india_china_industry_guide_2010?productid=3B1E5EF9-2D29-4DEB-984A-4F455F1CC716.
36 Available from http://marketing.rbc.ru/eng.
37 http://www.pwc.com/en_GX/gx/investment-management-real-estate/pdf/europe_et2007.pdf.
38 Panibratov 2010, 63–93.
39 http://www.yitgroup.com/docs/yit-group-documents/2011/04/07/YIT_Interim%20Report_1_9_2009.pdf?Status=Master.
40 Porter 1998.
41 Panibratov 2009, 210–28.

3 Exporting from Russia: the oil and gas industry

1 http://www.energy-market-research.info/research/EMAAABOR-Oil-and-Gas–Global-Industry-Guide—Datamonitor.shtml.
2 Bosquet 2009.
3 Badler *et al.* 2009.
4 http://www.eia.gov/ (2010).
5 http://www.euromonitor.com/ (2010).
6 https://www.cia.gov/library/publications/the-world-factbook/geos/rs.html (2010).
7 http://www.datamonitor.com/store/Product/oil_gas_bric_brazil_russia_india_china_industry_guide?productid=E0D29CFF-55C5-4244-A5BD-140D1828DF77.

8 Ibid.
9 Bosquet 2009.
10 Badler *et al.* 2009.
11 Ibid.
12 Goldman 2008.
13 http://www.datamonitor.com/store/Product/oil_gas_bric_brazil_russia_india_china_industry_guide?productid=E0D29CFF-55C5-4244-A5BD-140D1828DF77.
14 Ibid.
15 www.rosneft.com.
16 www.companiesandmarkets.com 2011.
17 http://www.datamonitor.com/store/Product/ojsc_rosneft_oil_company?productid=2FDE1F25-8852-4F72-A0CB-D2C0DD61BE0D.
18 http://www.rosneft.com/Downstream/petroleum_product_sales/servicestations/.
19 Datamonitor, 08.04.2009.
20 Lukoil 2008.
21 Ibid.
22 Ibid.
23 http://www.naturalgas.org/naturalgas/processing_ng.asp.
24 http://www.datamonitor.com/store/Product/oil_gas_bric_brazil_russia_india_china_industry_guide?productid=E0D29CFF-55C5-4244-A5BD-140D1828DF77.
25 http://www.tatneft.ru/wps/wcm/connect/tatneft/portal_eng/to_shareholders/equities_structure/.

4 Establishing partnerships: the high-tech sector

1 Crane and Usanov 2010.
2 Crane and Usanov 2010.
3 http://www.mbi.com.br/mbi/global/english/2007britto/2007%20Globelics-Paper Software_JorgeBritto.pdf.
4 Ibid.
5 http://business.highbeam.com/437189/article-1G1-191176691/russia-software.
6 Pronin 2009.
7 Crane and Usanov 2010.
8 Crane and Usanov 2010.
9 Crane and Usanov 2010.
10 http://www.luxoft.com/about/glance/fact_sheet.html.
11 Ibid.
12 http://www.kaspersky.com/about/contactinfo.
13 See the corporate website of Sitronics, www.sitronics.com, for further information on this company.
14 http://www.allbusiness.com/trade-development/economic-development-emerging-markets/12280260-1.html.
15 http://business-video.tmcnet.com/news/2009/12/20/4542631.htm.
16 http://us.generation-nt.com/sitronics-establishes-joint-venture-zte-corporation-press-1021511.html.
17 http://158.151.240.55/company-activities-management/company-strategy/5305622-1.html.

5 Opening subsidiaries: the banking industry

1 Steinherr 2004.
2 Steinherr 2004.
3 Economist Intelligence Unit 2009.

4 United Nations Conference on Trade and Development 2007.
5 This assessment is based on the data of the Central Bank of Russia: www.cbr.ru.
6 Jumpponen *et al.* 2004.
7 Jumpponen *et al.* 2004.
8 Kuznetsov 2009.
9 'Mergers and acquisitions in banking', in MA online: mergers and acquisitions, 2009, April 15, www.maonline.ru
10 http://alfabank.com/media/news/2001/03/21/.
11 http://www.rao-ees.ru/en/news/pub_uesr/show.cgi?300802tender.htm.
12 http://eng.spb-venchur.ru/news/2221.htm.
13 VTB 2009.
14 VTB 2009.
15 http://www.vtb-bank.kz/rus/web.html?l=321&s1=8507.
16 http://www.datamonitor.com/store/News/vtb_bank_launches_business_in_azerbaijan?productid=9F2F14D9-43C1-48F2-A739-B94C292DA4B8.
17 Humber 2006.
18 Sekhri 2009.
19 http://www.vtb.com/we/press-center/releases/21708/.
20 Humber 2006.

6 FDI from Russia: the metallurgy sector

1 http://www.rusal.ru/en/about/facts.aspx.
2 Further discussion of this company is based on information contained in its corporate website: www.rusal.ru.
3 http://www.africaneconomicoutlook.org/en/countries/west-africa/guinea/.
4 Finam 2009.
5 http://www.newmaterials.com/Customisation/News/Non-Ferrous_Metals/Aluminium/UC_Rusal_CEO_visits_Guinea_with_Russian_Government_delegation.asp.
6 Fedorinova 2009.
7 http://www.severstal.com/eng/businesses/resources/.
8 http://www.evraz.com/press/press_releases/080829_1H08%20results.pdf.

7 Acquiring the customer: the telecom industry

1 Anderson 2005.
2 http://www.networkworld.com/news/2008/091708-global-telecom.html.
3 http://english.corp.megafon.ru/ai/document/208/file/Annual_Report_2009.pdf.
4 http://www.mtsgsm.com/news/2007-12-18-26575/.
5 RBC 2008'.
6 http://www.eiu.com/index.asp?layout=ib3Article&article_id=824702667&pubtypeid=1162462501&category_id=775133077&country_id=1750000175&page_title=Forecast&rf=0.
7 http://www.vimpelcom.com.
8 C114 2009.
9 http://www.alfagroup.org/18/4/2007/122/126/19223/news.aspx.
10 Dzyadko'' 2007.
11 http://www.tadviser.ru/index.php?title=%D0%9A%D0%BE%D0%BC%D0%BF%D0%B0%D0%BD%D0%B8%D1%8F:%D0%92%D1%8B%D0%BC%D0%BF%D0%B5%D0%BB%D0%BA%D0%BE%D0%BC,_%D0%9E%D0%90%D0%9E&cache=no&ptype=product.
12 http://about.beeline.ru/media/About_eng/annual%20reports/ar2005.pdf.
13 cnews 2007.

14 http://www.alfagroup.org/16/4/2008/122/126/19595/news.aspx.
15 Dzyadko 2009''.
16 http://www.vimpelcom.com/media/Documents/Quarterly%20Reports%202009/consolidated%20financials%202009-2008-%202007.pdf''.

8 Born to global business

1 http://www.freelifeonearth.org/docs/PBMR%20SEIA%20comment%20ecoprogram%20A.pdf and http://ere.stanford.edu/pdf/IGAstandard/SGW/2011/goldstein1.pdf.
2 http://www.iea.org/Textbase/npsum/weo2010sum.pdf and http://www.iea.org/weo/docs/weo2010/weo2010_london_nov9.pdf.
3 Simonov 2011.
4 http://www.economy.gov.ru/minec/activity/sections/innovations/doc20101231_016?presentationtemplate=docHTMLTemplate1&presentationtemplateid=2dd7bc8044687de796f0f7af753c8a7e.
5 Communication from the Commission to the Council and the European Parliament, A Strategic Framework for International Science and Technology Cooperation, COM (2008) 588 final, Brussels, 24.09.2008, 7.
6 Vahtra 2010.
7 Ibid.
8 Ibid.
9 Ibid.
10 http://marchmontcapital.com/Technology-Innovation/Volga/17427-RUSNANO-invest-470m-five-projects-and-two-venture-funds.html.
11 http://www.sras.org/russian_internet_usage_increases.
12 Latukha (2010).
13 http://money.cnn.com/2009/02/10/technology/ioffe_russians.fortune/.
14 http://www.reuters.com/article/2010/07/26/us-online-search-market-idUSTRE66M3LI20100726.

9 Strategy emphasis: government stake or brand power?

1 http://www.iea.org/papers/2010/nuclear_foldout.pdf.
2 https://inlportal.inl.gov/portal/server.pt/community/nuclear_energy/277/nuclear_power_plants/7055.
3 http://articles.economictimes.indiatimes.com/2011-09-20/news/30180363_1_nuclear-power-nuke-accident-nuclear-reactors.
4 http://www.areva.com/EN/operations-809/milestones-in-the-history-of-areva-pierre-latte.html.
5 http://www.tractebel-engineering-gdfsuez.com/.
6 http://www.world-nuclear.org/info/inf45.html.
7 http://www.atomenergoprom.ru/en/corp/ and http://www.jmu.ru/ru/index.php?cid=48.
8 This information is contained in the company's 2007 annual report.
9 http://www.old.rosatom.ru/en/about/international_cooperation/.
10 http://www.atomstroyexport.ru/show/press/553.
11 Shah 2010.
12 http://en.rian.ru/mlitary_news/20110131/162393806.html.
13 http://www.brahmos.com/content.php?id=1&sid=2.
14 http://www.roe.ru/cataloque/air_craft/aircraft.pdf.
15 http://ey.mobi/Publication/vwLUAssets/Newsletter_Russia2009-EN/$FILE/Food-Beverage-2009-EN.pdf.
16 Ibid.

17 http://www.tpprf.ru/common/upload/documents/committee/kpr/monitor/2008040710355303.doc.
18 http://eng.baltika.ru/m/450/bhow_is_the_companys_export_business_developing__how_many_countries_are_baltika_products_deliver.html.
19 www.russianstandard.com/corporation/press_center/press_releases/22.smx.
20 http://www.wbd.com/profile/governance/documents/Offering%20Memorandum%20of%206%20February%202007.pdf.
21 http://rusmergers.com/en/mna/500-.html.
22 http://www.wbd.com/financial/annual/WBD%20AR%20fina%202006.pdf.
23 *RT magazine* 2009.
24 http://www.datamonitor.com/store/Product/spirits_in_russia?productid=88D12EF7-115A-46E4-BF68-9A4C9D92BD8E.
25 Ibid.
26 Suddath 2010.
27 Elamin 2007.
28 http://www.russianstandard.com/corporation/press_center/?From1=15&Page1=3.
29 *Drinks Media Wire* 2009.
30 Ahrend 2005.
31 Kalotay 2008a.

10 Boundaries of Russian MNEs

1 http://top.rbc.ru/finances/17/11/2008/261240.shtml.
2 Kalotay 2010.
3 Ibid.
4 Ibid.
5 Ibid.
6 http://www.banksdaily.com/info/sberbank.
7 http://www.magna.com/magna/en/about/.
8 http://media.gm.com/content/media/us/en/gm/news.detail.html/content/Pages/news/us/en/2011/Feb/0224_earnings.
9 http://www.fsz-industrie.de/471.html?&L=1.
10 http://www.vz.ru/economy/2009/6/1/292805.html.
11 http://newsru.net/finance/02jul2009/gref.html.
12 http://vz.ru/economy/2009/5/29/292174.html.
13 http://www.vz.ru/economy/2009/6/4/294106.html.
14 http://expert.ru/expert/2009/22/opel_dlya_naroda/.
15 http://www.gazeta.ru/auto/2009/09/10_a_3258988.shtml.
16 http://www.rbcdaily.ru/2010/06/24/finance/489111.
17 Johnson 2004.
18 Ketting 2006.
19 Zhuplev and Shtykhno 2009.
20 Information in this section is derived from Latukha *et al.* 2011.

Bibliography

Aervitz, I. (2009) 'Russia's investment forecast: mostly cloudy', *Russia Profile*, available: http://www.russiaprofile.org/business/a1236017589.html [accessed 21 September 2010].

Ageev, A., Gratchev, M. and Hisrich, R. (1995) 'Entrepreneurship in the Soviet Union and post-socialist Russia', *Small Business Economics*, 7: 365–76.

Ahrend, R. (2005) 'Sustaining growth in a resource-based economy: the main issues and the specific case of Russia', Geneva: United Nations Economic Commission for Europe, Occasional Paper 6.

Aloui, R., Ben Aïssa, M. and Nguyen, D. (2011) 'Global financial crisis, extreme interdependences, and contagion effects: the role of economic structure?', *Journal of Banking and Finance*, 35(1): 130–41.

Anderson, J. (2005) *Understanding Information Technology*, Piscataway, NJ: Interscience.

Åslund, A. (1995) *How Russia Became a Market Economy*, Washington, DC: The Brookings Institution, 1995.

Badler, D., Lippert, E., Seifert, E., Shockley, R., Teplitsky, M. and Traxler, J. (2009) 'Challenges in the Russian energy sector: consolidate or capitulate?' in *International Focus at Kellogg*, Kellogg School of Management, available: http://www.kellogg.northwestern.edu/Departments/International/InternationalFocus/Article/2007_Challenges_in_the_Russian_Energy_Sector.aspx [accessed 21 September 2011].

Bartlett, C. and Ghoshal, S. (1989) *Managing Across Borders*, Boston, MA: Harvard Business School Press.

Belousov, D. (2010) 'On the development of the crisis of the Russian economy in 2008–2009', *Studies on Russian Economic Development*, 21(1): 14–27.

Benito, G. and Narula, R. (eds) (2007) *Multinationals on the Periphery*, London: Macmillan.

Blasi, J.R. (1997) 'The hundred largest companies in the Russian Federation: a preliminary research note on ownership, governance and restructuring', paper presented at the conference on Restructuring Russian Enterprises, March 24–25, Moscow: Russian Finance Academy.

Blasi, J.R., Kroumova, M. and Kruse, D. (1997) *Kremlin Capitalism: The Privatisation of the Russian Economy*, New York: Cornell University Press.

Blomström, M., Kokko, A. and Globerman, S. (2001) 'The determinants of host country spillovers from foreign direct investment', in N. Pain (ed.), *Inward Investment, Technological Change and Growth*, Basingstoke: MacMillan.

Boddewyn, J.J. and Brewer, T.L. (1994) 'International-business political behavior: new theoretical directions', *Academy of Management Review*, 19(1): 119–43.

Bosquet, B. (2009) 'The role of natural resources in fundamental tax reform in the Russian Federation', *Policy Research Working Paper*, WPS2807, Washington, DC: The World Bank.

Boycko, M., Schleifer, A. and Vishny, R.W. (1996) 'A theory of privatisation', *The Economic Journal*, 106: 309–19.

Bulatov, A. (1998) 'Russian direct investment abroad: main motivations in the post-Soviet period', *Transnational Corporations*, 7(1): 69–82.

Bulatov, A. (2001) 'Russian direct investment abroad: history, motives, finance, control and planning', *Economics of Planning*, 34(3): 179–94.

Burawoy, M. and Hendley, K. (1992) 'Between perestroika and privatisation: divided strategies and political crisis in a Soviet enterprise', *Soviet Studies*, 44(1): 371–402.

C114 (2009) 'VimpelCom expands in Southeast Asia', available: http://www.cn-c114.net/576/a444589.html [accessed 22 September 2011].

Chubais, A. and Vishnevskaya, M. (1993) 'Main issues of privatisation in Russia', in A. Åslund and R. Layard (eds), *Changing the Economic System in Russia*, London: Pinter Publishers, 1993.

Clarke, S. and Kabalina, V. (1995) 'Privatisation and the struggle for control of the enterprise', in D. Lane (ed.) *Russia in Transition: Politics, Privatisation and Inequality*, London: Longman.

Clarke, S., Fairbrother, P., Borisov, V. and Bizyukov, P. (1994) 'The privatisation of industrial enterprises in Russia: four case-studies', *Europe-Asia Studies*, 46(2): 179–214.

cnews (2007) 'Beeline to test 3G in Tajikistan', available: http://eng.cnews.ru/news/top/indexEn.shtml?2007/02/09/235085 [accessed 10 October 2011].

Colton, T.J. and Holmes, S. (eds) (2006) *The State After Communism: Governance in the New Russia*, New York: Rowman and Littlefield Publishers.

companiesandmarkets.com (2011) 'OJSC Rosneft Oil Company – Oil & Gas – Deals and Alliances Profile', available: http://www.companiesandmarkets.com/Company-Profile/ojsc-rosneft-oil-company-%28rosn%29-oil-gas-deals-and-alliances-profile-546510.asp [accessed 21 September 2011].

Crane, K. and Usanov, A. (2010) 'Role of high-technology industries', in A. Åslund, S. Guriev and A. Kuchins (eds), *Russia After the Global Economic Crisis*, Washington, DC: PIIE Center for Strategic and International Studies.

Crane, K., Peterson, D.J. and Oliker, O. (2005) 'Russian investment in the Commonwealth of Independent States', *Eurasia Geography and Economics*, 46(6): 405–44.

Danilov, U., Yakovlev, A. and Simachev, Y. (2010) 'The Russian corporation: patterns of behavior during the crisis', Centre for Comparative Economics (CCE), Economics working paper 100.

Davies, K. (2010) 'Outward FDI from China and its policy context', *Columbia FDI Profiles*, Vale Columbia Centre on Sustainable International Investment, Columbia University, October 18, available: http://www.vcc.columbia.edu/content/outward-fdi-china-and-its-policy-context-ken-davies.

Desai, P. (1995) 'Russian privatisation: a comparative perspective', *The Harriman Review*, 8(3): 1–34.

Drinks Media Wire (2009) 'Russian Standard Vodka and Remy Cointreau Global travel retail enter into international duty free alliance', October 16, available: http://www.drinksmediawire.com/afficher_cdp.asp?id=5563&lng=2 [accessed 22 September 2011].

Dunning, J. (1993) *Multinational Enterprises and the Global Economy*, New York: Addison-Wesley.

Dzyadko, T. (2007) 'VimpelCom has dumping in Georgia', *RBC Daily*, available: http://www.rbcdaily.ru/2007/03/16/media/268367 [accessed 10 October 2011].

Dzyadko, T. (2009) 'World by calculation', *Vedomosti*, no. 188.

Earle, J.S., Estrin, S. and Leshchenko, L.L. (1996) 'Ownership structures, patterns of control, and enterprise behavior in Russia', in S. Commander, F. Qimiao and M.E. Schafer (eds), *Enterprise Restructuring and Economic Policy in Russia*, EDI Development Studies, Washington, DC: The World Bank.

Economist Intelligence Unit (2006) *The Russians are Coming: Understanding Emerging Multinationals*, report commissioned by Rusal.

Economist Intelligence Unit (2009) 'Russia: Fixing the banks?' in *Business Eastern Europe*, http://goliath.ecnext.com/coms2/gi_0198-572181/Russia-fixing-the-banks.html.

Elamin, A. (2007) 'Russian Standard attacks global market', *Food & Drink Europe*, available: http://www.beveragedaily.com/Markets/Russian-Standard-attacks-global-market [accessed 10 October 2011].

Elenkov, D.S. (1995) 'Russian aerospace MNCs in global competition: their origin, competitive strengths and forms of multinational expansion', *The Columbia Journal of World Business*, Summer: 66–78.

Expert Online (2009a) '«КамАЗы» с немецким акцентом' ('KamAz' with a German accent), http://expert.ru/expert/2009/46/kamazy_s_akcentom/ [accessed 21 September 2011].

Expert Online (2009b) 'КамАЗ заговорит по-итальянски' (KamAz will speak Italian), http://expert.ru/2009/10/09/kamazfiat/ [accessed 21 September 2011].

Fedorinova, Y. (2009) 'UC Rusal restructured its debts on US$16.8 billion', *Vedomosti*, December.

Filatotchev, I., Buck, T. and Wright, M. (2007a) 'Soviet all-union enterprises as new multinationals of the CIS', *The International Executive*, 35(6): 525–38.

Filatotchev, I., Strange, R., Piesse, J. and Lien, Y.-Ch. (2007b) 'FDI by firms from newly industrialised economies in emerging markets: corporate governance, entry mode and location', *Journal of International Business Studies*, 38(4): 556–73.

Filippov, S. (2008) 'Russian emerging multinationals: trends and issues', UNU-MERIT (United Nations University and Maastricht University), Working Papers, 062, Maastricht, the Netherlands.

Filippov, S. (2010) 'Russian companies: the rise of new multinationals', *International Journal of Emerging Markets*, 5:(3/4), 307–32.

Finam (2009) 'Rusal', in *Company news*, available: www.finam.ru.

Fischer, S. (1994) 'Russia and the Soviet Union then and now', in O.J. Blanchard, A. Root and J.D. Sachs (eds), *The Transition in Eastern Europe, Volume 1: Country Studies*, Chicago: The University of Chicago Press.

Frydman, R., Rapaczynski, A. and Earle, J.S. (1993) *The Privatisation Process in Russia, Ukraine and the Baltic States*, London: Central European University Press.

Gaddy, C.G. and Ickes, B.W. (1998) 'Russia's virtual economy', *Foreign Affairs*, 77(5): 53–67.

Gaddy, C.G. and Ickes, B.W. (2010) 'Russia after the global financial crisis', *Eurasia Geography and Economics*, 51(3): 281–311.

Globerman, S. and Shapiro, D. (2006) 'Outward FDI and the economic performance of emerging markets', in *International Conference on the Rise of Transnational Corporations from Emerging Markets: Threat or Opportunity?* New York: Columbia University.

Goldman, M. (1991) *What Went Wrong with Perestroika: The Rise and Fall of Mikhail Gorbachev*, New York: W.W. Norton.

Goldman, M. (1994) *Lost Opportunity: Why Economic Reforms in Russia Have Not Worked*, New York: W.W. Norton.

Goldman, M. (2003) *The Piratization of Russia: Russian Reform goes Awry*, London: Routledge.

Goldman, M.I. (2008) *Petrostate: Putin, Power and the New Russia*, New York: Oxford University Press.

Goldman Sachs (2003) 'Dreaming with BRICs', *Global Economics Paper*, 99.

Goldman Sachs (2005) 'How solid are the BRICs?', *Global Economics Paper*, 134.

Goldman Sachs (2010a) 'EM equity in two decades: a changing landscape', *Global Economics Paper*, 204.

Goldman Sachs (2010b) 'The long-term outlook for the BRICs and N-11 Post Crisis', *Global Economics Paper*, 192.

Goldstein, A. and Shaw, T.M. (2007) *Multinational Companies from Emerging Economies: Composition, Conceptualisation and Direction in the Global Economy*, London: Macmillan.

Golubchikov, O. (2007) 'Re-scaling the debate on Russian economic growth: regional restructuring and development asynchronies', *Europe–Asia Studies*, 59(2): 191–215.

Gregory, P.R. and Stuart, R.C. (1981) *Soviet Economic Structure and Performance*, New York: Harper & Row.

Hamilton, G. (ed.) (1986) *Red Multinationals or Red Herrings? The Activities of Enterprises from Socialist Countries in the West*, New York: St. Martin's Press.

Hanson, P. (2004) 'Putin and Russia's economic transformation', *Eurasia Geography and Economics*, 45(6): 421–8.

Heenan, D.A. and Keegan, W.J. (1979) 'The rise of third world multinationals', *Harvard Business Review*, 57(1): 101–9.

Huber, P. and Wörgötter, A. (1998) 'Observations on Russian business networks', *Post-Soviet Affairs*, 14(1): 81–91.

Humber, Y. (2006) 'VTB Chief Outlines Expansion', *The St Petersburg Times*, vol. 1149, no. 15, March 3.

Jensen, C. (2004) 'Localised spillovers in the Polish food industry – the role of FDI in the development process', *Regional Studies*, 38(5): 535–50.

Johnson, J.E. (2004) 'Factors influencing the early internalization of high technology start-ups: US and UK evidence', *Journal of International Entrepreneurship*, 2: 139–54.

Jumpponen, J., Liuhto, K., Sõrg, M. and Vensel, V. (2004) 'Banks' internationalization: Estonian and Russian banks' expansion to the foreign markets', Tallinn School of Economics and Business Administration, Tallinn University of Technology, Working papers, N 109.

Kalotay, K. (2001) 'The contribution of foreign direct investment to transition revisited', *The Journal of World Investment*, 2(2): 259–76.

Kalotay, K. (2004) 'Will foreign direct investment take off in the Russian Federation?', *Journal of World Investment and Trade*, 5(1): 119–38.

Kalotay, K. (2005) 'Outward foreign direct investment from Russia in a global context', *Journal of East–West Business*, 11(3/4): 9–22.

Kalotay, K. (2008a) 'How to explain the foreign expansion of Russian firms', *Journal of Financial Transformation*, 24: 53–61.

Kalotay, K. (2008b) 'Russian transnationals and international investment paradigms', *Research in International Business and Finance*, 22(2): 85–107.

Kalotay, K. (2010) 'The political aspect of foreign direct investment: the case of the Hungarian oil firm MOL', *The Journal of World Investment & Trade*, 11(1): 79–90.

Kalotay, K. and Sulstarova, A. (2010) 'Modelling Russian outward FDI', *Journal of International Management*, 16(2): 131–42.

Ketting, J. (2006) 'SMEs in EU and Russia: Developments and obstacles', http://thelighthousegroup.ru/client/lighthouse/uploads/presentations/13.%20SME%27s%20in%20the%20EU%20and%20Russia.pdf [accessed 22 September 2011].

King, R., Hill, M. and Cornforth, J. (1995) 'From "red multinationals" to capitalist entrepreneurs?', *European Journal of Marketing*, 29(13): 6–22.

Kuznetsov, A. (2009) 'Russian multinationals continue their outward expansion in spite of the global crisis', Report of Institute of World Economy and International Relations, Russian Academy of Sciences, and Vale Columbia Centre on Sustainable International Investment, Columbia University.

Kuznetsov, A. (2010) 'Industrial and geographical diversification of Russian foreign direct investments', *Publications of Pan-European Institute*, Turku, Finland: Turku School of Economics, 7, available: http://www.tse.fi/FI/yksikot/erillislaitokset/pei/Documents/Julkaisut/Kuznetsov.pdf.

Kuznetsov, A. and Kuznetsova, O. (1996) 'Privatisation, shareholding and efficiency argument: Russian experience', *Europe–Asia Studies*, 48(7): 1173–85.

Lall, S. (1983) *The Rise of Multinationals from the Third World*. New York: Wiley.

Latukha, M. (2010) 'Human Resource Management at Yandex', The European Case Clearing House (ECCH). 2010-410-101-1.

Latukha, M., Panibratov, A. and Safonova-Salvadori, E. (2011) 'Entrepreneurial FDI in emerging economies: Russian SME strategy for Brazil', *International Journal of Entrepreneurship and Innovation*, 12(3): 201–12.

Lenta (2006a) 'VimpelCom bought 90 per cent of Armenian internet-monopolist', available: http://www.lenta.ru.

Lenta (2006b) 'VimpelCom is buying the biggest telecom operator in Kyrgyzstan', available: www.lenta.ru.

Lima, L.A. and de Barros, O. (2009) 'The growth of Brazil's direct investment abroad and the challenges it faces', *Columbia FDI Profiles*, Vale Columbia Centre on Sustainable International Investment, August 17, available: http://www.vcc.columbia.edu/content/growth-brazil-s-direct-investment-abroad-and-challenges-it-faces-lu-s-afonso-lima-and-octavi.

Liuhto, K. and Vahtra, P. (2007) 'Foreign operations of Russia's largest industrial corporations – building a typology', *Transnational Corporations*, 16(1): 28–36.

Lucey, B.M. and Voronkova, S. (2008) 'Russian equity market linkages before and after the 1998 crisis: evidence from stochastic and regime-switching co integration tests', *Journal of International Money and Finance*, 27(8): 1303–24.

Lukoil (2008) *Annual Report*, available: http://www.lukoil.com/static_6_5id_218_.html [accessed 21 September 2011].

Luo, Y. and Tung, R.L. (2007) 'International expansion of emerging market enterprises', *Journal of International Business Studies*, 38: 481–98.

MA online (2009) 'Mergers and acquisitions in banking', April 15, available: www.maonline.ru.

McMillan, C. (1987) *Multinationals From the Second World: Growth of Foreign Investment by Soviet and East European Enterprises*, New York: St. Martin's Press.

Nove, A. (1992) *An Economic History of the USSR, 1917–1991*, London: Penguin Books.

Panfilov, V. (2009) 'Global crisis: its origin and implications for Russia's macroeconomic and social stability', *Studies on Russian Economic Development*, 20(3): 229–42.

Panibratov, A. (2009) 'Internationalisation process of Russian construction industry: inward investments perspective', *Journal for East European Management Studies*, 2: 210–28.

Panibratov, A. (2010) 'European FDI for emerging market: the German firm strategy in Russia', *Asian Case Research Journal*, 14(1): 63–93.

Panibratov, A. and Kalotay, K. (2009) 'Russian outward FDI and its policy context', *Columbia FDI Profiles*, Vale Columbia Centre on Sustainable International Investment, Columbia University, October 13, available: http://www.vcc.columbia.edu/content/andrei-panibratov-and-kalman-kalotay-0.

Porter, M.E. (1998) *Michael Porter on Competition*, Boston, MA: Harvard Business School Press.

Pronin, A. (2009) 'From Russia with software', *Programmer Magazine*, November, http://auriga.com/files/From_Russia_with_Software.pdf.

Puffer, Sh. and McCarthy, D. (2001) 'Navigating the hostile maze: a framework for Russian entrepreneurship', *The Academy of Management Executive*, 15(4): 24–38.

Ramamurti, R. (2009) 'What have we learned about emerging-market MNEs?', in R. Ramamurti and J.V. Singh (eds), *Emerging Multinationals from Emerging Markets*, Cambridge: Cambridge University Press.

RBC (2007) 'MTS acquires mobile operator from Bashneft', http://eng.cnews.ru/news/top/indexEn.shtml?2007/12/18/279984 [accessed 22 September 2011].

RBC (2008) 'Summa Telecom again in Beeline's way', available: http://www.cnews.ru/news/top/indexEn.shtml?2008/02/05/286595 [accessed 22 September 2011].

Restate (2007) available: www.restate.ru.

Robinson, N. (2007) 'So what changed? The 1998 financial crisis and Russia's economic and political development', *Demokratizatsiya: The Journal of Post-Soviet Democratisation*, 15(2): 245–59.

RosBusinessConsulting (2010) available: www.rbc.ru.

RT magazine (2009) 'Dairy productivity gets boost through technology', March 9, http://rt.com/business/news/dairy-productivity-gets-boost-through-technology/ [accessed 22 September 2011].

Rugman, A. and Verbeke, A. (2008) 'A regional solution to the strategy and structure of multinationals', *European Management Journal*, 26: 305–13.

Saleem, K. (2009) 'International linkage of the Russian market and the Russian financial crisis: a multivariate GARCH analysis', *Research in International Business and Finance*, 23(3): 243–56.

Satyanand, P. and Raghavendran, P. (2010) 'Outward FDI from India and its policy context', *Columbia FDI Profiles*, Vale Columbia Centre on Sustainable International Investment, September 22, available: http://www.vcc.columbia.edu/content/outward-fdi-india-and-its-policy-context-premila-nazareth-satyanand-and-pramila-raghavendran.

Sauvant, K., Maschek, W. and McAllister, G. (eds) (2010) *Foreign Direct Investment from Emerging Markets: The Challenges Ahead*, New York: Palgrave Macmillan.

Sekhri, R. (2009) 'Russia's VTB eyes string of Gulf deals', http://en.news.maktoob.com/20090000005816/Russia_sVTBeyesstringofGulfdeals/Article.htm [accessed 22 September 2011].

Sethi, D. (2009) 'Are multinational enterprises from the emerging economies global or regional?', *European Management Journal*, 27: 356–65.

Shah, A. (2010) 'World military spending', available: http://www.globalissues.org/article/75/world-military-spending [accessed 10 October 2011].

Shleifer, A. and Vasiliev, D. (1996) 'Management ownership and Russian privatisation', in R. Frydman, C.W. Gray and A. Rapaczynski (eds), *Corporate Governance In Central Europe and Russia*, vol. 2, Budapest: Central European University Press.

Simonov, A. (2011) 'Russia has recognised its index: The country innovation sector has got its estimate', *Russkaya Gazeta*, 5492(116), 1 June, available: http://www.rg.ru/2011/06/01/indeks.html [accessed 26 October 2011].

Steinherr, A. (2004) 'Russian banking since the crisis of 1998', CEPS (Centre for European Policy Studies) Working Document, 209.

Sterlin, A. (1993) 'The conditions for entrepreneurship in the CIS', in D.F. Adell and T. Köllermeier (eds), *Dynamic Entrepreneurship in Central and Eastern Europe*, The Hague: DELWEL Publishers.

Suddath, C. (2010) 'Russians and vodka', *Time Magazine*, January 5.

Tsang, E. and Yip, P. (2007) 'Economic distance and the survival of foreign direct investments', *Academy of Management Journal*, 50(5): 1156–68.

UNCTAD (United Nations Conference on Trade and Development) and UNECE (United Nations Economic Commission for Europe) (1998) 'The Russian crisis of 1998', report, October 1998, available: http://www.twnside.org.sg/title/1998-cn.htm [accessed 21 September 2011].

UNCTAD (United Nations Conference on Trade and Development) (2007) World investment report 2007, October 16.

UNCTAD (United Nations Conference on Trade and Development) (2008) World investment report 2008, September 24.

UNCTAD (United Nations Conference on Trade and Development) (2009) World investment report 2009, September 17.

UNCTAD (United Nations Conference on Trade and Development) (2010) World investment report 2010, July 22.

Vahtra, P. (2006) 'Expansion or exodus? The new leaders among the Russian TNCs', *Electronic Publications of Pan-European Institute*, Turku, Finland: Turku School of Economics, 1, available: http://www.tse.fi/FI/yksikot/erillislaitokset/pei/Documents/Julkaisut/Vahtra_12006.pdf.

Vahtra, P. (2010) 'The Rusnano corporation and internationalisation of Russia's nanotech industry', *Electronic Publications of Pan-European Institute*, Turku, Finland: Turku School of Economics, 11, available: http://www.tse.fi/FI/yksikot/erillislaitokset/pei/Documents/Julkaisut/Vahtra2.pdf.

Vahtra, P. and Liuhto, K. (2006) 'An overview of Russia's largest corporations abroad', in K. Liuhto (ed.), *Expansion or Exodus – Why do Russian Corporations Invest Abroad?* New York: International Business Press.

VTB (2009) *Annual Report 2008*, available: http://www.vtb.com/we/ir/disclosure/fannual/?sphrase_id=404536 [accessed 22 September 2011].

Wells, L.T. (1983) *Third World Multinationals: The Rise of Foreign Direct Investment from Developing Countries*, Cambridge, MA: MIT Press.

Witt, M.A. and Lewin, A.Y. (2007) 'Outward foreign direct investment as escape response to home country institutional constraints', *Journal of International Business Studies*, 38: 579–94.

World Bank (2009) *Russian Economic Report No. 19: From Crisis to Recovery*, available: http://web.worldbank.org/WBSITE/EXTERNAL/COUNTRIES/ECAEXT/RUSSIANFEDERATIONEXTN/0,contentMDK:22222555~pagePK:141137~piPK:141127~theSitePK:305600,00.html [accessed 9 October 2011].

Yakovlev, A. (2006) 'The evolution of business: state interaction in Russia: from state capture to business capture?', *Europe–Asia Studies*, 58(7): 1033–56.

Zhuplev, A. and Shtykhno, D. (2009) 'Motivations and obstacles for small business entrepreneurship in Russia: fifteen years in transition', *Journal of East–West Business*, 15(1): 25–49.

Index